CONCENTRATED CREATION

T&T Clark Studies in Edward Schillebeeckx

Series editors
Frederiek Depoortere
Kathleen McManus O.P.
Stephan van Erp

CONCENTRATED CREATION

Creation and Salvation in the Christology of Edward Schillebeeckx

Rhona Lewis

LONDON • NEW YORK • OXFORD • NEW DELHI • SYDNEY

T&T CLARK
Bloomsbury Publishing Plc
50 Bedford Square, London, WC1B 3DP, UK
1385 Broadway, New York, NY 10018, USA
29 Earlsfort Terrace, Dublin 2, Ireland

BLOOMSBURY, T&T CLARK and the T&T Clark logo are trademarks of
Bloomsbury Publishing Plc

First published in Great Britain 2023
Paperback edition published 2024

Copyright © Rhona Lewis, 2023

Rhona Lewis has asserted her right under the Copyright, Designs and Patents Act, 1988, to be identified as Author of this work.

All rights reserved. No part of this publication may be reproduced or transmitted in any form or by any means, electronic or mechanical, including photocopying, recording, or any information storage or retrieval system, without prior permission in writing from the publishers.

Bloomsbury Publishing Plc does not have any control over, or responsibility for, any third-party websites referred to or in this book. All internet addresses given in this book were correct at the time of going to press. The author and publisher regret any inconvenience caused if addresses have changed or sites have ceased to exist, but can accept no responsibility for any such changes.

A catalogue record for this book is available from the British Library.

Library of Congress Cataloging-in-Publication Data
Names: Lewis, Rhona, author.
Title: Concentrated creation : creation and salvation in the Christology of Edward Schillebeeckx / Rhona Lewis.
Description: London ; New York : T&T Clark, 2022. |
Series: T&T Clark Studies in Edward Schillebeeckx |
Includes bibliographical references and index. |
Identifiers: LCCN 2022036169 (print) | LCCN 2022036170 (ebook) |
ISBN 9780567708892 (hb) | ISBN 9780567708946 (paperback) |
ISBN 9780567708908 (epdf) | ISBN 9780567708939 (ebook)
Subjects: LCSH: Jesus Christ–History of doctrines–20th century. |
Schillebeeckx, Edward, 1914–2009.
Classification: LCC BT203 .L495 2022 (print) | LCC BT203 (ebook) |
DDC 230/.2092–dc23/eng/20221017
LC record available at https://lccn.loc.gov/2022036169
LC ebook record available at https://lccn.loc.gov/2022036170

ISBN: HB: 978-0-5677-0889-2
PB: 978-0-5677-0894-6
ePDF: 978-0-5677-0890-8
eBook: 978-0-5677-0893-9

Typeset by Newgen KnowledgeWorks Pvt. Ltd., Chennai, India

To find out more about our authors and books visit www.bloomsbury.com and sign up for our newsletters.

CONTENTS

List of Abbreviations … vii

INTRODUCTION … 1

Part I
SCHILLEBEECKX'S *RESSOURCEMENT*

Chapter 1
CHRISTIAN CREATION FAITH: AQUINAS AND SCHILLEBEECKX … 13

Chapter 2
CHRISTIAN ANTHROPOLOGY: IRENAEUS AND SCHILLEBEECKX … 43

Part II
QUESTIONS OF CONTINUITY AND CHANGE

Chapter 3
QUESTIONS OF CONTINUITY AND CHANGE … 73

Chapter 4
CONTINUITY AND CHANGE IN SCHILLEBEECKX'S
CHRISTOLOGY: THE EARLIER CHRISTOLOGY … 101

Chapter 5
CONTINUITY AND CHANGE IN SCHILLEBEECKX'S LATER
CHRISTOLOGY: SUFFERING AND SIN … 123

Chapter 6
CONTINUITY AND CHANGE IN SCHILLEBEECKX'S LATER
CHRISTOLOGY: THE PRAXIS OF THE KINGDOM OF GOD AND THE
HUMANITY OF JESUS CHRIST … 143

Part III
SCHILLEBEECKX'S IDEAS AND METHODS IN DIALOGUE WITH NEW CONTEXTS

Chapter 7
SCHILLEBEECKX'S IDEAS AND METHODS IN DIALOGUE WITH NEW
CONTEXTS: THE FEMINICIDE IN CIUDAD JUÁREZ   167

Chapter 8
SCHILLEBEECKX'S IDEAS AND METHODS IN DIALOGUE WITH NEW
CONTEXTS: THE CATHOLIC DIALOGUE SCHOOL IN FLANDERS   195

CONCLUSION   217

Bibliography   221
Index   231

ABBREVIATIONS

Works by Edward Schillebeeckx

Christ	*Christ: The Christian Experience in the Modern World*
Church	*Church: The Human Story of God*
Essays	*Essays: Ongoing Theological Quests*
Jesus	*Jesus: An Experiment in Christology*
CHF	*Church with a Human Face*
CSEG	*Christ the Sacrament of the Encounter with God*
FSG	*For the Sake of the Gospel*
G&M	*God and Man*
GAU	*God Among Us: The Gospel Proclaimed*
GFoM	*God the Future of Man*
GNEM	*God Is New Each Moment*
HT	*I Am a Happy Theologian: Conversations with Francesco Strazzari*
IR	*Interim Report on the Books* Jesus *and* Christ
JWC	*Jesus in our Western Culture: Mysticism, Ethics and Politics*
R&T	*Revelation and Theology*
SEG	*The Sacraments: An Encounter with God*
UF	*The Understanding of Faith: Interpretation and Criticism*
W&C	*World and Church*

Where two page numbers are given in a footnote, the first number is the one in the Bloomsbury, 2014 edition of eleven volumes of the Collected Works of Edward Schillebeeckx, and the second one, in square brackets, is the page number in the first published English translation.

INTRODUCTION

The quest for well-being

On an isolated beach on the east coast of England stands a small monument featuring three paddles. The unbroken paddles are a memorial to two brothers who, in September 1941, paddled for fifty-six hours in a kayak across the North Sea from the village of Katwijk to escape the Nazi occupation of the Netherlands. They wanted life, safety and to be able to work for their country from a base across the water.[1] When the brothers approached the beach at the hamlet of Sizewell the first person they saw was a policeman in uniform. One of the brothers shouted to ask if they might land and the policeman answered, 'No problem.' Because the brothers had to be screened to check that they were not spies, they were detained the first night at the police station in the neighbouring small town of Leiston. The elder brother later told his son that he never felt as free as he did that first night in a British jail.[2] The extreme circumstances of war highlight the lengths to which human beings go for the sake of life, freedom and purposeful work. Every day there are myriad diverse examples of people seeking and experiencing salvation – deliverance from suffering and sin and their consequences – from the mother at her wits' end with fractious children who takes them out into the park or countryside and finds that the best word for the soothing effect of nature on the children is 'salvation', to the homeless street vendor, greeted daily by one of the commuters who at Christmas time invites him to his place for dinner;[3] from an asylum seeker who is rehabilitated after suffering torture, to the person who has the courage to own up to a wrong and is met with spontaneous forgiveness; from the marginalized person suffering from mental illness who is drawn into a group

---

1. The broken paddle is a memorial to the twenty-four (out of thirty-two) who were killed or drowned as they attempted the crossing to freedom and relative safety by kayak.
2. Laurence Cawley, *World War Two: The Brothers Who Fled Nazi Occupation by Kayak*, BBC News website, 21 September 2021.
3. Paul Logan, who became homeless, rebuilt his life and sold copies of *The Big Issue*, a street newspaper which exists to offer homeless people the opportunity to earn a legitimate income. He told his story in an article published in *The Big Issue* 1486, 1 November 2021, 46.

of friends, to a child living in a remote rural area whose sight is restored by doctors in a mobile clinic.

The gamut of concepts to denote profound well-being runs from rescue and safety to healing and flourishing in fullness of life. At the heart of the Jewish and Christian faiths and religious practice is a confidence that living in relationship with God is the way to well-being or salvation in the fullest sense. In his extensive theological writings Edward Schillebeeckx endeavours to reframe the quest for well-being and to write about salvation in Christ. He bases a soteriological Christology on Christian creation faith. He was doing theology in broad cultural contexts in which 'religious faith is upbraided as meaningless, or worse, as an outright impediment to human development and freedom'.[4] His life's work was to elucidate how fullness of humanity, salvation or well-being in its widest and deepest sense, is to be achieved in the world in relationship with God, mediated through Jesus Christ. This task involved for Schillebeeckx a radical rethinking and a new expression of the meaning of salvation in and through Christ.

Purpose and structure

The primary purpose of this book is to show how Edward Schillebeeckx formulates a theology of salvation by linking salvation to creation faith. The structure of the book falls into three parts. In the first section Schillebeeckx's *ressourcement* of tenets of the creation faith of Thomas Aquinas and of Irenaeus is examined. By linking salvation to the Creator God's purposes for human beings and the creation, purposes which are concentrated and find their culmination in Jesus Christ, Schillebeeckx's development of a soteriological Christology is investigated. In the second section, Aquinas' distinction between a reality and a statement about that reality provides the foundation on which to analyse the question of continuity and change in Schillebeeckx's theology. In the analysis, which uses the threefold model of change of the *Annales* school of French historiography, the primary focus is on Schillebeeckx's Christology. The third section explores how some of Schillebeeckx's methods and ideas are brought to play and developed in two very different contemporary contexts: the feminicide of Ciudad Juárez in Mexico and the Catholic Dialogue School in Flanders. Nancy Pineda-Madrid's theological analysis of how salvation is sought and found in the midst of the suffering of the feminicide in Ciudad Juárez parallels Schillebeeckx's thinking about resistance to suffering in order to bring about the reign of God. Lieven Boeve's exposition of the theological principles which underlie the project of the Catholic Dialogue School is found to be helpful in tracing how Schillebeeckx's thinking can be developed in a specific educational situation within a postmodern, secularized society.

---

4. Philip Kennedy, *Schillebeeckx* (London: Chapman, 1993), 1 (henceforth *Schillebeeckx*).

The connection between creation and salvation

In Western Christianity the dominant soteriology has for centuries focused on Christ crucified on the cross. The unintelligibility and abhorrence of Jesus' execution by the torture of crucifixion demands attempts to explain it. By the time of Anselm (*c.* 1033–1109) not only was the crucifixion becoming the primary focus of the theology of God's saving action, but it was tending to become the explanation for the Incarnation itself. In his logically structured interpretation of the crucifixion, Anselm vigorously refutes the idea of the devil's 'rights' over humanity, averring that the idea that the devil was deceived by God was an affront to God: it is impossible for God, who is truth, to be a deceiver.[5] He argued, rather, that the Incarnation was necessary in order that the *God-man* might fulfil humanity's need to make adequate satisfaction for its sin because,

> Only the God-man has something [of infinite value] to offer [the infinite God]; being without sin, Christ is exempt from the need to undergo death, and hence can freely offer the gift of his life as a work of reparation for the whole human race ([Cur Deus Homo], 2.6-7,11, 14, 18-19).[6]

Intense soteriological focus on the crucified Christ led to a stark narrowing of the understanding of God's saving action. Gerald O'Collins points out that in *Cur Deus Homo* Anselm makes 'only a brief closing reference to the divine mercy' and he observes two notable omissions, namely, the resurrection 'with the gift of the Holy Spirit and that major patristic theme, the divinization of the redeemed' and also 'the full significance of Jesus' life and public ministry'.[7] Nevertheless, Anselm's interpretation of the crucifixion as a reparation for humanity's sin took root in Western Christianity. It, and the distortions his interpretation suffered and caused in theological thinking (such as that of penal substitution) continue to be evident to this day.

To isolate the crucifixion from the life story of Jesus and to interpret it in terms of a propitiatory sacrifice ignores the priority of creation faith. Without

---

5. In the early centuries of the Christian era, the first wave of interpretation by the patristic theologians tended to be based on an understanding of the Genesis account of the fall of Adam and Eve as historical and causative. Paradoxically, this led to interpretations in quasi-mythical terms of the crucifixion of Jesus Christ as part of a cosmic battle between Satan and God. On the one hand, Christ's death was seen as a ransom paid to Satan, the lord of sin and death, in order that humanity be freed from his tyranny; on the other hand, however, God won the final victory over Satan by raising Jesus from the dead. Satan was tricked because, hidden in the human body of Christ, was the 'hook' of his divinity by which Satan was caught.

6. Gerald O'Collins, *Jesus Our Redeemer: A Christian Approach to Salvation* (Oxford: Oxford University Press, 2007), 135.

7. Ibid., 136.

God's creative action there is nothing, either of humanity or of the world and the universe in which it finds itself. God's creative action has implications. An exploration of its implications leads to God's saving action and finds that the two are inseparable: God is Creator and Saviour of all.

The need to test conceptions of the saving significance of Jesus' death

Schillebeeckx writes that believing Christians must 'seek to test Christian conceptions of the saving significance of Jesus' death in order to see if a Christian soteriology ties us to concepts like "ransom", "propitiation", "substitution", "satisfaction", et cetera'.[8] To test such Christian concepts is not to diminish the significance of the crucifixion nor is it, in any way whatsoever, to belittle the fact that Jesus' love for people led to his dying by crucifixion for them. Testing seeks, rather, to place Jesus' death in the light of what is consistent with other beliefs about the person and nature of Jesus and with beliefs about God the Creator. There is a variety of problems associated with atonement theory. Based on taking the Genesis story of Adam and Eve's fall and their expulsion from Eden, at least to some extent as an historical account, atonement theory sees the creation that we live in as no longer essentially as God intended it to be. Human beings are thought to be part of a creation that is spoilt and intrinsically flawed. The belief in a flawed creation opens the way to dualism and separates nature from God's saving grace. Death and the limitations of human finitude are not acknowledged for what they are, the natural conditions of human creaturehood, but are assumed to be divine punishments. Adam and Eve's sin of disobedience, the underlying argument goes, severed friendship with God to such an extent that the Incarnation and a sacrifice of propitiation became necessary for the reconciliation of humanity with God. The Incarnation is said to be God's response to the dilemma that humanity brought upon itself by sinning: God had to send the Son to earth to make a propitiatory sacrifice of himself on the cross to God the Father. This theory generates severe theological problems: God becomes a God who, in the wake of an original sin, ceased to be intimately present to humanity until after an atoning sacrifice should be made; the Incarnation becomes contingent upon sin; if a propitiatory sacrifice is deemed necessary, violence is sacralized to be a reality within God which compromises any experience or idea of God as a God of love. Further, the unity of God the Father and God the Son is sundered because they are positioned on opposing sides of a legalistic transaction; if God is thought to have required or even masterminded the 'sacrifice' of Calvary, the freedom of Jesus and of his persecutors in the free decisions that, in fact, led to his execution is abrogated and

---

8. Edward Schillebeeckx, *Jesus: An Experiment in Christology*, trans. Hubert Hoskins, ed. and revised by Joanna Dunham and reread by Marcelle Manley, The Collected Works of Edward Schillebeeckx 6 (London: Bloomsbury, 2014), 285 [318] (henceforth *Jesus*).

God is reduced to the status of a puppeteer. Finally, atonement theory has tended to reduce God's saving action to the locus of the cross.

Schillebeeckx's starting point in his theology is no less than God the Creator. Reflecting theologically about salvation from the basis of creation faith, he finds that the scope of God's saving action is as wide as God's creative action.

An exploration of salvation

In the ressourcement of Thomas Aquinas' creation faith

Schillebeeckx, in his regard for 'the creation as the foundation of all theology',[9] considers that in the second part of the twentieth century there was still 'so much talk of the history of salvation that there [was] need to reflect anew on the concept of creation'.[10] He starts from basic tenets of creation faith, as articulated by Thomas Aquinas, identifying their corollaries. The implications of those corollaries provide the essential principles of his Christology. God's creative action, in Thomist terms, is a free sharing of divine bounty, 'simply an expression of love'[11] and that self-giving love of God finds its fullest and most explicit expression in the life, death and resurrection of Jesus of Nazareth. Jesus is the culmination of the self-revelation of God's love. The more the understanding of Jesus Christ is informed by the elements of Christian creation faith, the clearer it becomes that God gave his Son 'because he so loved the world'[12] and he desires human beings to enjoy the abundance of life that becomes possible in reliance on God through Jesus Christ. Jewish and Christian creation faith declares that the creation is 'very good'; it is not intrinsically flawed (in distinction to any collapse in its systems caused by the despoliations of human greed). Far from seeking escape from, or chafing at, the conditions of human finitude, creation faith 'sets us free for our own task in the world',[13] the task of building a world and making a history that is in accordance with God's will and the coming of God's kingdom. Whereas contingency and finitude may ultimately render life meaningless to an existential atheist, Christian faith in God as Creator sees finitude's and contingency's ultimate source and ground to be in the Living God. Seen in the light of creation faith, Jesus' intimate prayer life with his Father and his total involvement with people, irrespective of their condition or status, means that his whole life on earth brought salvation from God and was a spiritual worship of God.

---

9. Edward Schillebeeckx, *I Am a Happy Theologian: Conversations with Francesco Strazzari*, trans. John Bowden (London: SCM Press, 1994), 47 (henceforth *HT*).

10. Ibid.

11. Fergus Kerr, *After Aquinas: Versions of Thomism* (Oxford: Blackwell, 2002), 39 (henceforth *After Aquinas*).

12. Jn 3.16.

13. Edward Schillebeeckx, *God Among Us: The Gospel Proclaimed*, trans. John Bowden (London: SCM Press, 1983), 94 (henceforth *GAU*).

An exploration of salvation

In the ressourcement *of Irenaeus' Christian anthropology*

While Schillebeeckx draws on Aquinas for truths about the Creator, and the distinction and the relation between creature and Creator, he reaches to an earlier theologian, Irenaeus, for a *ressourcement* of Christian anthropology. Human beings are made with a capacity to respond to the transcendent Creator God who makes himself known to them by his very immanence. God reveals himself to them through the medium of the concrete world of material things in which they find themselves. God's self-revelation in place and time is his invitation to human beings, with their capabilities and vulnerabilities, to get to know him and to share more deeply in his own life.

Both Irenaeus and Schillebeeckx have an implicit and integral Trinitarian foundation to their theology of the manner in which the transcendent God works immanently with human beings. Irenaeus suggests an image of God the Father working on the moist clay of the heart of each human being with his two hands which correspond to the Son and the Holy Spirit. Schillebeeckx starts with the Son, the historical, flesh and blood person of Jesus of Nazareth, and stresses his absolute unity with his Father, in the power of the Spirit. Followers of Jesus Christ, in whatever historical context they find themselves, are called, like Jesus, to draw from an empowering relationship with the Father and, filled with the Spirit, to work with him to build God's kingdom. Schillebeeckx's expression, the 'praxis of the reign of God', denotes the 'indivisible interplay'[14] between 'an intensive form of experience of God' or 'an intensive form of prayer', and 'an intensive form of social commitment' or 'socio-political involvement' carrying out the concrete actions needed to help build God's kingdom as a place of well-being and salvation.[15]

For both Irenaeus and Schillebeeckx the distinction and the relation of Creator and creature have the same fundamental implications for human beings. The prime one is a twofold need, not merely the necessary dependence on God for biological existence itself but, equally importantly, a need to flourish in relationship with God in whom the deepest meaning is to be found and to whom gratitude can be expressed for the gifts of life. Human beings as temporal creatures are intended to grow to ever fuller humanity in their progress towards God, a growth which is watered, so to speak, by conversation with God in prayer complemented by action for others. The theme of glory is common to both theologians: growth into the full humanity that God intends for each person redounds to God's glory. Jesus Christ both embodies the mystery and divinity of God as a human being and, at the same time, embodies the mystery of what it is to be human. On earth he was both the

---

14. Kennedy writes, 'The word "praxis", a neologism in English, connotes an indivisible interplay between an action and a theory'. *Schillebeeckx*, 114.

15. Martin G. Poulsom quotes these definitions in *The Dialectics of Creation: Creation and the Creator in Edward Schillebeeckx and David Burrell* (London: Bloomsbury, 2014), 122 (henceforth *Dialectics*).

splendour of God and, simultaneously, he glorified him in his perfect humanity. Raised to heaven he is, and does, the same. For both Irenaeus and Schillebeeckx, the cornerstone of the three phases of salvation history is Jesus Christ. The time of the Old Testament prepared for Christ's arrival on earth, Jesus on earth is God enfleshed, and after his death and resurrection Christ lives and is present, in his Spirit, explicitly in the members of the Church.

Questions of continuity and change

Schillebeeckx's soteriological Christology both breaks from Anselmian atonement theory and is, at the same time, in continuity with the dogmatic tradition of the Church. Just as he wrote that Christians must 'seek to test Christian conceptions of the saving significance of Jesus' death'[16] so his soteriological Christology must be tested to see whether it is in continuity with Chalcedon and the dogmatic tradition of the Church. Acknowledging that Schillebeeckx's soteriological Christology cuts loose from the bonds of atonement theory to comprise a far wider concept of salvation, a method must be found to test whether it is, nevertheless, in continuity with Scripture and tradition. The French *Annales* threefold model of cultural–historical change provides an appropriate tool to analyse the component elements of Schillebeeckx's soteriological Christology, before and after Vatican II. This model identifies cultural change as taking place at three different levels or on three different planes, namely, ephemeral, conjunctural and structural, and allows for those changes to take place asynchronously. Use of the model can show how change at one level is sometimes necessary for continuity at another level. In addition to structural dogmatic elements of Schillebeeckx's Christology, three structural grids or frameworks for his Christological thinking are identified: first, he always places his Christology in the context of creation faith; secondly, it is through their experiences that God is revealed to human beings and that they come to know God and, thirdly, the basis of Jesus Christ's mediation of God is through his humanity.

Christology is concentrated creation

In Jesus Christ, 'human nature is assumed in such a way *as to be the person* of the Son of God,'[17] and on earth he was 'known as man, professed as Son of God.'[18]

---

16. Schillebeeckx, *Jesus*, 285 [318]. Cf. p. 4.
17. See Kennedy, *Schillebeeckx*, 104, for a discussion of the critical textual variation for this phrase. The majority of manuscripts have 'in quo humana natura asumpta est ad hoc quod sit *persona* Filii Dei', which translates as above. The Leonine edition of Aquinas' works has, 'in quo humana natura assumpta est ad hoc quod sit *personae* Filii Dei' which translates as, 'in whom [Christ] human nature is assumed so as *to belong to the person* of the Son of God'.
18. Ibid., 105.

Raised from the dead by God, his human body is glorified and he sits at his Father's right hand. Both on earth and now in heaven, he was and is the visible embodiment of God's whole purpose in creation, namely, to give the revelation of God's unfathomable and faithful love to humanity, a love that both creates and saves, and to live the perfect human response to God. In living out his perfect response to his Father, those who met Jesus while he was on earth, and who were not hostile to him, understood and experienced him 'to be the very essence of final salvation'[19] which comes from God. As Kennedy writes,

> Everything that is good in creation is seen most clearly in Jesus. The meaning of creation as the manifestation of God's nature, as the beginning of salvation, and, in biblical categories, as the inauguration of God's kingdom, receives its amplest clarification in Jesus.[20]

The sequence of chapters

Chapter 1 places Schillebeeckx in the historical context of his grounding in the philosophy and theology of Thomas Aquinas and examines his *ressourcement* of Aquinas' creation theology. An analysis is made of Schillebeeckx's development of the corollaries of certain basic Thomist tenets of creation faith, seen in the light of contemporary concerns, and how these feed into his Christology. Chapter 2 examines how Schillebeeckx's Christian anthropology draws on a *ressourcement* of Irenaeus to reach an understanding of Jesus Christ not only as the fullest revelation of God but also as the perfect expression of what it is to be human. Chapter 3 considers the issue of continuity and change in theology and of the need, sometimes, for change at one level if continuity is to be preserved. The crucial difference between a reality (God) and the statements about that reality is elucidated and the role of faith in theology is analysed. Continuity and change in Schillebeeckx's method are examined. Chapters 4, 5 and 6 use the French *Annales* school threefold model of historico-cultural change in order to determine whether Schillebeeckx's soteriological Christology is in continuity with Chalcedon and to determine in what sense Jesus is salvation. In Chapter 4 his earlier Christology is analysed; in Chapters 5 and 6 his later Christology is examined with a focus on suffering and sin (Chapter 5) and the praxis of the kingdom of God and the humanity of Jesus (Chapter 6). In Chapters 7 and 8 Schillebeeckx's ideas and methods in dialogue with new contexts are explored. In Chapter 7, Nancy Pineda-Madrid's analysis of suffering and salvation in Ciudad Juárez is examined and found to develop central themes of Schillebeeckx. In her words, 'We can understand salvation only through our communion with one another, with God, and with creation. Without a love for community, without an active drive to make more visible and vital the many ways

---

19. Schillebeeckx, *Jesus*, 33 [50].
20. Kennedy, *Schillebeeckx*, 94.

we are interrelated, salvation is impossible'.²¹ She speaks of the social interpretation of salvation as bringing 'the crucified peoples down from the cross' and argues that 'through their public actions, those who have suffered feminicide in Ciudad Juárez have laid claim to their religious birthright, revealing community driving toward salvation'.²² In Chapter 8 Lieven Boeve's account of the Catholic Dialogue School is examined. In a postmodern secularized society identity construction is an assignment or task. The Catholic Dialogue School engages religious, philosophical and ideological plurality to propose a way of (re-)discovering identity in a 'new, different and challenging way'.²³ It is a project which brings the Christian voice into the conversation. In a plural field 'each person is already a participant and in relation to other positions. Identity and difference go hand in hand'.²⁴ As a Catholic school the Dialogue School is based on the fundamental experience of faith and recognizes that the 'deepest mystery of reality is love [which is the] guideline for educating, for living and for living together'.²⁵

Schillebeeckx's statement 'Christology is concentrated creation' is found to mean that God's purposes in creation are perfectly and fully expressed in Jesus Christ: 'everything that is good in creation is seen most clearly in Jesus'²⁶ and 'the condensation of all that is entailed in creation' is found in Jesus Christ.²⁷ When he lived on earth, people experienced in Jesus a wonderful fullness of life, salvation directly from God. Now that Jesus has been raised and sits at God's right hand, people experience fullness of life and salvation in the power of his Spirit. Jesus Christ is the one in whom 'all things in heaven and earth were created' and 'in whom all things hold together'.²⁸ On earth, God's invitation to humanity is to discover God and work with the risen Jesus to continue bringing in God's kingdom.

---

21. Nancy Pineda-Madrid, *Suffering and Salvation in Ciudad Juárez* (Minneapolis, MN: Fortress Press, 2011), 152.
22. Ibid.
23. Lieven Boeve, 'Faith in Dialogue: The Christian Voice in the Catholic Dialogue School', *International Studies in Catholic Education* 11 (2019): 37–50 (40).
24. Ibid.
25. Ibid., 38.
26. Kennedy, *Schillebeeckx*, 94.
27. Ibid., 10.
28. Col. 1.16, 17.

Part I

SCHILLEBEECKX'S *RESSOURCEMENT*

Chapter 1

CHRISTIAN CREATION FAITH: AQUINAS AND SCHILLEBEECKX

In the first part of this chapter the circumstances of Schillebeeckx's grounding in the theology and philosophy of Thomas Aquinas are given. The second part of the chapter identifies elements of Schillebeeckx's creation faith. It is found to be rooted in basic tenets of Aquinas' creation faith. The way in which Schillebeeckx develops corollaries of these basic tenets and how his development of them feeds into his Christology is explored.

Neo-Thomism

In 1879 Leo XIII had published the encyclical *Aeterni Patris* in which he directed Catholics to the philosophy of St Thomas Aquinas, so promoting a revival of Thomism at the end of the nineteenth century and in the first half of the twentieth century. Leo XIII's exhortation was a consolidation of the tendency of his predecessor, Pius IX, to centralize authority in the Holy See in order to ensure uniformity of theological method and doctrinal teaching within the Church in the face of the rapid and radical political and social changes of the time. By the early twentieth century a Thomistic revival was fully entrenched. The Roman Catholic Code of Canon Law in 1917 'required that the study of philosophy and theology in all institutes of higher education, including seminaries, must be carried out "according to the arguments, doctrine, and principles of St. Thomas which they are inviolably to hold".[1]

Schillebeeckx joined the Dominican order in Ghent in 1934. The backbone of the initial three-year period of study, the *philosophicum*, was a detailed examination of the bases of Aquinas' philosophy, and it was followed by the *theologicum*, four years devoted to a systematic reading of Aquinas' theology with a parallel study of commentaries on the texts. This Thomist curriculum was universal for those

---

1. Francis Schüssler Fiorenza, 'The New Theology and Transcendental Thomism', in *Modern Christian Thought: The Twentieth Century*, ed. James C. Livingston, Francis Schüssler Fiorenza with Sarah Coakley and James H. Evans, Jr (Minneapolis, MN: Fortress Press, 2006), 197–232 (197).

in training for the priesthood in the Catholic Church, yet different teachers might convey their special interests to their students. Dominicus De Petter, for example, who taught at Ghent, profoundly influenced Schillebeeckx's epistemological thinking with his own development of an epistemology of the 'implicit intuition of totality'.[2]

Two slightly older contemporaries of Schillebeeckx's, Karl Rahner and Hans Urs von Balthasar, had entered the Society of Jesus in Germany, in 1922 and 1929, respectively, where the same Thomist curriculum was in force.[3] From the Thomist base of their studies these three men, who were to become major theologians of the twentieth century, each developed their theology in a singular way. Borgman plots Schillebeeckx's position in relation to Rahner in the landscape of twentieth-century theology. He writes that 'in the period after the Second World War the terms "salvation history" and "economy of salvation" resounded through Catholic theology'.[4] He describes how, in the attempt to take account of the growing sense that human existence was 'historical' and bound up with space and time, Rahner's 'philosophical and theological reflections on the "historicity" of human existence played a key role'.[5] Schillebeeckx himself took up the term 'salvation history' and Borgman suggests that 'there is a striking affinity in development between Rahner and Schillebeeckx'.[6] He first describes the considerable level of agreement between the two theologians. He says that Rahner's view is of 'human existence as orientated on God in longing', a longing which is fulfilled by a Christian acceptance of a 'particular word spoken in human history' as God's word, a word that has no human foundation but rests only on a 'free action of God, on God's free decision to disclose himself'.[7]

The fundamental difference, however, between Rahner and Schillebeeckx, according to Borgman, is that in Rahner 'all the emphasis [is] on the basic structure – in technical philosophical terms the transcendental structure – of the human consciousness' whereas for Schillebeeckx the active, dynamic longing for salvation and happiness in God is through concretely formed and situated human longing.[8] For Rahner, human beings are more fully themselves when they are transcending their limited horizons; for Schillebeeckx, human beings are more fully

---

2. Erik Borgman, *Edward Schillebeeckx: A Theologian in His History. Volume 1: A Catholic Theology of Culture (1914–1965)*, trans. John Bowden (London: Continuum, 2003), 42 (henceforth *Edward Schillebeeckx*). Also, Kennedy, *Schillebeeckx*, 18–19.

3. Karl Rahner, b. 1904, Hans Urs von Balthasar, b. 1905, Edward Schillebeeckx, b. 1914. Balthasar was Swiss but entered the Society of Jesus in Germany because it was still banned in Switzerland: Fergus Kerr, *Twentieth Century Catholic Theologians* (Oxford: Blackwell, 2007), 121.

4. Borgman, *Edward Schillebeeckx*, 166.

5. Ibid., 167.

6. Ibid., 170.

7. Ibid.

8. Ibid., 170–1.

themselves when they are entering most deeply into those situations of limitation. As Kennedy writes, Schillebeeckx avers that 'humankind's factual state of being is interwoven with a supernatural order'; he does not posit a Rahnerian 'supernatural existential'.⁹ Maureen Patricia Carroll expresses Schillebeeckx's position by saying that, rather than presenting a transcendental analysis of human development, he sees 'the process of human transformation by grace as originally historical, social, and embedded in the Christian narrative tradition'.¹⁰ Schillebeeckx himself went so far as to say that 'he finds [a notion of a] supernatural existential "useless" ("nutteloos") and "meaningless" ("zinloos")'.¹¹ Martin Poulsom encapsulates Schillebeeckx's approach in these words: 'Schillebeeckx is not a transcendental thinker. ... He is a markedly situational thinker, and, as far as the particular debate about the knowledge of God in Catholic theology goes, found his inspiration and guide in the approach taken by Dominic de Petter rather than Joseph Maréchal.'¹²

Although in *Aeterni Patris* Leo XIII calls for a return to ' "the golden wisdom of St. Thomas" he does not specify *what* interpretation of the wisdom is to be preferred'.¹³ He does, however, insist that 'the doctrine of Thomas be drawn from his own fountains, or at least from those rivulets which, derived from that very fount, have thus far flowed, according to the established agreement of learned men, pure and clear (para. 31)'.¹⁴ Among the 'rivulets' which subsequently flowed from the Thomist source, in the late nineteenth century and first half of the twentieth century, Philip A. Egan identifies three which 'became increasingly discrete and internally sundered: traditional Thomism, neo-Thomism and transcendental Thomism'.¹⁵ McGinn, however, uses four general categories in which to allocate twentieth-century Thomisms, adding that they are not to be thought of as discrete

---

9. Philip Kennedy, *Deus Humanissimus: The Knowability of God in the Theology of Edward Schillebeeckx* (Fribourg: University Press Fribourg, 1993), 105 (henceforth *Deus Humanissimus*).

10. Maureen Patricia Carroll, 'Framework for a Theology of Christian Conversion in the Jesus-Project of Edward Schillebeeckx' (unpublished doctoral dissertation, Catholic University of America, 1985), Abstract in *Dissertation Abstracts International* 46 (1985), 1007-A, ProQuest Dissertations & Theses A&I, http://0-search.proquest.com, Abstract, paragraph 2 of 4.

11. Kennedy, *Deus Humanissimus*, 105.

12. Poulsom, *Dialectics*. He refers here to William L. Portier, 'Interpretation and Method', in *The Praxis of the Reign of God: An Introduction to the Theology of Edward Schillebeeckx*, 2nd edn, ed. Mary Catherine Hilkert and Robert J. Schreiter (New York: Fordham University Press, 2002), 19–36 (21). Poulsom, on p. 7 of *Dialectics*, is the source of the material from Patricia Carroll and Kennedy in *Deus Humanissimus*.

13. Bernard McGinn, *Thomas Aquinas' Summa Theologiae: A Biography* (Princeton, NJ: Princeton University Press, 2014), 171.

14. Ibid.

15. Philip A. Egan, *Philosophy and Catholic Theology: A Primer* (Collegeville, MN: Liturgical Press, 2009), 50.

because some theologians span more than one type of Thomism.[16] His categories are Strict-Observance Thomism, Revived Thomism (which used a historical approach), Metaphysical Thomism (which used a philosophical approach) and Transcendental Thomism.[17] The Strict-Observance or Traditional Thomism known as neo-scholasticism was the one that was mandatory in seminaries and universities. Francis Schüssler Fiorenza says that this neo-scholasticism was intended to contest the rationalism of the Enlightenment and also the emphasis on sentiment, feeling and experience of nineteenth-century Romanticism. It sought to provide an independent rational foundation for supernatural revelation. He points out the irony that neo-scholastic fundamental theology 'assumed some of the same philosophical foundations as the Enlightenment in order to combat it'. It fought Romanticism 'as a naturalistic and subjectivistic emptying of religious belief and truth of its objective realism'.[18] Any appeal to experience and history was rejected by the Congregation of Studies.[19] Aquinas' theology and philosophy constituted the prescribed syllabus but, rather than students studying the original texts, 'an ambitious handbook tradition and the republication of prominent scholastic thinkers' were stipulated.[20] As McGinn says, 'the philosophical and theological manuals employed in seminaries circa 1880 – 1960 were generally based on Thomas, or at least purported to be *secundum mentem S. Thomae*, whatever that was taken to mean'.[21] Some of the manuals were 'baroque' in the sense that they dated from the era of the Spanish Counter-Reformation when a form of neo-scholasticism known as Suarezianism after Francisco de Suarez's commentary was established.[22]

Reginald Garrigou-Lagrange (1877–1964) was the foremost exponent of this Traditional Thomism which was taught from about 1910 until 1935.[23] It is intriguing that one of Garrigou-Lagrange's outstanding students was Marie-Dominique Chenu who, in contrast to his doctoral dissertation supervisor, espoused and established a quite different way of reading Aquinas, namely, by approaching his theology with an exploration and understanding of his historical and intellectual context. He was later to meet and have a great influence on Schillebeeckx during the time when the latter attended his classes at the Sorbonne in 1946–7.[24] There were other theologians who either had been or were at the time applying an historical

---

16. McGinn, *Thomas Aquinas' Summa Theologiae*, 187.

17. The most noticeable overlap was between Revived Thomism, which took a historical approach, and Metaphysical Thomism.

18. Fiorenza, 'The New Theology and Transcendental Thomism', 198–9.

19. Egan, *Philosophy and Catholic Theology*, 50.

20. Jürgen Metterpenningen, *Nouvelle Théologie New Theology: Inheritor of Modernism, Precursor of Vatican II* (London: T&T Clark, 2010), 20.

21. McGinn, *Thomas Aquinas' Summa Theologiae*, 174.

22. Egan, *Philosophy and Catholic Theology*, 50.

23. McGinn, *Thomas Aquinas' Summa Theologiae*, 180.

24. Schillebeeckx, *HT*, 8.

approach to the texts and thought of Aquinas. Foremost among them were Jacques Maritain (1882–1973) and Etienne Gilson (1884–1978) who spearheaded the move 'back to the texts' or *ressourcement*.[25] This approach sought

> to renew Thomist thought from within by identifying accretions and eschewing the various corruptions that over time had crept into the tradition. The aim was to explore the thought of Thomas in greater depth within its original context in order to expound its brilliance.[26]

As Master of Students and teacher of anthropology and philosophy at the Dominican House in Ghent (from 1931 to 1939), De Petter steered a distinctive course through the Thomist syllabus. He thoroughly examined the philosophical bases of Aquinas' philosophy with the student priests and, exceptionally, he also encouraged them to complement the ideas of Aquinas with the ideas of modern and contemporary philosophers.[27] Schillebeeckx was steeped in Aquinas and also read philosophers such as Kant, Hegel, Husserl and Merleau-Ponty.[28] He 'fell in love with philosophy' and it became a lifelong interest.[29] De Petter not only influenced Schillebeeckx with his approach to epistemology which aimed to 'overcome philosophical conceptualism and dualism [the dualism that divides, too sharply, objective reality from subjective reality]'.[30] In broader terms, it was thanks to De Petter that Schillebeeckx was able to distinguish 'between a Thomistic theology and doing theology on "purely Thomistic principles", favouring the latter'.[31]

Two Thomist principles to which Schillebeeckx adhered

Kennedy draws attention to two Thomist principles which inform and guide Schillebeeckx's theology throughout his career. One is an epistemological principle and the other concerns the understanding of explicit affirmations of faith. The first

---

25. Cajetan O'Reilly wrote of Ambrose Gardeil,

> No-one realized more clearly than he that St. Thomas, keenly alive to the needs of his own day, wrote the *Summa Theologica* to meet the demands of the thirteenth century. ... Père Gardeil had no peer in making St. Thomas actual for our times, in clothing His thought in terms suitable to the modern mind, in showing points of contact between medieval and modern problems. 20. www.dominicanajournal.org/wp.../dominicanav17n1peregardeilappreciation.pdf.

26. Egan, *Philosophy and Catholic Theology*, 51.
27. Kennedy, *Schillebeeckx*, 18.
28. Ibid., 19.
29. Schillebeeckx, *HT*, 5.
30. Kennedy, *Schillebeeckx*, 40.
31. Borgman, *Edward Schillebeeckx*, 240.

principle is Aquinas' statement that 'while human beings cannot know or define God's essence, they can at least make explicit affirmations about the divine because God is manifested in effects, that is, through creation (Aquinas' *Summa Theologiae*, 1, q. 1, a. 7, ad 1)'.[32] In other words, it is through the concrete reality of the creation that human beings are able to know and articulate something about God. Schillebeeckx writes, 'God is ineffable. And it is only possible to talk about him as creator in an indirect way through the medium of the world, i.e. our contingent nature and history'.[33] As Kennedy puts it, Schillebeeckx 'transposes' Aquinas' creation-based epistemological principle to say that 'the divine discloses itself in relation to human experiences of creatureliness (or contingency)'.[34] In his later work it is the basic human experience of resistance to suffering that Schillebeeckx regards as the pre-religious condition for 'a cognitive experience of God'.[35] The second Thomist principle is one which is vital to guarantee 'the continuity in substance between new-born interpretations of faith' and it states, 'The act of the believer does not terminate at a statement (of faith) but at the reality (*actus credentis non terminatur ad enuntiabile sed ad rem*)' (*Summa Theologiae*, II-II, q. 1, a. 2, ad 2).[36] This principle of Aquinas' theology is examined in some detail in Chapter 3.

Kennedy also memorably suggests that a Schillebeeckian catechism would run something like this:

> Who is God? God is Creator and saviour of all. What is reality? Reality is a divine creation. Who is Jesus Christ? He is the condensation or … encapsulation of the reality of creation. What are human beings? They are creatures living in a divine creation. What is the ecosphere? It is part of a divine creation.[37]

He is making the point that 'creation is the mainspring and master concept of his theological corpus'.[38]

This assessment is not unchallenged.[39] Robert J. Schreiter, for example, proposes that the soteriological has primacy in Schillebeeckx's work. He writes, 'The four focal points of [Schillebeeckx's] commitment are: working inductively; the narrative

---

32. Kennedy, *Schillebeeckx*, 35–6.
33. Schillebeeckx, *GAU*, 94.
34. Ibid., 36.
35. Ibid., 128.
36. Kennedy, *Schillebeeckx*, 58.
37. Ibid., 10.
38. Ibid.
39. Martin G. Poulsom writes, 'It must be said … that how this balance [between creation and salvation] is achieved and whether creation or salvation is prior in Schillebeeckx's theology are contentious matters in the secondary literature', Footnote 6, p. 2 in '"The Distinction" and "The Relation": Creation and Creator in Burrell and Schillebeeckx' (Doctoral Dissertation, University of Oxford, 2008).

character of experience; the mystery of suffering and contrast; and the primacy of the soteriological.'[40] In what follows, three basic tenets of Aquinas' creation faith, as presented by Fergus Kerr and Brian Davies, are taken. Schillebeeckx's creation faith is found to be a development of corollaries of these tenets, and the place of soteriology within his creation faith is explored. Belief in creation raises questions: Does belief in God the Creator have implications for understanding the world and humanity? How are belief in God the Creator and a true understanding of humanity linked? How does creation faith inform Christology?

Some Thomist tenets and Schillebeeckx's development of their corollaries

A first Thomist tenet: God the Creator creates his creation, freely, neither internally nor externally coerced

A corollary of the freedom of God's creative action: Contingency

Aquinas writes,

> When we affirm that God created all things by his Word we exclude the error of those who claim that God produced things ex necessitate naturae – by postulating a procession of love it is shown that God did not produce creatures in virtue of any neediness on his part nor because of any alien cause extrinsic to him, but on account of love of his own goodness (ST 1.32.1, citing Genesis 1:3-4 as so often).[41]

Schillebeeckx affirms God's freedom in creation when he states, 'God freely creates men and women', and he describes God's freedom in his creative action as 'sovereign'.[42] God's total freedom in his creative action means that the creation is contingent.

What are the deeper implications of the freedom of God's creative action which comes about on account of love of his own goodness? Kerr suggests that Aquinas

---

40. Robert J. Schreiter, 'Edward Schillebeeckx: His Continuing Significance', in *The Praxis of the Reign of God: An Introduction to the Theology of Edward Schillebeeckx*, 2nd edn, ed. Mary Catherine Hilkert and Robert J. Schreiter (New York: Fordham University Press, 2002), 185–94 (186). Donald J. Goergen, without according primacy to the soteriological in Schillebeeckx's work, notes, 'An ongoing theological concern for Schillebeeckx is: "In what does salvation consist?"'. Donald J. Goergen, 'Spirituality', in *The Praxis of the Reign of God: An Introduction to the Theology of Edward Schillebeeckx*, 2nd edn, ed. Mary Catherine Hilkert and Robert J. Schreiter (New York: Fordham University Press, 2002), 117–31 (129).

41. Fergus Kerr, *After Aquinas: Versions of Thomism* (Oxford: Blackwell, 2002), 39 (henceforth *After Aquinas*).

42. Schillebeeckx, *GAU*, 104.

was committed 'to curing Christians of the temptation to think that the world (as he would put it) might be the result of some external pressure on the creator or some compensatory expression of the creator's need'.[43] He avers that many people of Aquinas' time did not believe that the creation (or world) is a free sharing of divine bounty, unforced and 'unnecessary', 'simply an expression of love'.[44] It is not altogether idle to speculate how many people in contemporary times believe the creation to be simply an expression of love. Theologically, a keen sense of the freedom of God's creative action entails an awareness of the sheer bounty, gratuity and giftedness of created life. It engenders a sense that human life, existence itself, is an undreamt of, undeserved sharing somehow in Life itself, the Source and End of all life. What Aquinas calls 'God's love of his own goodness',[45] Schillebeeckx refers to as 'God's unfathomable love',[46] and he emphasizes the unconditional nature of it.[47] Through his love expressed in creation, God not only knows and shapes all human hearts but he also wants human beings in their own freedom to grow in awareness of, and respond to his gift of life and so to enter into a conscious and living relationship with him that leads to an ever deepening sharing in his life.

When Schillebeeckx homed in on the contingency of creation, he might well have been taking his cue from many people's feelings of pervasive angst about the world that were prompted by the Second World War and later caused by the rapid social changes of subsequent decades. The idea of contingency struck a deep chord with him. In his year in Paris, in the bleakness of the aftermath of the Second World War, Schillebeeckx came face to face with existentialism, predominantly in the writings of Sartre and Camus, with their twofold emphasis on the human individual's freedom to choose while standing in an absurd and meaningless world. Schillebeeckx takes the fact of contingency, experienced as absurd by the post-war French existentialists, and reflects on it in the light of Christian creation faith. The concept of contingency is, strictly speaking, a philosophical rather than a theological idea but it is one which Schillebeeckx charges with theological meaning. He focuses on two aspects of it: the contingency of the universe itself and contingency within the world in which we find ourselves and which we know. He writes, 'everything might just as well not have been or could have been other than it in fact is' and 'contingency is the essential characteristic of man and the world'.[48] He expands the point:

---

43. Kerr, *After Aquinas*, 39.
44. Ibid.
45. Aquinas, *ST*, 1.32.1.
46. Edward Schillebeeckx, *Church: The Human Story of God*, trans. John Bowden, checked by Ted Schoof, The Collected Works of Edward Schillebeeckx 10 (London: Bloomsbury T&T Clark, 2014), 179 [181] (henceforth *Church*).
47. Edward Schillebeeckx, *Interim Report on the Books Jesus and Christ*, trans. John Bowden, checked and in parts ed. Ted Schoof, The Collected Works of Edward Schillebeeckx 8 (London: Bloomsbury T&T Clark, 2014), 116 [134] (henceforth *IR*).
48. Schillebeeckx, *GAU*, 95.

[Contingency] applies to every phenomenon in this world, in nature and in history. Even institutions, specific historical forms like languages, cultures and civilizations, and even the forms of religions, are mortal: they come and go, so none of us need be surprised that the day comes when in fact they do go. Nothing about this is non-contingent.[49]

Aquinas holds that in creating human beings God communicates his likeness to them in two ways, 'not just in their existing at all, but, "as far as acting is concerned", God creates "so that created things may also have their own actions" (3.69.14)'.[50] Human actions are not free in the way that God's action is free but they are free within the restraints of human finitude. Frederick Christian Bauerschmidt emphasizes the Thomist point that the dependence of the human creature on God does not preclude freedom, that 'creatures are not simply "occasions" for God's exercise of causality, but are genuine causes'.[51] He writes, 'this dependence of creatures on the primary causality of God does not vitiate the causal capacity of creatures, and Aquinas takes Aristotle to have given a compelling account of this capacity in his metaphysics of act and potency'.[52] Drawing on Aquinas' doctrine of double agency, Schillebeeckx develops the idea of the contingency of human actions which is the fact that human beings in their freedom may act one way or the other. By looking at human free will in terms of contingency, Schillebeeckx throws a piercing light on the power and potential of human freedom for openness to God or otherwise. Even if human beings allow themselves to sleep in their freedom, their inaction and its consequences are contingent. Schillebeeckx argues forcefully against fatalism, predeterminism and the avoidance of human responsibility by drawing out the implications of the contingency of human free will. He goes so far as to say that to use God, in a fatalistic way, as an explanation of how things and events are what they are (e.g. to say that disease is a punishment from God or to say that war is inevitable because of how God makes us human beings) would either mean, on the one hand, that any attempt to change things or situations would be blasphemous, or, on the other hand, it would be to turn 'human beings and our whole world into a puppet-show in which God alone holds the strings in his hands behind the screen: human history as a large-scale Muppet show!'.[53] Schillebeeckx understands God's act of creation as the origin of human freedom. He avers, 'Because of God's act of creation, the divine origin of human freedom is essentially incarnate in a bodily life which brings men's freedom into contact with the world of men and things.'[54] He develops the idea of human freedom and the contingency

49. Ibid.
50. Kerr, *After Aquinas*, 45.
51. Frederick Christian Bauerschmidt, *Thomas Aquinas: Faith, Reason, and Following Christ* (Oxford: Oxford University Press, 2013), 50.
52. Ibid.
53. Schillebeeckx, *Church*, 227 [230].
54. Edward Schillebeeckx, *World and Church*, trans. N. D. Smith, The Collected Works of Edward Schillebeeckx 4 (London: Bloomsbury, 2014), 210 [273] (henceforth *W&C*).

of human free will as gifts to be deployed in the world and human society: 'People themselves are the principle of what they do and what they will make of the world and human society – and of what might not have been, yet is, thanks to contingent human free will.'[55] In Christian creation faith the autonomous self-determination of human beings is exercised in 'direct personal relationship with God'.[56] It is 'a responsibility *for* something in that relationship with God'.[57]

Schillebeeckx emphasizes that creation faith does not provide an explanation of how the universe came into being or for the contingencies of the natural world. Natural phenomena might pan out one way or the other and it is the task of human science to observe, explain and predict.[58] In a pre-scientific age, mishaps of nature were attributed to God, most often as punishments inflicted on human beings and sometimes as 'lessons'. The disciples of Jesus ask of the man born blind, 'Who sinned, he or his parents?' to which Jesus answered, 'Neither he nor his parents sinned but [he was born blind] in order that the works of God might be made visible in him.'[59] Even in the scientific age, Schillebeeckx gives the example of a pope, at the beginning of the nineteenth century, who 'condemned the practice of inoculation against smallpox, an illness which at that time was interpreted as a divine punishment … because of a mistaken conception of [the theology of] creation as explanation'.[60] More recently in England, when a bolt of lightning struck York Minster in 1984 and caused a fire that destroyed the roof of the south transept, 'some church goers feared the fire was a sign from God in response to the consecration at the Minster three days earlier of the Bishop of Durham, David Jenkins'. David Jenkins had been reported in the news 'for saying that he did not believe in the physical resurrection of Christ'.[61] After subsequent tests at the Minster, the conclusion reached was that 'the fire was "almost certainly" caused by lightning striking a metal electrical box inside the roof'.[62]

The contingency of facts, as shown, consists of two strands, the events of natural phenomena and the actions of human free will, and these two are intertwined. The natural world and human beings are symbiotic. God creates 'man as the principle of his own human action, who thus himself has to develop the world and its future and bring them into being within contingent situations'.[63] For a healthy symbiosis, to the advantage both of the environment and of humanity, human beings must

---

55. Schillebeeckx, *GAU*, 95.

56. Schillebeeckx, *W&C*, 210 [273].

57. Ibid.

58. Contingency as it relates to natural phenomena is probably the way in which the idea of contingency is mainly understood and used today.

59. Jn 9.3.

60. Schillebeeckx, *GAU*, 96.

61. Lauren Potts, 'Remembering the York Minster Fire 30 years on', BBC News, York and North Yorkshire, 9 July 2014.

62. Ibid.

63. Schillebeeckx, *GAU*, 95.

use their freedom intelligently and unselfishly. Not only is nature contingent but, as a creation, it has limits. Schillebeeckx writes,

> I would say that within all contingency, one concern for humanity is: For what sort of humanity are we ultimately making a choice? ... We have learnt, from irresponsible behaviour, the specific implications of this finitude of nature. ... development is not unlimited, as we have learnt to our shame and to our hurt.[64]

Implications of contingency for Christology

Schillebeeckx's exposition of contingency feeds directly into his Christology. The train of thought, or sequence of ideas, starts with the contingency-of-being of the creation and the concomitant contingency of the actions of human free will; human beings are free for their own task in the world. As Schillebeeckx expresses it,

> Belief in creation sets us free for our own task in the world. Enjoying and loving what is worldly in the world, what is human in man, is enjoying and loving what is divine in God. God's honour lies in the happiness, in the well-being of man in the world, who seeks his honour in God.[65]

Schillebeeckx specifies God's task for humanity as a 'transformation of the world'. He writes, 'The transformation of the world, the development of a better and more tolerable human society and a new earth has been given over into the hands of contingent man.'[66] He then observes that some Christians and others, sometimes and somehow, expect God to solve human problems as though he were a magician.[67] He writes that human beings

> cannot expect God to solve their problems. Given a proper belief in creation, we cannot shift on to God what is our task in the world. ... To overcome suffering and evil wherever we encounter them with all possible scientific and technological means, with the help of our fellow human beings and, if necessary, perhaps (when all other means are exhausted), by rebellion, is our task and our burden within all our finitude and contingency.[68]

This is not a Pelagian rallying cry, rather, it is to apply the fact of the distinction between creature and Creator to an understanding of the sphere and task of humanity. The transformation of the world expressed in New Testament terms is for it to become the kingdom of God. In Schillebeeckx's Christology, Jesus acted in his contingent humanity, in his oneness with God the Father, and transformed the

---

64. Ibid., 99.
65. Schillebeeckx, *IR*, 101 [115–16].
66. Ibid., 96.
67. This raises the question of the nature of petitionary prayer.
68. Schillebeeckx, *Church*, 229 [231]. Cf. *IR*, 103 [118]; *GAU*, 96.

lives of people who needed freeing from one form of oppression or another. Just as we are not muppets, Jesus was not a divine automaton. He had to work out, in his contingent human freedom, which way to act and what to say.

Schillebeeckx avers that it is important to remember the 'sovereign free decision and choice of Jesus'.[69] To forget them can lead to a 'kind of Christology of paradox, between the extreme of the human and the extreme of the divine, passing over the actual narrative of the Gospels'.[70] In this Christology of paradox 'there is often an abstract dialectic between "weak humanity" (*forma servi*, the form of a slave) and the all-powerful God (*forma Dei*), viewed in an unhistorical way'.[71] Jesus was sovereignly free in his human decisions and choices, anguished though these may at times have been for him. The gospels tell of the critical consequence of Jesus' lifelong exercise of his freedom when, in Gethsemane, he knows his enemies are seeking to have him killed and are closing in on him. A man in such circumstances, if he had not gone into hiding before, could have made a last-ditch attempt to escape. Jesus, however, chooses, at this twelfth hour, not to attempt escape and, in human dread at the prospect of his death, does the one thing left to him and prays. He prays that, 'if it were possible, this hour might pass him by. "Abba!" he said, "Everything is possible for you. Take this cup away from me. But let it be as you, not I would have it." '[72]

In the light of Schillebeeckx's caution against a Christology of paradox, what does Jesus' prayer in Gethsemane say about his divinity and humanity and his contingent freedom? Is his divinity one with, united with, his humanity, or, in a conflicted state, does Jesus want one thing in his humanity and another thing in his divinity? To argue *sequela* Schillebeeckx, in the first half of the prayer, Jesus expresses his faith in his Father ('Everything is possible for you'). He does not want to die ('Take this cup away from me'), nor does God the Father want his Son to die a premature death by execution. Contrary to an Anselmian view in which the Father requires the sacrifice of his Son for the reconciliation of humanity to himself, Father and Son are absolutely one in not wanting the horrendous death which awaits Jesus (and, indeed, God is absolutely opposed to anyone's horrendous death). Jesus' is not a prayer of a weak humanity opposed to the Father's will. However, in voicing the second part of the prayer, 'yet not what I want, but what you want', Jesus admits that, if he is to remain faithful to the life that he has lived so far, to escape the consequences of that life and the consequences of the opposition to the message he has consistently proclaimed (by his actions as well as his words) is not an option. It is not an option because it would render everything he has said and done up to that point meaningless. What is it the Father would have him do? It is to live a life consistently witnessing to the truth of God's love to the end, no matter what. Jesus chooses in Gethsemane to remain faithful to his Father and

---

69. Ibid., 123 [124].
70. Ibid.
71. Ibid.
72. Mk 14.35-36.

bear witness to the freely chosen course that led him there, suffering the human consequences of his and his Father's love (they are one) to death. In his prayer his will is one with his Father's, aligned with it, despite his dread at his impending death. The prayer shows a Christology of relational dialectic between the divine and the human rather than a Christology of paradox.

Schillebeeckx shows how Jesus exercised his freedom to 'subject ... both past and present to prophetic criticism' to speak and to act according to God's truth.[73] So, for example, Jesus 'certainly did support the Law as a revelation of God's will [but], in actual fact – when faced with materially concrete demands and circumstances – [he] sometimes overrode its formal requirements, even that of keeping the Sabbath holy, out of humane considerations'.[74] Schillebeeckx describes Jesus 'as a free man whose sovereign freedom was never used to his own advantage but to the advantage of others, specifically as an expression of God's free and loving concern for men'.[75] His was a 'freedom-in-the-service-of-others' which 'was liberating for some people but shocking for others'.[76] Jesus, in his freedom towards the Law and the Sabbath, became a thorn in the flesh of those who imposed the Law with a merciless strictness.[77]

Schillebeeckx's stress on the contingent freedom of Jesus is important for at least two reasons. First, it shows how human freedom was used by Jesus, and is to be used *sequela Jesu*, by his followers to fulfil their human task in this world. Jesus by his words and actions, by his very being, was, in himself, God's salvation: healing, forgiving, liberating the oppressed and imparting a fullness of life. Men and women are no more automatons than Jesus of Nazareth was. God endows them with freedom so that they, like Jesus, may respond to him in that freedom and align their wills with his. Thus, in their own way, they can be vehicles or instruments of God's saving action.

Secondly, Schillebeeckx shows how Jesus, in the way he acted in his sovereign freedom, antagonized the members of the religious establishment of his day to such an extent that they sought to kill him. His execution was not a sacrifice of atonement required by God the Father. Rather, the compassion that Jesus showed to the suffering, including those spurned by the religious establishment, was an indictment of those who imposed the religious rules oppressively and inhumanely. While people flocked to Jesus, members of that establishment became inflamed with anger and with jealousy of Jesus to the point that they found a way to have him put to death.[78] Jesus is the one who embodies, in his words, actions and life, human freedom used to bring in the kingdom of God, 'a new world of suffering removed, a

---

73. Schillebeeckx, *Jesus*, 120 [140].
74. Ibid., 142 [164].
75. Schillebeeckx, *GAU*, 50.
76. Ibid., 51.
77. Ibid., 50–1.
78. Mk 14.1.

world of completely whole or healed men and women'.[79] The work of transformation is for all human beings in their contingent freedom: in every smallest attempt in apparently insignificant situations as well as in obviously critical ones. At the most critical point of Jesus' life, it was in the intimacy of his Sonship with God the Father that he was able to pray in his human agony in Gethsemane, 'But let it be as you, not I, would have it.'[80] Likewise Christians draw their inspiration for discernment in how to use their freedom in the work of transformation from the very heart of their relationship with God: where they find people suffering, they are called to remove or, at least, alleviate that suffering; where there are established systems that cause oppression, they are called to have the courage to use their freedom in living a way of life that is a countercultural critique of those systems.

A corollary of God's creative action: The finitude of the creation

God, for both Aquinas and Schillebeeckx, is Creator and therefore the cause of there being anything not-God, that is to say, anything created. That the universe and human beings within it are created may sound so obvious an article of Christian creation faith and theology as hardly to need remarking on. Schillebeeckx, however, turns the beam of his enquiry onto the implications of the creatureliness or finitude of the created. For Schillebeeckx finitude is a theological idea. He develops the implications of the finitude of the world in two main ways. First, he avers that the limitations of finitude are not flaws and examines what this means. Secondly, he turns the spotlight on the fact that the finitude of the world means that there is nothing that can be introduced between the world and God to interpret their relationship. He looks at what this, in turn, tells us about the Creator God and humanity.

Schillebeeckx gives two main descriptions of what finitude is.[81] The first description is that it is a 'coming and going, mortality, failure, mistakes and ignorance' which are 'part of the normal condition of our humanity'.[82] In the second description Schillebeeckx includes the same content but adds that finitude 'brings with it the burden of subjection and … suffering'.[83] Mortality is the starkest proof of human finitude and creatureliness. The themes of creatureliness and dependency are hardly mainstream in our societies today. Kevin Dillon, writing about the question of the spiritual growth of people with intellectual disabilities, describes the values of modern societies as personal power, independence and

---

79. Edward Schillebeeckx, *Jesus in Our Western Culture: Mysticism, Ethics and Politics*, trans. John Bowden (London: SCM Press, 1987), 19–20 (henceforth *JWC*).

80. Mk 14.36.

81. The word 'descriptions' is used here because the style of Schillebeeckx's theology is not to give definitions. It is, rather, discursive and at the same time multilayered and tightly woven.

82. Schillebeeckx, *GAU*, 92.

83. Ibid., 93. The context of a discussion of finitude suggests that 'subjection' means to be subject to limitations.

self-sufficiency.[84] He draws on Deborah Creamer who writes that 'limits are an intrinsic element of being human' and quotes Stanley Hauerwas who makes the point that our creatureliness necessitates human dependence on each other (quite apart from the question of our dependence on God):

> We are creatures. Dependency, not autonomy, is one of the ontological characteristics of our lives. That we are creatures ... is but a reminder that we are created for and with one another. We are not just accidentally communal, but we are such by necessity.[85]

When listed together the limits of human finitude that Schillebeeckx identifies may, on the one hand, make for a gloomy sense of powerlessness. It is such a sense of powerlessness in the face of finitude that may lead to dualism or atheistic existentialism. On the other hand, in the light of Christian creation faith, the gift of life comes with its conditions of finitude which are seen as the very material for realizing the potential of full humanity. They are the hard, dry clay out of which human beings work, in dependence on God, to transform lives and the world with creative inventiveness. The hard clay is watered, so to speak, by human love and ingenuity as the antidote to need and ignorance. In Christian creation faith, the direction and purpose of human love, inventiveness and perseverance is to bring about God's kingdom in the light of that faith in order to further human flourishing. When the consequences of bereavement, failure, mistakes and ignorance seem overwhelming, Christian hope and trust in God is the fuel of transformation which shows the way through.

It is precisely in recognizing their limits that human beings may have intimations of the divine. In Christian creation faith, human limits are responded to with an understanding of our creaturely relation to, and relationship with God. In dependence on God, trust is placed in his Spirit as the source of empowerment to work creatively within the constraints of finitude. Schillebeeckx avers that 'the basic mistake of many misconceptions about creation lies in the fact that finitude is felt to be a flaw, a hurt which as such should not really have been one of the features of this world'.[86] The distinction between the limits of finitude and sin and its consequences is crucial. Human finitude, the limits of being human, are not in themselves sinful although a failure to recognize human finitude can give rise

---

84. Kevin Dillon, 'The Spiritual Growth of People with Intellectual Disabilities: Jean Vanier and John of the Cross' (unpublished doctoral dissertation, Heythrop College, University of London, 2016), emailed to Rhona Lewis, 13 June 2016, p. 63.

85. Dillon, 'The Spiritual Growth of People with Intellectual Disabilities', p. 64. Deborah Creamer, *Disability and Christian Theology* (New York: Oxford University Press, 2009), 31; Stanley Hauerwas, 'Timeful Friends: Living with the Handicapped', in *Critical Reflections on Stanley Hauerwas' Theology of Disability: Disabling Society, Enabling Theology*, ed. John Swinton (New York: Routledge, 2004), 11–25 (16).

86. Schillebeeckx, *GAU*, 92 (cf. *IR* 99).

to a hubristic and, therefore, sinful attitude. The fact that some human beings 'do not want to accept their finitude [but] hanker after that which is not finitude, after immortality and omniscience, so that they can be like God', Schillebeeckx says, is the 'so-called primal sin of mankind' which is described in the Genesis story.[87] In the same breath Schillebeeckx underlines the goodness of creation: 'Humanity and the world are not the result of a fall, an apostasy from God, nor are they a failure, much less a testing ground in expectation of better times.'[88] Human beings are limited by the constraints of finitude and may, also, too often become enmeshed in the consequences of their sinful actions, which affect the world, but the creation is not flawed.

In contrast to a view in which the world and humanity are seen as intrinsically flawed, Schillebeeckx vehemently and laconically affirms the worth of the world. Human ambition should be 'simply [to] want to be human beings in a world which is simply the world'.[89] Or elsewhere, 'We may and must simply be human beings in a living world which is simply the world: fascinating, but also mortal, failing, suffering.'[90] A conception of the world as flawed may cause a retreat from the world into a kind of spiritual escapism which has 'often brought [Christians] to a dead end, above all in the sphere of Christian action'.[91] The dead end to which Schillebeeckx refers is a kind of privatized piety which barely ventures into acts of charity let alone seeks to change oppressive social structures. Creation faith, 'truly experienced, in no way encourages a privatized view'.[92]

The immediacy of God's presence: Creatio ex nihilo

In a sentence in which Schillebeeckx seems to be using the terms 'finitude' and 'contingency' interchangeably, he writes, 'Finitude or contingency mean that people and the world are in and of themselves in a complete vacuum. There is nothing that can be introduced between the world and God to interpret their relationship.'[93] For the existentialist, apart from the world, there is only a vacuum: there is no God in or beyond it (to use the human language of place to talk about God). The material world with the limit of its finitude, and the suffering and ravages caused by destructive human behaviour, is the sum of reality. Patrick McCarthy writes of the popular version of existentialism which Schillebeeckx encountered in Paris and which made Sartre and Camus famous, 'Since life made no sense … each man must give [his own] meaning to his individual existence.'[94]

87. Ibid.
88. Ibid., 93.
89. Ibid., 92.
90. Ibid., 93.
91. Ibid., 91.
92. Ibid., 102.
93. Ibid., 93.
94. Patrick McCarthy, *Camus: A Critical Study of His Life and Work* (London: Hamish Hamilton, 1982), 202.

Existentialism predisposes to limitless pessimism. Albert Camus affirms that 'in existentialist philosophy there is a tendency to depict an actionless, reactionless anguish where the man of anguish never transcends the anguish, which is his highest achievement'.[95] But for Schillebeeckx human apprehension of the vacuum of contingency and finitude has the reverse effect in Christian creation faith: the belief that 'nothing can be introduced between the world and God to interpret their relationship' means the opposite of anguish and limitless pessimism. Rather, God's creative action ex nihilo means that he is absolutely present in and with the finite. Creation is a theological concept and means God's nearness and involvement with our reality, not just that God was the force that started it. To keep created things in existence is, at the same time, to provide what is needed for existence. In a God-centred (*theologaal*)[96] intersubjective relationship of faith with God, the link between God's creative action and saving action is experienced as, and proves to be, a creative spring that leads to fuller life. The more a person grows in a *theologaal* relationship with God, the more (s)he becomes whole or saved. God's creating for Schillebeeckx is not a 'chronological beginning moment in human history' but, on the contrary, is an ongoing reality 'by which the personal presence of God is established [non-pantheistically] in all things'.[97] Kennedy describes the ontological relation of finite human creatures to the transcendent God in these words:

> Human beings can never live outside the divine creation. By their very nature as creatures, they live in God, as it were: In reality 'we are taken up into a living communion with God, we live, have our being, and move in the rhythm of the divine life. We dwell in God, as in our own house'.[98]

As Schillebeeckx expresses it elsewhere, '[Creation faith] has this finitude taken up into the presence of God, without relieving the world and man of their finitude or regarding these as hostile'.[99] Schillebeeckx calls this presence of God 'the absolute presence of God' and 'the absolute saving presence of God'.[100] In the inseparable linking of creation with the 'absolute saving presence of God' Schillebeeckx gives equal weight to God's creative action and his saving action.

The idea of God's absolute presence with his creatures in their finitude as the inseparable and reverse side of the coin of creation, so to speak, sounds somewhat cerebral. Schillebeeckx, in reading Aquinas, understands the language of metaphysics that Aquinas uses, and he engages in his world of abstract categories

---

95. Ibid., 252.
96. Schillebeeckx uses the word *theologaal*, a neologism in both Dutch and English.
97. Kennedy, *Deus Humanissimus*, 104.
98. Ibid., 104–5, quoting Edward Schillebeeckx in *Revelation and Theology*, trans. N. D. Smith, The Collected Works of Edward Schillebeeckx 2 (London: Bloomsbury, 2014), 291 [109] (henceforth *R&T*).
99. Schillebeeckx, *GAU*, 93.
100. Ibid., and in Schillebeeckx, *Church*, 229 [231].

of Aristotelian causation. What may seem singularly lacking to a contemporary person in reading Aquinas' account of creation faith, and even Schillebeeckx's development of the ideas of contingency and finitude, is a sense of God's love as a motive and mark of his creative action. The word 'love' is famously multivalent in today's English. How does the love of the Creator, powerfully and repeatedly given expression in the Old Testament in personalistic terms, feature in Aquinas' account? Brian Davies compares the human idea of love with God's divine love. He says human love normally suggests a preoccupation, emotional involvement and some sort of need for the one(s) loved. Aquinas, he says, 'would find it absurd or even blasphemous to suppose that God is affected by or in need of anything other than what is divine'.[101] God creates not from need, to have creatures to love or to be loved, but 'by no other act than the pure act he is as *ipsum esse* for no other act is capable of such a singular effect'.[102] For Aquinas, 'will, of its nature, involves love':

> For the first motion of will, indeed of any power of appetition, is love … It is like their very root. No one desires an object or rejoices in it unless it be a good that is loved … On this account wherever there is appetite or will there must be love; take away the foundation and nothing else is left.[103]

Despite the human limitations in talking about God's divine love for human beings, Aquinas writes,

> But God's love evokes and creates the goodness in things. The lover in loving the good of the beloved and planning and working for it as though the beloved was himself, is transported out of himself into the beloved; and we must dare to say with pseudo-Denys that in the abundance of his loving kindness and providence for everything that exists, God too is ecstatic with love.[104]

Encrypted, as it were, within Schillebeeckx's statement that the creative action of God is 'balanced by the absolute presence of God in and with the finite' is God's limitless, unconditional, ecstatic and constant love for humanity which wills the happiness of human beings. That happiness increases in an ever-strengthening sense of the 'living communion [we have] with God', in whom 'we live',[105] which, in turn, is a mark of the growing closeness of our human relationship with him.

---

101. Brian Davies, *The Thought of Thomas Aquinas* (Oxford: Clarendon Press, 1992), 150.

102. Thomas G. Weinandy, *Does God Suffer?* (Notre Dame, IN: University of Notre Dame Press, 2000), 132–3.

103. Davies, *The Thought of Thomas Aquinas*, 150, quoting *ST*, 1a. 20.1.

104. St Thomas Aquinas, *Summa Theologiae*, A Concise Translation, ed. Timothy McDermott (Notre Dame, IN: Christian Classics, 1991), 54 (henceforth *ST*, ed. McDermott).

105. Kennedy, *Deus Humanissimus*, 104–5.

Implications of the finitude of creation for Christology

How do these two aspects of the finitude of the creation (that it is not flawed and that there is nothing that can be introduced between the world and God to interpret their relationship) feed into Schillebeeckx's Christology? That finitude is not a flaw means that the creation is not a place of punishment and separation from God. This in turn means that understandings of the Incarnation must break out of an Anselmian soteriology. Sin did not cause the Incarnation although, through it, human beings experience God's mercy in the concreteness of Jesus' forgiveness of sinners. In his Incarnation in Jesus Christ, God reveals his love most explicitly. In and through the humanity of his Son, God lifted, and lifts, men and women out of the entanglements of sin and shows the extent and depth of his saving purposes. St John gives the reason for the Incarnation as love: 'God so loved the world that he gave his only Son.'[106] It is about God's love for humanity, and his desire that it should flourish and enjoy life in all its fullness and happiness, through forgiveness of sin and working with God for the transformation of the world.

Secondly, that the absolute presence of God is the inseparable, reverse side of the coin of God's creative action is embodied in Jesus Christ. Schillebeeckx writes that in Jesus the earliest Christians experienced salvation and new life equally. Of God's saving presence experienced in Jesus, Schillebeeckx writes, '[In the New Testament] Christians expressed their belief in the decisive, God-given salvation in Jesus which they had experienced.'[107] He reiterates this claim when he writes, 'In the New Testament ... we have the testimony of people who found salvation – or grace – explicitly imparted by God in Jesus of Nazareth.'[108] So true and radical was these people's experience of God's salvation in Jesus that Schillebeeckx uses the metaphor of enchantment to convey the nature of their fellowship with him: 'the factors inspiring the tradition about Jesus [recorded in the New Testament] lie in his personal fellowship with his disciples during his lifetime, ... who came under the spell of his person, message and ministry'.[109] Of the new life that Jesus, after his resurrection, continued, and continues, to give, he writes,

> The only knowledge we possess of the Christ event reaches us via the concrete experience of the first local communities of Christians, who sensed a new life present in themselves, which they regarded as a gift of the Pneuma, the Spirit: an experience of new life in the ambience of the Spirit, but in remembrance of Jesus.[110]

---

106. Jn 3.16. Raymond E. Brown points out that 'in 1 John the love is oriented toward Christians ("we") while in John iii.16 [here] God loves the world. In all other examples in John, God's love is directed to the disciples'. *The Gospel According to John I-XII*, a new translation with introduction and commentary by Raymond E. Brown, The Anchor Bible 29 (New York: Doubleday, 1966), 133.
107. Ibid., 18 [36].
108. Ibid., 83 [103].
109. Schillebeeckx, *Jesus*, 52 [72].
110. Schillebeeckx, *Jesus*, 28 [45].

It is in the power of that same new life that Christians continue to experience God's saving forgiveness and power in Jesus Christ.

A note on Schillebeeckx's use of the terms contingency and finitude

It is helpful to note that the way in which Schillebeeckx uses the two words *contingency* and *finitude* is the cause of some debate. Does Schillebeeckx use the terms interchangeably, as synonyms? Or, for him, do the terms *contingency* and *finitude* denote different things? Or, does he pair them as different aspects of one thing? Each of these positions can be argued from what he writes about creation. As noted above, he gives two similar descriptions of *finitude*. Meantime he slips in the term *contingency* without any introduction to its meaning. At first Schillebeeckx could be said to appear to use the terms interchangeably, for example, '[Christian creation] belief means that we do not need altogether to transcend our contingent or finite nature and to escape from it or regard it as a flaw'.[111] Real confusion, or inconsistency, seems to start when he next writes of contingency 'as the essential characteristic of man and the world' and, two sentences later, writes, 'Here the most essential aspect of all historicity is neglected, i.e. finitude: everything might just as well not have been or could have been other than it in fact is.'[112] The definition, 'everything might just as well not have been or could have been other than it in fact is' is patently a definition of what is commonly understood to be contingency. It is the first time Schillebeeckx gives such a definition in the chapter on God the Creator in *God Among Us*. It is difficult to see, however, how it can be argued to be a definition of finitude especially when measured against Schillebeeckx's own descriptions of what he means by finitude given earlier in the chapter. For those who argue that Schillebeeckx uses the terms *finitude* and *contingency* interchangeably, the last sentence quoted, within its original context, provides evidence. For those who argue that Schillebeeckx does not do so, there are three ways of dealing with this sentence: either to say that it is a mistake or a misprint, or to argue that Schillebeeckx was being relaxed in the way that he was using the terms, or to argue that for Schillebeeckx one of the two (contingency and finitude) perhaps encompasses the other.

Two scholars take different positions on the question of how Schillebeeckx uses the terms *finitude* and *contingency*. Kennedy considers that Schillebeeckx uses the terms interchangeably. In 1993 he wrote, 'To speak of finitude, contingency or immanence, is simply to refer to human beings' experiences of their limitations or mortality.'[113] By 2002, Kennedy avers, 'In effect, the terms *finitude* and *contingency*

---

111. Ibid., 93.
112. Ibid., 95.
113. Kennedy, *Schillebeeckx*, 80. 'Immanence' is here being used in a philosophical as opposed to a theological sense to mean 'finite, limited, historical human existence is the only existence which prevails, for there are neither supernatural potencies, nor values nor a personal Creator-God existing apart from and beyond the worldly, profane existence in which human beings find themselves'. Ibid.

serve as synonyms in his [Schillebeeckx's] writings and are freely interchanged.'[114] Kennedy, however, does not give an argument to support his position. Poulsom, on the other hand, comes to a different conclusion and presents a convincing case to support his position. He argues that Schillebeeckx proposes 'a relational dialectic of finitude and contingency' in dialogue with his atheistic, secular humanist interlocutors. He writes that in the first stage of the dialogue, Schillebeeckx uses the terms *finitude* and *contingency* interchangeably. 'He is willing to say that considering the world and humanity in and of itself (which is all that the atheist is willing to do) finitude and contingency mean living suspended over the gulf of absolute nothingness.'[115] When, however, Schillebeeckx goes on to express 'what contingency and finitude mean "from a Christian perspective"', Poulsom explains that in speaking of finitude, Schillebeeckx 'no longer brackets out the active presence of the Creator in creation [which] means that both the experience and the Christian concept of finitude have a depth-dimension that contingency does not have, one that depends on "the relation" of creation'.[116] What Schillebeeckx, therefore, does is to use the terms for two different stages of dialogue; in the first stage he uses them interchangeably but, in the second stage of his dialogue, finitude, as understood by Christians, has a depth dimension that the term 'contingency' does not have.

A second Thomist tenet: Every created thing is intrinsically good

Kerr states how 'Thomas repeatedly insists on the goodness of the created order. Again and again, he resists views which he suspects of Catharist dualism.'[117] Davies tells how at the heart of Aquinas' thinking is the conclusion that everything that exists is good. He quotes Aquinas,

> For everything, inasmuch as it exists, is actual and therefore in some way perfect, all actuality being a sort of perfection. Now ... anything perfect is desirable and good. It follows then that, inasmuch as they exist, all things are good.[118]

Josef Pieper describes how Aquinas makes a strong theological affirmation of the material world including, above all, the human body, and defines himself against both the 'spiritualistic, symbolistic unworldliness of [his] age's traditional theology' and the 'radical, secularistic worldliness of heterodox Aristotelianism'.[119]

114. Kennedy, 'God and Creation', in *The Praxis of the Reign of God: An Introduction to the Theology od Edward Schillebeeckx*, ed Mary Catherine Hilkert and Robert J. Schreiter (New York: Fordham University Press, 2002), 37–58 (48).
115. Poulsom, *Dialectics*, 137.
116. Ibid., 138.
117. Kerr, *After Aquinas*, 86.
118. Davies, *The Thought of Thomas* Aquinas, p. 86, quoting *ST*, 1a. 5. 3.
119. Josef Pieper, *Guide to Thomas Aquinas*, trans. Richard and Clara Winston (San Francisco, CA: Ignatius Press, 1991), 131–2.

Rudi te Velde writes that what seems to him most characteristic of Aquinas' view of creation is

> his conviction that any devaluation of the world of creatures means, in fact, derogation of the power of the Creator himself. Thinking disparagingly of creatures, even if this happens with a view to highlighting God's greatness and perfection, actually comes down to demeaning God.[120]

A corollary of the goodness of the material creation: The world in its worldliness is the place of spiritual worship of God

In order to explore Schillebeeckx's understanding of 'the world' and 'worldliness' it is helpful to examine what he writes in a lecture that he gave on Church liturgy.[121] He chose not to give his lecture the simple title 'Church Liturgy' but instead he called it 'Secular Worship and Church Liturgy'.[122] This pairing by Schillebeeckx of what, at first glance, may appear to be opposites (secular and Church) indicates precisely the special character of Schillebeeckx's theological thinking and writing. Poulsom, in an investigation of the philosophical components of Christian creation faith, analyses the pattern of Schillebeeckx's thinking as 'relational dialectic', a term which he devises. He writes, 'In Schillebeeckx's relational dialectic, the constituent elements are not considered as polar opposites but aspects, allowing them to be described as mutually co-constitutive.'[123] Schillebeeckx, in his characteristic resistance to the distorting polarization of a question under debate, sees Church liturgy as being in a relational dialectic with what he calls 'secular worship'.

Schillebeeckx first argues, citing quotes from New Testament epistles, that 'Christian life in the world, being concerned with the world, and practising human solidarity must ... be for the Christian, *worship* of God, glorifying God's name.'[124] The first scriptural quote in support of his argument is St Paul's exhortation to the Christians of Rome that 'they should present their lives "as a living sacrifice, holy and acceptable to God" and as "spiritual worship"'.[125] The word 'lives' in St Paul's Greek is 'bodies', *sōmata*, in the 'Semitic sense of all that belongs to man, the human person with all its secular implications. As a "body" man is with others in the world. This totality, the "world", as St. Paul said, is the place of "spiritual worship".'[126]

---

120. Rudi te Velde, *Aquinas on God: The 'Divine Science' of the Summa Theologiae* (Farnham: Ashgate, 2006), 123.

121. Schillebeeckx gave his lecture on liturgy on his lecture tour in the United States in 1967. As a result of repeated requests, he published all the lectures of that tour and they appear in *God the Future of Man*, trans. N. D. Smith, The Collected Works of Edward Schillebeeckx 3 (London: Bloomsbury, 2014) (henceforth *GFoM*).

122. Ibid., 55.

123. Poulsom, *Dialectics*, 96.

124. Schillebeeckx, *GFoM*, 59 [99].

125. Ibid., 59 [98].

126. Ibid., 59 [98–9].

Secondly, Schillebeeckx argues from a statement in the Epistle to the Hebrews. He writes that the death of Jesus on the cross was not a Church liturgy but the execution of Jesus who 'gave his life for his own in a secular combination of circumstances'.[127] He avers that 'Calvary was … an hour of human life, which Jesus experienced as worship', an hour of the human life of Jesus 'situated in history and in the world'.[128] The words 'experienced as worship' are condensed. They do not mean that Jesus' death was liturgical worship. Least of all do they mean that Jesus' death was a sacrifice required by God the Father. Schillebeeckx himself writes that we are redeemed 'despite the crucifixion'.[129] By the words 'experienced as worship' Schillebeeckx means that the excruciating torture that Jesus suffered in his passion and death was the culmination and the consequence of the way he lived his life in total faithfulness to his Father. His life, lived from day to day in the world of his time, in its very faithfulness was worship of God; his death, a direct consequence of the way he lived his life in faithfulness to God, therefore, was also worship of God. It was part and parcel of a life lived wholly in accordance with God's will and, in that sense, something made holy, a 'sacrifice'. Schillebeeckx explains that the author of Hebrews applied to Jesus' death the cultic categories of Jewish religion under the Old Law and it was in this way that 'the new concept of worship came into being'. Life as lived in the world, and death, the inevitable experience of every human being, were 'endowed with their sacred character'.[130]

The crux of Schillebeeckx's argument, therefore, is that daily life lived in the world, that is, secular life, must itself be a 'spiritual worship'. From the Christian point of view, worldly activity is an intrinsic part of the Christian's whole-life worship of God. Any 'cleavage between worldly activity and liturgical worship is a disaster, and … this gap must be bridged'.[131] The world is God-given. 'God is, after all, the creator of the secular sphere, and he does not take back with his left hand what he has given to us with his right.'[132] The world that is his creation is his precious gift to humanity, to be treated as such by his human creatures. 'A religion which is not at the same time secular [i.e. worldly], then, can hardly be called authentic.'[133]

Aquinas and Schillebeeckx both see the world, prayer and the Church's worship as inextricably linked. For Schillebeeckx prayer and the Church's liturgy must be rooted in the realities of life. The realities of life (the world) are the very materials

---

127. Ibid., 59 [99].

128. Ibid.

129. Edward Schillebeeckx, *Christ: The Christian Experience in the Modern World*, trans. John Bowden, checked by Ted Schoof, new section trans. Marcelle Manley (London: Bloomsbury, 2014), 722 [729] (henceforth *Christ*).

130. Schillebeeckx, *GFoM*, 59 [100].

131. Ibid., 57 [96].

132. Ibid., 58 [98].

133. Ibid.

out of which prayer and the Church's worship (from the human end) are made. Schillebeeckx supports this argument of his by quoting Aquinas:

> Thomas Aquinas could say that 'visiting widows and orphans' (the typically medieval form of social concern for one's fellow-men, which could be translated into modern terms as help for the underdeveloped countries, Christian protest against racial discrimination and all forms of injustice) was itself worship, the glorifying of God's name.[134]

Schillebeeckx writes that for Aquinas 'holiness and prayer are essentially identical with concern for one's fellow-men in the world'.[135]

Implications for Christology of the world in its worldliness being a place of spiritual worship of God

How does Schillebeeckx's understanding of the dialectic of the secular and the sacred inform his Christology? The creation is God-made and good. In his sustaining creative action God is constantly present to, and intimately involved in his creation although we cannot see him in a directly visible way. Before Jesus' time, the place of encounter with God for the Jewish people was the Temple. When Jesus came, he himself was the presence of God among us. As Schillebeeckx writes, 'Jesus replaces the Temple as the medium of a relationship with God. … Just as the Temple was God's presence on earth, so Jesus Christ becomes God's presence among us.'[136] Jesus came not to perform a sacrifice of atonement within a spoilt creation but to be, and, through his words and actions, to bring God's actual saving presence, effective among all the men and women whom he met and who were open to him. In the three years of his public ministry, he engaged with people and involved himself in their lives within the fabric of the world. His task, in biblical shorthand, was to bring in his Father's kingdom which in longhand means that he forgave sinners, healed the sick and afflicted, brought in the marginalized, rescued the condemned, engaged with the ostracized, the poor, the rich and the in-between. In short, he saved people from the weight of their oppression and set them free into fullness of life. He taught people how to do things in God's way, preaching powerfully in parables drawn from nature and the common activities of human life. He lived in community with his disciples, he enjoyed friendships with men and women, he noticed and included children, he observed the widow entering the Temple and emptying her purse into the offering box. He challenged religious hypocrites who, with their rigid insistence on obeying the rules to the letter, made life a misery for some of the Jewish faithful. His involvement with people in all their worldly activities and conditions, so that he removed their suffering, in accordance with his Father's will, was a continual, spiritual sacrifice

---

134. Ibid., 65 [107–8].
135. Ibid., 65 [108] with footnote 28 reference to *ST* II-II, q. 81, a. 8.
136. Schillebeeckx, *Jesus*, 217 [245].

in praise of God.[137] From his unique and indivisible unity with the Father, Jesus of Nazareth gives the fullest revelation of God's nature and activity. Jesus' words and actions were the expression and enactment of God's overriding concern for human beings. In Jesus, God sets his seal on the worth of every human being, whatever their particular context within the world, so that they may be freed to offer their daily life in spiritual worship of God.

After the resurrection, God continues to enact his salvation in and through Christ. St Paul uses the metaphor of the Church as the Body of Christ, in order to say that Christ is effecting his salvation in and through his followers who are, as it were, 'his fingers and muscles, the cells of his body'.[138] Christ's saving action is present in the world through the power of the Holy Spirit, operative through his followers, members of the Church, who aim to live their lives, *sequela Jesu*, as a 'living sacrifice holy and acceptable to God which is [their] spiritual worship'.[139] This way of life means engaging as wholeheartedly with the worldliness of the world, each in his or her context, as Jesus did: sensing the sacredness of the world, with all its resources, as a gift from God to be appreciated and protected and working to overcome suffering wherever it is encountered.

A third Thomist tenet: Createdness is simply the relatedness of creatures to the Creator as source of their being

In Aquinas' time a keenly debated question among theologians was whether the world was eternal or had a beginning.[140] Aristotle, who held that 'an unchanged changer or unmoved mover' must be the cause of the existence of the world, 'also argued that there was no temporally first event – that the world had no beginning in time'.[141] In his response to the question, Aquinas melds an article of faith with philosophy. Basing the theological part of his answer on his interpretation of the Genesis account of creation, he says, 'That God is the creator of a world that began to be is an article of faith,' and he adds, '[It] is held through revelation alone, and cannot be demonstrated'.[142] Philosophically the question could not be settled. Frederick Christian Bauerschmidt states that 'the [faith] claim that the world is created is first and foremost a claim about its relation to God, and not about its life history'.[143] Aquinas writes,

137. Rom. 12.1.
138. C. S. Lewis, *Mere Christianity* (New York: HarperCollins, 2001), 63–4.
139. Rom. 12.1.
140. The question of the world's beginning was much discussed at the University of Paris during the thirteenth century. Davies, *The Thought of Thomas* Aquinas, 37, citing John F. Wippel, *Metaphysical Themes in Thomas Aquinas* (Washington, DC: CUA Press, 1984), 192 f.
141. Davies, *The Thought of Thomas* Aquinas, 36.
142. Ibid., Reference *ST*, 1a.46.2.
143. Bauerschmidt, *Thomas Aquinas*, 112.

> [When we think and talk of creation] making and being made are more appropriate terms than changing and being changed, since what they directly signify is the relatedness of cause to effect and effect to cause, with change implied only on one side. The createdness of creatures is simply their relatedness to their Creator as source of their being.[144]

As Kerr explains, 'creatures are really related to God in the sense that we are totally dependent on God as the one who keeps us in being.'[145]

Aquinas, in his discussion of the relatedness of the Persons within the Trinity, writes, 'The very idea of relatedness involves over-againstness one to other, and thus distinctness.'[146] McDermott's translation of *oppositio* as 'over-againstness' deliberately avoids the polarizing import of 'opposition'. It is 'over-againstness' one *to* other, not one *against* the other/another. If the ideas of relatedness and its concomitant *oppositio* are transferred from discussion of the Trinity to the Creator and creatures, it means that the relatedness of creature to Creator, which involves a distinction, is the ontological framework which makes relationship possible. A down-to-earth, horticultural image that could be useful here is of a cold frame (a structure which, in fact, protects from hostile cold). The frame represents the ontological relatedness of Creator to creature. It provides the light and warm air necessary for seeds to germinate and grow into plants. Similarly, the relatedness of creatures to Creator is the framework which provides the setting for the germination of faith and its growth into relationship between God the Creator and his human creatures. 'Over-againstness one to another' has an antiphonal ring to it and suggests the to and fro of God calling out his invitation to humanity and humanity's answering. What is generated in the interaction between the Creator and the creature is a germination of faith, a growth of new life.

Robert Sokolowski summarizes the wider and fuller sense of creation by pairing relationship with the distinction of the Creator and the creature. He posits creation as the starting point for understanding what he calls the relationship between the world and God (he conflates the distinct ideas of relation and relationship in the one word relationship):

> We can discuss [creation] not in its character of being a beginning, but as establishing a distinction and a relationship, a distinction and relationship that remain after the beginning. We can discuss creation as that which defines how we are to understand God, how we are to understand the world, and how we are

---

144. Thomas Aquinas, *ST*, ed. McDermott, 85–6.
145. Fergus Kerr, *Thomas Aquinas: A Very Short Introduction* (Oxford: Oxford University Press, 2009), 54.
146. Thomas Aquinas, *ST*, ed. McDermott, 67.

to understand the [relation and ensuing] relationship between the world and God.[147]

A corollary of the relatedness of the creature to the Creator: The relationship of dialogue between God and the human person and how it informs Christology

Schillebeeckx, along with Aquinas, professes the relatedness of God the Creator to created human beings, a sine qua non of creation faith. Schillebeeckx avers that God's creative action, with its inbuilt ontological relatedness of creatures to Creator, of its very self initiates a relationship between God and human beings. He says, '[humanity's] creation is the beginning of a relationship of dialogue between God and the human person. This creation is unique, an absolutely new beginning which calls into being a direct relationship with God.'[148] Schillebeeckx's understanding of the relatedness of Creator and creature and its potential and intended fulfilment in relationship feed straight into his Christology. In three paired statements he makes clear and stresses the indissoluble link between God-Creator and humanity as expressed supremely in the life, death and resurrection of his Son, Jesus. The pairs of statements are as follows:

Creation: God-Creator	Christology: God-Man
Creation is an act in which God places us in our finite, non-divine state.	At the same time, God gives himself in unselfish love.
Creation is an act in which God destines us for true humanity.	At the same time God gives himself as our salvation and our happiness, the supreme content of true and good humanity.
God freely creates men and women for their own salvation and happiness.	In the same creative action God wants to be the deepest meaning, the salvation and happiness of human life.[149]

The first statement in each pair is an articulation of an element of creation faith. Each of the second, corresponding statements tells how God the Creator fulfils his purpose in creation through his Incarnation in the creaturely limited, historical humanity of Jesus. In the first pair of statements above, Jesus is understood as embodying God the Creator's giving of himself in unselfish love. Jesus expresses the self-gift of God in creation. The ontological relatedness of God's creative action in which he gives us life and places us in our finite, non-divine state becomes in Jesus, Son of God, a human life given wholly and utterly to God's care and concern for people, to the point of giving his life. Schillebeeckx writes, 'All that matters to

---

147. Robert Sokolowski, 'Creation and Christian Understanding', in *God and Creation: An Ecumenical Symposium*, ed. David B. Burrell and Bernard McGinn (Notre Dame, IN: University of Notre Dame Press, 1990), 179–92 (179).
148. Schillebeeckx, *W&C*, 187 [244].
149. These statements come from Schillebeeckx, *GAU*, 104.

Jesus is people in their relationship to God, and God in his care and concern for people.'[150]

In the first statement of the second pair, God the Father creates us in order that we grow into true and full humanity; this is his destiny for us. Jesus is the person in whom this creative purpose of God is realized. He is the human embodiment of what God destines all human beings for: true and good humanity. In his own contingent historical context, Jesus lived a life that was supremely true and good in its humanity. In living the most human of lives Jesus Christ brings salvation and happiness from God. Schillebeeckx repeatedly stresses the beneficent effect that Jesus had on those who were drawn to him. Compared with the tenor of the rest of his theological language, the words Schillebeeckx uses to describe the effect of Jesus on those who were not hostile to him are poetically metaphorical: Jesus enchanted them, people were spellbound by him.[151] In using these words Schillebeeckx is not referring to the kind of adulation that Jesus experienced on Palm Sunday or to the kind of celebrity worship that is common today. The enchantment or spellbinding effect of Jesus is earthed concretely in what he says, in what he does and in who he is and, at the same time, it intimates undreamt of, genuine happiness.[152] He always pointed away from himself towards his Father. What makes for or constitutes the supreme content of true and good humanity in Jesus? It is his relationships in two directions: the relationship, within the divine source of both his divine and his human being, that is, with his Father, and the relationships he had on earth with those whom he knew. If we, in our turn, are open to God, the creative source of our being, through the medium of friendship with Jesus Christ, we are on the road to salvation and happiness. The relationship of friendship with Jesus on earth, and with the Spirit of the risen Christ, makes possible 'the supreme content of true and good humanity', each in our own context, which is the purpose of God's creative action.

In the third pair of statements, God creates men and women for their own salvation and happiness and he wants to be that salvation and happiness for them in their human lives. Jesus on earth revealed the salvation and happiness that is the meaning of God the Father's creative action. Again and again Schillebeeckx says that those who knew Jesus, or who came across him, experienced salvation, and

---

150. Schillebeeckx, *Jesus*, 130 [151].

151. Ibid., 180 [205].

152. Jesus pointed not only from himself to God the Father but also from his mother to God the Father. Once, when he was speaking to crowds of listeners, a woman was so moved by what he was saying, and by whom that revealed him to be, that she raised her voice and blessed his mother: 'Blessed the womb that bore you and the breasts you sucked.' Jesus answered, 'Rather, blessed are those who hear the word of God and keep it.' Lk. 11.27-28. Joseph A. Fitzmyer, in his comment on these verses, describes the woman as 'being charmed by his eloquence'. *The Gospel According to Luke*, ed. Joseph A. Fitzmyer, The Anchor Bible 28A (Garden City, NY: Doubleday, 1985), 927.

the happiness that goes with it, in him, from God.[153] His life provided the deepest human meaning which was, at the same time, religious meaning: In Jesus people 'began to recognize God's face'.[154] In Jesus Christ relatedness to God becomes relationship with God which is the deepest meaning, the salvation and happiness of human life.

Conclusion

Schillebeeckx found the sources of Christology in his contemplation of Thomist tenets of creation faith. That the creation is good, and that the finitude of creation and humanity within it is not a flaw, obviates a dualistic understanding of the world. God gave his Son to the world not to fight some abstract force of evil but to make himself present and bring salvation in the humanity of Jesus of Nazareth. On earth the culmination of the expression of Jesus' love for humanity was his death by crucifixion. Jesus in his contingent humanity, with his contingent free will, acted to bring in his Father's kingdom, a new world of oppression removed and sin forgiven. Just as the absolute saving presence of God is inseparable from his creative action, so, in Jesus, those who did not resist him had an extraordinary experience of new life inseparable from their being made whole. In Jesus' living of his life in the world of his time and place, he showed the world to be a place of spiritual worship of God and set God's seal on humanity as something sacred. In Jesus is seen the supreme and unique form of human relationship with God. By the very relatedness of the creature to Creator every human being is invited, through Christ, into a close and living relationship with God in order to experience, through salvation and happiness, the deepest meaning of human life.

---

153. For example, 'Christians [of Jesus' time] expressed their belief in the decisive, God-given salvation-in-Jesus which they had experienced' (*Jesus*, 18 [36]). 'Living contact with this person [Jesus] who proclaimed the kingdom of God was experienced as God-given salvation' (*Jesus*, 507 [545]).

154. Schillebeeckx, *Church*, 8.

Chapter 2

CHRISTIAN ANTHROPOLOGY: IRENAEUS AND SCHILLEBEECKX

In the previous chapter, it was found that Schillebeeckx's Thomist creation faith is the seedbed of his Christology. From the springboard of Thomist metaphysical tenets of creation faith (as identified in the analyses of Fergus Kerr and Brian Davies), Schillebeeckx explores truths about the condition of humanity in creation and the implications of the relation of creature to Creator. It was shown how these truths and implications inform his Christology. The main task in this chapter is an investigation into a source of Schillebeeckx's Christian anthropology. Philip Kennedy avers that Schillebeeckx's fundamental theological lineage can be traced further back than Aquinas to Irenaeus.[1] He writes that 'he often quotes St. Irenaeus (*c.*115–190) for whom it is not necessary to negate the honour of humanity in order to affirm the honour of God'.[2] A critical assessment is made of the degree to which Schillebeeckx's theology can be said to be based on and shaped by theological foundations and preoccupations which absorbed Irenaeus and, in particular, how his theology of the human being is a theological anthropology rooted in the theology of Irenaeus. To what extent does Schillebeeckx's understanding of humanity derive from a *ressourcement* of the theological anthropology of Irenaeus and inform his soteriological Christology?

Common ground in Irenaeus for Balthasar and Schillebeeckx

Just as Thomist tenets were identified from independent authors, a different independent source is used to identify Irenaean themes, namely, Hans Urs von Balthasar, a theologian who is not normally thought even to belong in the same theological group as Schillebeeckx.[3] After Vatican II, and to some extent in the run-up to it, two dominant streams of thought formed in the Roman Catholic

---

1. Kennedy, *Schillebeeckx*, 93.
2. Ibid., 7.
3. Partly because Balthasar does not write thematically, what he says will be supplemented with what Julie Canlis writes because not only does she draw on Balthasar but what she writes is germane to Irenaeus and the theological anthropology as traced out by Balthasar.

Church. These are well represented by the two Roman Catholic post-Vatican II periodicals, *Concilium* and *Communio*. Schillebeeckx, together with Karl Rahner and others, was a *Concilium* founder, author and regular editor, and Balthasar, together with Joseph Ratzinger and others, was a *Communio* founder and author. Francis Fiorenza summarizes the different emphases of the two periodicals by writing that whereas *Concilium* 'represented a progressive interpretation of the renewal called for by Vatican II', *Communio* 'insisted on Vatican II's affirmation of the tradition'.[4] Using Balthasar as the touchstone for key themes in Irenaeus helps to show that Schillebeeckx is not simply reading back into a patristic author, eisegetically, themes that he wants to develop after Vatican II. If Balthasar and Schillebeeckx can be shown to agree about cardinal points of Irenaeus' theology then two theological claims can be made: first that Schillebeeckx is engaging in genuine Irenaean *ressourcement* and may therefore be legitimately claimed to be Irenaean in his theology, and, secondly, that common ground can therefore be established between the *Concilium* author and the *Communio* stream of thought. This may be helpful in overcoming a tendency towards polarization which is now evident in Roman Catholic thinking fifty-five years after Vatican II. Robert Schreiter follows Timothy Radcliffe and others in agreeing 'that at this time in the early twenty-first century, we are seeing two distinctive approaches within the Roman Catholic Church about what makes the Church "Catholic", and both see themselves as representing the best of the Catholic tradition'.[5]

One of these conceptions, as Schreiter explains, is the understanding of catholicity 'as the fullness of faith'. He describes it as seeing the Church as 'the depository and guarantor of the full and living faith that has been passed down by Christ to the apostles and through them to the Church in the course of history, down to the present time'.[6] This is the dominant conception of the theological idea of catholicity underlying Balthasar's approach. The other conception is of the Church as '*kath'holou*, that is, to be found throughout the whole world'. Schreiter says that this 'catholicity ... is defined principally by its extension throughout the world [which] embraces both its role and its mission'. Its role is to be the bearer of the Good News of Jesus Christ 'bringing the gospel of healing, redemption and reconciliation to every creature' (Mt. 28.19-20).[7] Both these conceptions of catholicity lie at the heart of Schillebeeckx's theology. The strain or tension between the *Concilium* and *Communio* emphases lies in the approach to the formulation and reformulation of dogmatic formulae of the theological tradition. Schillebeeckx

---

4. Fiorenza, 'The New Theology and Transcendental Thomism', 256.
5. Robert Schreiter, 'Pastoral Theology as Contextual: Forms of Pastoral Catholic Theology Today', in *Keeping Faith in Practice: Aspects of Catholic Pastoral Theology*, ed. James Sweeney, Gemma Simmonds and David Lonsdale (London: SCM Press, 2010), 64–79 (65) (henceforth *Pastoral Theology*).
6. Ibid., 67.
7. Ibid.

considered that human beings, because of their historicity, are '*in a tradition*', and that 'it belongs to man's very being to be within a tradition while re-activating it'.[8]

Deane-Drummond avers that Balthasar 'in particular ... was hostile to influences of Enlightenment thought that seemed to undercut the distinctive approach of the church in its mission'.[9] She writes that 'he was ... critical of what he saw as implicit uncritical acceptance of the assumptions of modernity and the ideal of progress'.[10] Schillebeeckx himself emphatically disowned secular ideals of progress or ideologies because he was keenly aware of humanity's capacity for repeated, calamitous exploitation of, and violence against itself. Deane-Drummond does not name the 'assumptions of modernity', the uncritical acceptance of which Balthasar was critical. What can be said, however, is that Schillebeeckx's dialogue with the issues of modernity is of its very nature critical. When culture moves in a critical way towards the new, he constantly analyses and assesses what the issues are, while at the same time searching for common ground on which to meet his contemporaries, in the way that St Paul did in Athens when he found the altar dedicated to the unknown god and used it as his starting point.[11] He does not see the Catholic faith as something besieged in a fortress by enemies called secularization and modernity. The world is God's world and for Schillebeeckx the truths of the Catholic Christian faith, the 'fulness of the faith', are to be taken to the world, for the world, and interpreted in each age and context within the world. Aquinas had engaged with and 'employed logical modes of argument based directly or indirectly on Aristotle' in order 'to achieve a new synthesis of the faith for the changing world of the thirteenth century'.[12] Schillebeeckx shares with Aquinas a critical openness to intellectual currents belonging to his own time in order to see whether they need refuting or how they can be used to strengthen Christian theology. Far from entering a dialogue in which he simply searches for the lowest common denominator with his interlocutors, Schillebeeckx engages in a strenuous and arduous dialogue that leads to him showing how God, the Creator of Heaven and Earth, reveals himself most fully in his humanity in the saving power of Jesus Christ. The whole purpose of Schillebeeckx's dialogue with the

---

8. Schillebeeckx, *GFoM*, 18 [27].

9. Deane-Drummond, Celia E., 'Hans Urs von Balthasar (1905–1988) A Theo-Drama', in *Creation and Salvation, Vol. 2: A Companion on Recent theological Movements*, ed. Ernst M. Conradie, Studies in Religion and the Environment 6 (Zürich: Lit Verlag, 2012), 71–6 (71).

10. Ibid.

11. Acts 17.23, 'Men of Athens, I have seen for myself how extremely scrupulous you are in all religious matters, because I noticed, as I strolled round admiring your sacred monuments, that you had an altar inscribed: To An Unknown God. Well, the God whom I proclaim is in fact the one whom you already worship without knowing it' (Jerusalem Bible translation). In this sentence I am using the word 'issues' to mean important topics of debate rather than the now more common, colloquial meaning of 'problems'.

12. Schreiter, *Pastoral Theology*, 68.

issues of modernity and pluralism is in order to see how to understand them and work with them in God's way.

If it can be shown that Schillebeeckx's identification of Irenaean themes is similar to Balthasar's, then it can be concluded that his Irenaean roots go much deeper than the mere use of Irenaeus' famous maxim *Gloria Dei, vivens homo: vita autem hominis visio Dei* (God's glory is a human being that is alive, the aliveness of a human being is in seeing God).[13] Among other intellectual influences, Schillebeeckx was imbued with Irenaeus' theological vision. It was one of the elements which provided a route through the straits of atonement theory to explore what soteriology means in the light of the Christian creation faith.

Balthasar's essay on Irenaeus

In his essay on Irenaeus, Balthasar analyses and illustrates how the theology of Irenaeus is shaped. He indicates that there are 'three main points of articulation of Irenaeus' theology'. The first is 'God, hidden and revealed in his unity and trinity'. The second is 'the relation between God and creature, being and becoming, especially God and man'.[14] This topic is a theological anthropology that is based on, and grows out of, what it is to be a creature. The third point concerns 'the relation of time and eternity patterned according to the order of salvation (*dispositio*): Old Covenant, Gospel and Church'.[15] Themes in Schillebeeckx's writing will be compared with these 'points of articulation' to see how far his theology is in tune with that of Irenaeus as presented by Balthasar. Inevitably there will be some overlap of theological ideas with those of Aquinas but the assessment which follows aims to avoid repetition because it is dealing with a different theological context (the writings of Irenaeus) with a particular focus (the human being).

Balthasar's first point of articulation: God, hidden and revealed in his unity and trinity

This point, in what Balthasar calls the all-encompassing 'broad, unbroken sphere' of truth, is about the transcendence and immanence of God.[16] He notes the

---

13. Irenaeus, *Adversus Haereses*, IV.20.7; own translation.
14. Hans Urs von Balthasar, *The Glory of the Lord: A Theological Aesthetics; Volume II: Studies in Theological Style: Clerical Styles*, trans. Andrew Louth, Francis McDonagh, Brian McNeil, ed. John Riches (Edinburgh: T&T Clark, 1995), 58. Balthasar cites Irenaeus from Books 1, 2, 4 and 5 of Harvey's edition *Sancti Irenaei, Episcopi Lugdunensis*, and Book 3 from the critical edition of François Sagnard, in both cases by page.
15. Ibid.
16. Ibid., 43.

apparent paradox that 'in reaction to the fashionable Gnostic transcendence' of his time 'which stamps the highest God as absolutely unknowable, Irenaeus is himself forced to stress this unknowability'.[17]

God's transcendence and immanence

Balthasar quotes a wonderful description by Irenaeus of God's transcendence as Creator which states that the 'God of all is the free majesty which "encompasses all, but is alone encompassed by no-one, he the former, he the founder, he the deviser, he the creator, he the Lord of all things. And neither outside him nor above him does anything else exist."'[18] Schillebeeckx makes a similar point about the complete otherness of God the Creator in more philosophically couched words, 'There is nothing that can be introduced between the world and God to interpret their [relation]. This is what people mean when they speak in symbolic language of "creation out of nothing."'[19] Schillebeeckx's creation faith is in absolute accordance with Irenaeus' expression of God's transcendence. He, like Balthasar, talks of it in terms of hiddenness: 'The main task of theology is to preserve the transcendence of God who loves men, hidden and yet so near.'[20] These words sound a caution because while the task of theology is to make statements about God, it must not presume that God can be defined, a point which Irenaeus makes with polemical edge when he writes,

> Do not transcend God himself, for he cannot be transcended. Do not look above the creator, for you will find nothing. He who formed you cannot be defined … your thought cannot encompass him, but if you think against nature you will become a fool.[21]

17. Ibid., 59.
18. Ibid.
19. Schillebeeckx, *GAU*, 93. The word 'relation' is here given to translate the word *verhouding* of the original Dutch (in *Evangelie Verhalen* [Baarn: H. Nelissen, 1982], 93) although the published English translation has 'relationship'. Poulsom differentiates between *verhouding* ('relation') and *relaties* ('relationship') in translating into English (*Dialectics*, 69–71). He notes that Erik Borgman, a native Dutch speaker, observes that the two are often used interchangeably in Dutch (Martin Poulsom, comment in conversation, 10 August 2015). Martine van den Poel, a native Flemish speaker and fluent English speaker, avers that *verhouding* in Flemish is definitely 'relation' as in, say, a mathematical relation, and *relaties* is definitely a 'relationship' as between two people (conversation with Rhona Lewis, 21 June 2015). Despite his years in the Netherlands, Schillebeeckx's Dutch, unsurprisingly, still retained Flemish characteristics. On p. 108 of *EV*, Schillebeeckx uses both *verhouding* and *relaties* in the same sentence: 'The kingdom of God is a new *verhouding* of man to God, and its tangible and visible side is a new kind of liberating *relaties* between human beings within a peaceful and reconciled society.' Although the *GAU* translation gives both words as 'relationship', it is preferable in this instance to treat them differently.
20. Schillebeeckx, *GAU*, 253.
21. Balthasar, *The Glory of the Lord*, 59, citing *AH* I.344.

For Schillebeeckx not only is the transcendence of God's existence and creative power unfathomable, so too is his love of his human creatures. He writes, 'In God one experiences that in absolute freedom he is essentially creator, the lover of the finite, loving with the absoluteness of a divine love which is unfathomable to us.'[22]

For Irenaeus and Schillebeeckx, however, God's immanence and intimacy in his creation are in direct proportion to his transcendence as Creator. Denis Minns writes that 'the concept of the absolute transcendence of God with respect to his creation and the consequent immediacy of his presence to it, which Irenaeus elaborates with the aid of … Platonic distinction, underlies the whole of his theological conception'.[23] Irenaeus frequently refers to the hand, or hands, of God when speaking of God the Creator[24] in an image that conveys his absolute and sustaining presence to his creatures. Schillebeeckx expresses this same Irenaean idea of the direct proportion of God's transcendence and immanence when he writes,

> God is … the mystery with which no thing or person or image or power, nothing in the world, or even the world in its entirety, can be identified. On the other hand, the living God is transcendent to the degree that he dwells in the utmost depths of ourselves, and we are like fish in divine water. He is more intimately close to us than we are to ourselves.[25]

God's self-revelation through the medium of the world and its history

The interchangeability of what Irenaeus and Schillebeeckx say about the immanence of God being made known by his self-revelation through the medium of the world and history is striking. The observation that God's self-revelation to humanity is to be found in history and not somewhere beyond is a leitmotif of Schillebeeckx's theology and Balthasar paraphrases Irenaeus as making the same point about the accessibility or self-revelation of God through history in these words, 'The triune God is accessible to us only where he makes himself accessible to us, so that it is the greatest possible slight to God to disparage the historical self-revelation of his immeasurable love and to look behind it for a non-existent access to the unknown God.'[26] Brian Daley in turn writes of Balthasar that

---

22. Schillebeeckx, *Church*, 179 [181].

23. Denis Minns, *Irenaeus* (London: Geoffrey Chapman, 1994), 34. Cf. *AH* IV.19.2;20.1; *Dem* 45.

24. See Ibid., 35, note 13.

25. Edward Schillebeeckx, 'Prologue: Human God-Talk and God's Silence', in *The Praxis of The Reign of God: An Introduction to the Theology of Edward Schillebeeckx*, 2nd edn, ed. Mary Catherine Hilkert and Robert Schreiter (New York: Fordham University Press, 2002), ix–xviii (xii).

26. Balthasar, *The Glory of the Lord*, 61.

He sees in Irenaeus' struggle against Valentinian Gnosticism the first appearance of a centrally important theological sensitivity: the recognition that the ordinary world – the world of concrete things, of religious institutions, of daily moral responsibilities, of the vulnerable human body – is the place in which the Creator God has revealed himself as the God of salvation. In other words, God reveals himself as the God who is other than the world, yet is its author and provident guide, working in the world to allow humanity ultimately to share his own life.[27]

For both Irenaeus and Schillebeeckx, it is only through a right understanding of God's self-revelation in history that God's transcendence and immanence can be understood as belonging together. Each human being's experience within, and of, their own historical context is the medium through which God may become known. Human beings are shaped by their contexts in time and place. Schillebeeckx refers to the human attempts, throughout the history of the church, to put the transcendent God's self-revelation into words as a 'stammering'. He writes, 'Theology is always a "stammering" in the face of the transcendent mystery of faith: "*balbutiendo ut possumus excelsa Dei resonamus*" ("by stuttering out the great truths of God as best we can echo them").'[28] Balthasar summarizes the way Irenaeus holds together the immeasurability of God with the concreteness of his presence in the following words:

> What is made known through the love of God is the manifestation of his unknown (because immeasurable) greatness: his love itself is the inconceivable, the indescribable; benignitas ejus inerrabilis [his unerring kindness]. This inconceivability is an attribute of the fact of his concrete presence which cannot go unnoticed or unperceived by any created thing.[29]

For Irenaeus and Schillebeeckx, the Creator, infinite in his transcendence, creates precisely in order to reveal himself through concrete historical contexts to his human creatures. In the eyes of both, human beings are made with a capacity for a sense of the transcendent which can only be detected through the concrete medium of the world.[30] God's immanent transcendence is, in Schillebeeckx's words, his 'absolute saving presence among men and women in their history'.[31]

---

27. Brian E. Daley, 'Balthasar's Reading of the Church Fathers', in *The Cambridge Companion to Hans Urs von Balthasar*, ed. Edward T. Oakes and David Moss (Cambridge: Cambridge University Press, 2004), 187–206 (198).

28. Schillebeeckx, *R&T*, 114 [176]. The Latin citation is from Thomas Aquinas, *ST* 1a 4, 1 ad 1.

29. Balthasar, *The Glory of the Lord*, 62.

30. In this respect Schillebeeckx differs from Rahner as was made clear in the previous chapter.

31. Edward Schillebeeckx, *Jesus in Our Western Culture: Mysticism, Ethics and Politics*, trans. John Bowden (London: SCM Press, 1987), 7.

It is 'only in a secular history in which men and women are liberated for true humanity [that] God [can] reveal his own being'.[32] God's presence in history was most concentrated and fully revealed in his Son, Jesus of Nazareth. For Christians, the ordinary world and its history is God's saving history 'to the degree that it liberates men and women for true and good humanity in deep respect for one another'.[33]

The trinitarian basis of Irenaeus' and Schillebeeckx's theology of God's self-revelation in history

Balthasar avers that Irenaeus' theology of how the 'unknown' or transcendent God reveals himself through the Son and the Spirit is basically a 'trinitarian formula' which is repeated constantly.[34] Minns draws attention to the fact that Irenaeus was writing 'before debates about the proper understanding of the God of our salvation pushed the Trinitarian theology of the Great Church into metaphysics'.[35] He avers, however, that 'although there are the beginnings of a metaphysical theology of the Trinity in his writings, he presents us, for the most part, with a highly developed economic theology of the Trinity'. Irenaeus' concern is more with 'the ways in which Father, Son and Holy Spirit are related to us, rather than the ways in which they are related to one another'.[36] Stephan van Erp surmises that it might surprise some that Schillebeeckx 'argues for a Trinitarian foundation of theology, which will point all theological speculation to its Christocentric focus, because according to him, speculative theology is methodologically Christocentric, although its object is theocentric'.[37] In a reconstruction of Schillebeeckx's trinitarian theology in three stages of his work, van Erp aims to 'clarify why the complex relationship of revelation and experience in Schillebeeckx's metaphysics and hermeneutics according to himself needs a personalist and soteriological foundation, expressed and systemized in a doctrine of the Trinity'.[38] He adds that Schillebeeckx 'thinks a well-balanced Trinitarian theology is needed to safeguard theology against an exclusive focus on either divine or human immanentism'.[39]

---

32. Schillebeeckx, *Church*, 7 [007].
33. Ibid., 10 [010].
34. Balthasar, *The Glory of the Lord*, 60.
35. Minns, *Irenaeus*, 38.
36. Ibid.
37. Stephan van Erp, 'From Speculation to Salvation: The Trinitarian Theology of Edward Schillebeeckx', https://core.ac.uk/download/pdf/34634940.pdf (accessed on 22 May 2018), pp. 1 and 3. On p. 3 van Erp is referring to Edward Schillebeeckx, *Revelation and Theology*, trans. N. D. Smith, The Collected Works of Edward Schillebeeckx 2 (London: Bloomsbury, 2014), 91 [138].
38. Ibid., 1.
39. Ibid., 3.

Irenaeus and Schillebeeckx, therefore, base their theology of the revelation of the transcendent God on a trinitarian formula. While Irenaeus wrote before a metaphysical theology of the Trinity was fully developed, Schillebeeckx writes in the wake of one. At times Schillebeeckx speaks explicitly about the Trinity but 'although he does not treat it as a separate doctrine, [yet he] considers it integral to all dogmatic theology'.[40] Van Erp observes,

> Schillebeeckx explicitly applies the doctrine of the Trinity in his fundamental theology to safeguard the two foundations of revelation, which he describes as 'manifestio Dei in Christo'; the Trinity offers the right equilibrium of a theocentric theology and a soteriological and therefore Christological orientation.[41]

Each theologian approaches the Trinity in a concrete, non-metaphysical way. While Irenaeus most strikingly uses an image of a potter at work, Schillebeeckx uses a concrete starting point in the person of Jesus. In Irenaeus' image, perhaps inspired directly from Isaiah's image of God as the potter,[42] the Son and the Holy Spirit correspond to each of God's hands working on the moist clay of each human being.[43] The physicality of God's creation and his involvement in it is conveyed: God's creative action is expressed in terms of flesh and blood hands plying clay with the deftness, and varying strength and gentleness exerted in a potter's hands. The hands are an intrinsic part of the potter: Father, Son and Spirit are one. Schillebeeckx, for his part, argues for a concrete starting point, namely, the flesh and blood person of Jesus of Nazareth, in order to talk about the Trinity:

> We should not understand Jesus [by] taking the Trinity as our starting but vice versa: only when we start with Jesus is God's fullness of unity (not so much a unitas trinitatis but a trinitas unitatis) to some extent accessible. Only in light of Jesus' life, death and resurrection do we know that the Trinity is the divine mode of God's perfect unity of being. Only on the basis of Jesus of Nazareth, his Abba experience – source and soul of his message, ministry and death – and his resurrection can we say anything meaningful about Father, Son and Spirit.[44]

The supreme meaning of Jesus is that his humanity reveals God as triune: Jesus is one with the Father in the Spirit. Van Erp remarks that

> for critics of Schillebeeckx's theology, claiming that he develops a natural theology grounded on experience or reason alone, this Trinitarian starting point of his Christology [i.e. starting with Jesus to reach the Father and thence to the

---

40. Ibid., 6.
41. Ibid., 3.
42. Isa. 64.8.
43. Irenaeus, *AH* IV. Pref.4.
44. Schillebeeckx, *Jesus*, 617 [658].

Spirit] is important to take into account, because it entails that Schillebeeckx's *Deus humanissimus*, the God with a human face Who is concerned with humanity and engaging with human history and experience, is only known by the triune and personal divine revelation in Christ.[45]

The relationship between Jesus Christ and God the Father is one of absolute unity and in the resurrection of Christ, the Spirit is given as eschatological gift, a gift from the Father and the Son. As Schillebeeckx succinctly expresses the Trinity of the unity of God, 'God, Jesus Christ and the Spirit are indissolubly bound together in the Christian understanding of God.'[46]

In the first point of articulation in Irenaeus' theology, as identified by Balthasar, it is shown that Schillebeeckx makes his own three fundamental features of Irenaeus' theology, together with their implications for humanity. First, Schillebeeckx believes that it is central to Christian theology to hold the transcendence of God together with his intimacy in creation. It is appropriate for human beings freely to recognize their dependence on God as the source of their life and to discover that, in relationship with him, he answers their deepest need for meaning. Human beings must talk about God's revelation of himself even though their attempts will be 'stammering' because he is beyond expression in his transcendence, while at the same time he is more closely intimate to them than they are to themselves. Secondly, like Irenaeus, Schillebeeckx avers that God is only accessible to us when he reveals himself as the God of salvation in place and time, that is, in the world and its history. The implication for human beings is that it is through the world of material things, in the daily living, experiencing, making and interpreting of history, that God's revelation is to be found. Thirdly, Schillebeeckx, like Irenaeus, has a trinitarian concept of the God who reveals himself in history. Balthasar writes, 'In the last resort Irenaeus knows no other doctrine of the Trinity (and here he keeps to Scripture) than that of the act of revelation and the historical content of revelation.'[47] Van Erp points out that a criticism sometimes addressed to Schillebeeckx is that his theology is exclusively concerned with the history of salvation and therefore neglects the mystery of revelation.[48] According to Schillebeeckx, however, theology 'at the same time confirms God as transcending the history of salvation and leading an independent intratrinitarian life, which theology can only affirm through the history of salvation'.[49] The implication of the trinitarian foundation of Irenaeus' and Schillebeeckx's theology is the personal dynamic between God and human beings: the Son Jesus and the Holy Spirit, the

---

45. Van Erp, 'From Speculation to Salvation', 4.
46. Schillebeeckx, *JWC*, 41.
47. Balthasar, *The Glory of the Lord*, 60.
48. Van Erp, 'From Speculation to Salvation', 3.
49. Ibid. Schillebeeckx writes, 'To study a pure history of salvation is to neglect in principle the aspect of mystery proper to history, just as to study pure theology is to disregard the fact that God revealed himself as God only in a historical plan of salvation or a saving event.' *R&T*, 280 [093–4].

hands of God in Irenaeus' image, bring salvation from God to work with and in human beings, drawing them into closer friendship with him.

Balthasar's second point of articulation: The relation between God and creature, being and becoming, especially God and man[50]

Balthasar's second point of articulation is the core of a theological anthropology. It is a theology of what it is to be a creature. Julie Canlis writes 'anthropology is theology viewed from another angle'.[51] With specific reference to Irenaeus she says that 'his definition of the creature is guided by his prior definition of the Creator'.[52] She proposes that Irenaeus' is always 'first and foremost a *theological* anthropology' because he 'remains steadfast in his focus on God, God's gifts, God's sustenance and only then on humanity's appropriation of these things'.[53] She does, however, note that 'at times Irenaeus focuses on the gift, at other times on the giver … but this should never tempt us to separate them, for they are "inséperable" in Irenaeus'.[54] The same is true of Schillebeeckx. Sometimes he writes with a focus on God, at other times with a focus on human beings. When he speaks of human beings it is always in their relation to God. To speak of either, God or human beings, is also a way of saying something about the other.

Dialectics to describe the relation of creatures to Creator

In Balthasar's explication of Irenaeus' understanding of the relation between God and creature, he writes that 'all "communion" between God and creature is based on a fundamental opposition of nature, creating and being created'.[55] Schillebeeckx, in writing about the connection between God and creature, shifts the emphasis away from considering the nature of the Creator and the creature in an oppositional, Barthian dialectic, to consider how the fact of their distinction simultaneously involves a relation in a relational dialectic.[56] Although Schillebeeckx consistently

---

50. Balthasar, *The Glory of the Lord*, 58.

51. Julie Canlis, 'Being Made Human: The Significance of Creation for Irenaeus' Doctrine of Participation', *Scottish Journal of Theology* 58 (2005): 434–54 (445).

52. Ibid., 445.

53. Ibid.

54. Canlis, 'Being Made Human', 445, quoting the French from Adhémar d'Alès, 'La Doctrine de L'Esprit en S. Irénée', *Recherches de Science Religieuse* 14 (1924): 530.

55. Balthasar, *The Glory of the Lord*, 62. Balthasar's description of the distinction between God and humanity as an 'opposition' is an example of his dialectic at work. His dialectic works (at least partly) on the notion of a *complexio oppositorum*, a methodology profoundly influenced by Barth, whose dialectic is also oppositional (Poulsom, conversation, 10 August 2015).

56. Poulsom analyses Schillebeeckx's theological thinking as based on a relational dialectic in which 'the constituent elements are not considered as polar opposites but aspects, allowing them to be considered as co-constitutive'. *Dialectics*, 96.

explores the connection in terms of a relational dialectic, he does not do so explicitly. His purpose is to hold firmly to the distinction and, at the same time, to explore what this implies for the relation. In interpreting the Irenaean theme of the relation of creature to Creator, Balthasar's and Schillebeeckx's approaches, in the late twentieth century, are equally valid although they use two different forms of dialectic. According to Irenaeus and Schillebeeckx, there are fundamental implications for human beings of the distinction and relation between themselves and God. In Canlis's words, 'God has structured creation for participation, not autonomous completion.'[57] The prime implications of Christian creation faith are that God wants to share his life, giving his human creatures both biological existence and a superabundance of life in relationship with God the Creator, source of all life.

Human dependence on and need of God

Human dependence on, and need of God, in combination with human freedom, is a key element of Irenaeus' Christian anthropology. Balthasar quotes Irenaeus' statement that the human creature is 'fundamentally dependent on God, in need of him'.[58] The connotations of the words 'dependence' and 'need' suffer, in contemporary north-western culture, from negative associations. Dependence is associated with an inability to think or do things for oneself, perceived as dehumanizing, whether it be applied to individual people, categories of people or nations. Need has even more unfavourable connotations. It is tinged with a sense of failure, shame and even uselessness. Those materially in need are often wrongly blamed for their plight; those who are labelled 'emotionally needy' are often half dismissed as hopeless cases. In the light of Christian creation faith the understanding of dependence and need takes on new meaning.

Schillebeeckx deals with the fundamental dependence of human beings on God in two ways. One way, as seen in the last chapter, is that he examines the implications of dependence in terms of finitude. He refutes the argument that finitude, the condition of human creaturehood and dependence, is a flaw. Rather, the conditions of finitude are, as it were, the clay of Irenaeus' scriptural image of God as the artist working with his two hands.[59] The clay of finitude is the material in and through which God works in his creation. The second way that Schillebeeckx deals with the fundamental dependence of human beings on God is to point out that, in those who profess a Jewish or Christian creation faith, a failure to acknowledge this fundamental dependence on God is sinful. He writes,

57. Canlis, 'Being Made Human', 445.
58. Balthasar, *The Glory of the Lord*, 63.
59. Cf. Balthasar's quotation of Irenaeus' image of God as the artist working with his two hands to form the clay of the heart of the human being, pp. 74–5. In this vivid scriptural imagery, which suggests God as a potter, Irenaeus refrains from applying the word 'potter' to God, perhaps because God creates the very material he uses as an artist whereas a potter does not create his own clay.

The Genesis story in the Old Testament sees the so-called primal sin of mankind not in the fact that human-beings simply want to be human beings in a world which is simply the world, but rather in the fact that they do not want to accept their finitude or contingency; they hanker after that which is not finitude, after immortality and omniscience, so that they can be like God.[60]

Minns describes how for Irenaeus disobedience, the attitude of not accepting, in human dependency, God's goodness and what he wants to bestow, is the 'archetypal, the paradigmatic' sin. He writes of Irenaeus, 'The only proper attitude of the creature before God is one that acknowledges … that God infinitely transcends his creation, that humankind is immediately dependent on God for everything.'[61] An inability of human beings to reflect on and acknowledge dependence on the Source of Life, which is outside of themselves, is an avoidance of what it is to be human.

Giving thanks to God, the Giver of life, the appropriate response to God's gifts

Human beings are not suppliers of their own lives. Their lives, and the fruits and the harvests of the earth needed to sustain them, are a gift from God and, as such, invite response and a return in giving. The context of the reference that Balthasar gives for Irenaeus' statement of the human need of God is a discussion of the Eucharist. Irenaeus avers that as surely as God does not need the things which come from us, human beings have a need to offer something to God.[62] Irenaeus does not elaborate, with what would be an anachronistic focus on human psychology, on the nature of this human need.[63] He simply makes clear that human beings' homage to God given in the Eucharist is not confined to liturgical activity but is made up also of 'good works'.[64] The thanks given to God in the Eucharist sanctify his creation[65] and this sanctification of the creation is implemented in concrete works such as feeding the hungry, taking in the stranger and going to the prisoner.[66] The mysticism of prayer and the practicality of good works are co-constitutive in the human activity of thanking God and sanctifying his creation.

How did Schillebeeckx understand human need of God? In the religious context of Irenaeus' time there was a religious pluralism and hardly any concept

---

60. Schillebeeckx, *GAU*, 92.
61. Denis Minns, *Irenaeus* (London: Geoffrey Chapman, 1994), 62.
62. Irenaeus, *AH*, IV.xviii.6 (Keble, 361).
63. One contemporary manifestation of the human instinct to worship is, perhaps, the cult of celebrity.
64. *bonas operationes nostras* (Harvey's edition of *AH*, 209).
65. *sanctificantes creaturam* (Harvey's edition of *AH*, 209).
66. Irenaeus quotes the verses from Mt. 25.34-36 in which the Kingdom which God has prepared for those who build his kingdom on earth is mentioned (Harvey's edition of *AH*, 209).

of the separation of religious from secular.[67] It is probable that most people acknowledged a dependence on divine powers beyond their own control and, in the case of Jews and Christians, central to their confession was (and is) dependence on the transcendent divine power of Yahweh-God. In the post-Enlightenment context of Europe and North America of the second half of the twentieth century Schillebeeckx set out to analyse 'why God has become a problem for Western men and women'.[68] He was profoundly aware of the need and desire of 'believers in crisis' subjectively to own their religious position, 'to the point of saying "yes" to the heart of the gospel'.[69] No longer was it possible or enough to swim along in a collective tide of religious practice. Along with Irenaeus, as presented by Balthasar, Schillebeeckx holds that human beings, over and above their fundamental dependence on God for existence itself, have a need of something more, something peculiar to their human nature, in order to live fully human lives. Schillebeeckx intimates that this need is for finding meaning in a relationship with God. He goes a level deeper than the outward expression of humanity's need to return thanks for life. He describes God as wanting 'to be the deepest meaning of human life':

> [God] gives himself in unselfish love as our God: our salvation and our happiness, the supreme content of true and good humanity. God freely creates men and women for their own salvation and happiness; but in the same action, in sovereign freedom, he wants to be the deepest meaning, the salvation and happiness of human life.[70]

To talk of God in very human terms, it could be said that, of all created things, human beings have the deepest meaning for God. They have been given the capacity to respond in freedom to God, to heed him, and play their part in a dynamic whereby the relation of creature to Creator becomes a relationship. According to Schillebeeckx the dynamic of human relationship with God is twofold. It consists of the same kind of intangible and real elements, such as reciprocal delight, gratitude and trust which give meaning to a relationship between human beings. He writes, 'God, the creator, the one in whom we can trust, is love that liberates men and women in a way which fulfils all human, personal, social and political expectations and indeed transcends them.'[71] Such qualities as trust and delight experienced in a relationship with God are mystical. With trust and delight goes the need that

---

67. Lucretius, in *De Rerum Natura*, shows that there was a concept of the non-religious in the time of Irenaeus although the Epicureanism that he describes did not deny the existence of gods. Irenaeus refers to the Epicurean kind of god(s): *c'est le Dieu d'Epicure qu'ils trouvent ainsi, un Dieu qui ne sert à rien, ni pour lui ni pour les autres, – un Dieu sans Providence.* Irénée de Lyon, *Contre les Hérésies Livre III* (trans. F. Sagnard, Editions du Cerf, 1952), 403.

68. Schillebeeckx, *Church*, 45 [46].

69. Schillebeeckx, *IR*, 33 [39].

70. Schillebeeckx, *GAU*, 104.

71. Ibid., 106.

Irenaeus remarks on, namely, a need to express thanks, a need to offer something in return to God, which is why Irenaeus connects this need with the Eucharist. In the Eucharist participants are joined with Christ in thanksgiving and reciprocal self-giving to God. Intrinsic to relationship with God, however, is also a practical element. The practical element is, in Schillebeeckx's words, 'a relational dynamic with [one's] fellow human beings' or, the praxis of the reign of God. It is what Irenaeus spoke of, in more scriptural terms, as giving bread to the hungry and visiting those in prison. Schillebeeckx, like Irenaeus, sees both the mystical and the caritative building of the kingdom of God as one in the dynamic of human relationship with God.

Human freedom

Just as the ideas of dependence and need are commonly narrowed to notions of human inadequacy or limits, so currently the concept of human freedom is frequently limited to a superficial idea of choice. Poulsom, writing about divine and human freedom, remarks on how Burrell 'is extremely wary of understanding freedom in terms of choice. He prefers to define the freedom of a creature as [choice operating at a profound level]: "the power to accept or reject what it itself is: its ontological status, if you will".'[72] Eric Osborn writes that

> Irenaeus argues that free will, the ability to choose, is part of being human and that all may choose or reject. Man's autonomy existed from the beginning and was never threatened by God, for it was part of the divine image. In free and frail humanity God brings to righteousness the free will which he has placed in man as he leads him on towards immortality and eternal obedience (5.29.1).[73]

For Schillebeeckx a keen awareness of human dependence on God as Creator and source of life has a startling consequence. In direct proportion to an awareness of human dependence on God a sense of the corresponding human freedom pervades his writing. Poulsom highlights this as

> a Schillebeeckian relational dialectic [in which] autonomy could be spoken of as 'relational autonomy', stressing that it is not only compatible with but correlates with the absolute dependence of the creature on the Creator. Commitment to self-realization then becomes a way of expressing a commitment to the Creator, who is, after all, the end, the goal, of that self-realization, as is made clear by the idea of participation.[74]

---

72. Poulsom, *Dialectics*, 196.

73. Eric Osborn, *Irenaeus of Lyons* (Cambridge: Cambridge University Press, 2005), 235 (henceforth *Irenaeus of Lyons 2005*).

74. Poulsom, *Dialectics*, 196.

Schillebeeckx writes, 'I am myself in dependence on God: the more I am God's, the more I become myself in transcending myself. In this constitutive relationship to God, who is a mystery, I am a mystery.'[75]

There is nothing controlling about God's love, nothing constraining. It invites in freedom. Balthasar elucidates how Irenaeus holds that God's guidance does not curtail human freedom,

> If man is to be able to follow God's lead, he must be free, and one of the principal places where this freedom can be seen is in that guidance itself, which always takes the form of gentle suggestion (suasoria) and never of compulsion.[76]

Growing into fullness of life

The human creature's dependence on God for existence is a glorious prerequisite for any life as well as life in all its human fullness. Canlis points out that 'by deepening the distinction between God and humanity' Irenaeus 'could then relate the two non-competitively, even allowing the creature "promotion into God"'.[77] In among Irenaeus' anti-Gnostic polemic, scathing, mocking and even parodying in turn, a leitmotif is his delight in humanity's God-given freedom which allows men and women, on their part, to draw near to God and to share more fully in the glory of his life. From the human side, men and women draw near to God not by any self-promotion but by allowing themselves to be prompted by the Holy Spirit of God in coming to recognize the transcendent Creator. In this way men and women are not only related to the Creator but enter into a relationship of growth, or a 'becoming more alive', in God. This 'promotion into God' is described by Schillebeeckx as a sharing in God's love for men and women 'delighting in and for men and women'.[78] As John Behr puts it, 'Freedom, therefore, along with temporality, is a pre-condition for creatures to be capable of becoming "other" than what they were created: for creatures to enter into communion with God, and so be transfigured'.[79] This transfiguration is *theiosis*.

Balthasar highlights how Irenaeus develops the theme of the temporality of human beings in contradistinction to the timelessness of God. He quotes the following sentence as the one which gives the greatest force to this idea:

> *Deus quidem facit, homo autem fit; et quidem qui facit semper idem est, quod autem fit, et initium et medietatem et adjectionem et augmentum accipere debet.*

---

75. Edward Schillebeeckx, *God and Man*, trans. Edward Fitzgerald and Peter Tomlinson (London: Sheed and Ward, 1969), 215 (henceforth *G&M*).
76. Balthasar, *The Glory of the Lord*, 66.
77. Canlis, 'Being Made Human', 124.
78. Poulsom, *Dialectics*, 188.
79. John Behr, *Asceticism and Anthropology in Irenaeus and Clement* (Oxford: Oxford University Press, 2000), 44.

[God makes, but man is made, and the one who makes is always the same but the thing that is made has to accept a beginning, a middle state, addition and increase.][80]

'God is being which is, and [is] therefore eternal',[81] and, in his timelessness, he transitively 'makes' (*facit*), while humankind, in its temporality, intransitively 'becomes' (*fit*). Irenaeus describes human beings not only as recipients of life but also as creatures 'becoming' something. They are creatures born in time, who pass through time and who change with the passage of time. They are in a process of becoming. For Irenaeus, therefore, the human being is properly related to God, both as a creature, which is what s/he is, and also as the creature which, in his or her freedom, s/he may in the course of time become. A little further on, in the same context as the words quoted above, Irenaeus explains that humanity, 'being found in God, will continually get on [that is, make progress] towards God'.[82] In his Christian anthropology, human beings' growth or progress is towards God in a deepening participation in his life.

Irenaeus' idea (as Balthasar expresses it) that 'human nature is seen all along as embedded in time and becoming'[83] reads as a blueprint for Schillebeeckx's theological conviction that human beings are temporal. He states explicitly that 'man has a *temporalized* existence'.[84] He makes the point that true humanity cannot dispense with any one of the three dimensions of time, whether future, present or past. He writes that these three dimensions are

> intrinsically held together by our time-conditioned humanity itself: a being that knows that it is on the way. In the last resort, we can only experience these

---

80. Balthasar, *The Glory of the Lord*, 62–3. Balthasar's Irenaean quote is from *AH* 2.175 and the translation is given in footnote 167, p. 63. When, further along on p. 63, Balthasar writes, 'the creature which comes into being ... necessarily has a beginning, middle and end, *i.e. time*' (italics added), he has taken words that Irenaeus uses about the divine economy and applied them mistakenly to the life of human beings. Irenaeus in his *Deus quidem facit* statement makes no mention of an end to the existence of the human creature, thus implying that the human creature is eternally held in being by God. The reference to Irenaeus that Balthasar gives for the words 'end, *i.e.* time' is *AH*, III.24.1 (footnote 175, S, 398). In III.24.1 Irenaeus is writing of 'the beginnings', 'the middle times' and 'the end' as the different stages that make up the whole of God's economy (*AH*, III, trans. and annotated by Dominic J. Unger, with an introduction and further revisions by Irenaeus M. C. Steenberg, *Ancient Christian Writers* 64 (New York: The Newman Press, 2012), 2110).
81. Balthasar, *The Glory of the Lord*, 63.
82. Irenaeus, *AH* IV.11.2: *homo in Deo inventus, semper proficient ad Deum*, trans. John Keble, *Five books of S. Irenaeus, Bishop of Lyons: Against Heresies*, trans. John Keble (Oxford: James Parker, 1872).
83. Balthasar, *The Glory of the Lord*, 66.
84. Schillebeeckx, *Christ*, 803 [807].

three dimensions as meaningful if on the one hand we express our temporal awareness, and on the other hand also allow God a place in what we say here.[85]

Schillebeeckx goes on to say that in order to allow God a place faith requires a fundamental decision of a person to '*entrust* [themself], others and the whole of history to God'.[86] The human trust in God that he describes is the hallmark of a profound relationship with God and is strongly reminiscent of the image in Irenaeus of the human 'clay' of a person who entrusts himself to God to be shaped and fashioned by God's 'hands' of Son and Spirit. This shaping by God of the human being requires the human being to allow him/herself to be held in God's hands, to entrust him/herself to God and to keep the clay of his/her heart 'soft and pliable',[87] that is, responsive over the course of his/her life. At the same time as being an image of human trust in the hands of God, Balthasar says that the 'two hands' passage is about the central concept of glory, the 'mutual glorification of God and man'.[88] He writes,

> Man, who preserves God's art in himself and obediently opens himself to its disposing, glorifies the artist and the artist glorifies himself in his work. 'You do not create God; God creates you. Therefore if you are God's work, wait patiently for the hand of your artist, who does everything in due proportion, and in due proportion as regards you who are being made. Offer him your heart soft and pliable, and preserve the form which the artist forms out of you: preserve it by keeping it moist, so that you do not dry out and harden and lose the trace of his fingers. Keeping the form that has been impressed on you, you will move towards perfection'.[89]

Schillebeeckx, in a development of this image, extends the scope of the one who entrusts him/herself to God to an entrusting also of others and of the whole of history to God. He writes, 'Anyone who believes in God knows that, in some way or other, he holds us in his hand'.[90] The person who does not tug away from God's hands has made a 'fundamental decision [… to *entrust*] himself', but not just him/herself writes Schillebeeckx, also 'others and the whole of history to God and in so doing knows that he is reconciled with himself, with others and with history – present, past and future – because the believer has come to terms with God's incomprehensible actions'.[91]

85. Ibid.
86. Ibid., 804 [808].
87. Irenaeus, *AH* IV.39.2 (Harvey's edition, 299; Keble's translation, 440).
88. Balthasar, *The Glory of the Lord*, 74.
89. Ibid., 74–5, quoting from Irenaeus, *AH* 2.99.
90. Schillebeeckx, *Christ*, 804 [807]. Here Schillebeeckx is also drawing on biblical imagery.
91. Ibid. By 'incomprehensible actions' Schillebeeckx suggests that because God is transcendent and incomprehensible to us in himself, his actions, which are no-other-than-God, are also incomprehensible to us, at least directly. We, as finite creatures, cannot think

Schillebeeckx writes, 'Progress towards God' is another way of expressing the increasing closeness to God that brings with it a 'true, good and happy mode of life',[92] that is, salvation. Humanity's 'progress towards God' is the result of God's 'pedagogy of salvation' which is one of the major themes in the writing of Irenaeus. Osborn summarizes Irenaeus' stages by which God accustoms himself to humanity: 'Between creation and incarnation God accustoms himself to man and man is accustomed to God. … In Christ, man is able to see God, to contain God, to accustom himself to participate in God while God is accustomed to live in man (3.20.2).'[93] It would seem, from the way that Irenaeus writes, that 'God's pedagogy of salvation' applies to individuals as well as to whole groups of people (such as Israel) as they appear in time.[94] Schillebeeckx, likewise, broadens the idea of individual Christian human growth in response to God as also belonging to human beings collectively in that they make history *sequela Jesu*, according to God's purposes. Osborn also writes,

> The economy [God's plan of salvation as described by Irenaeus] thus describes the ascent of man. Irenaeus' human optimism has long excited enthusiasm. At the Renaissance he inspired Erasmus. In the twentieth century he enthused those who, like Teilhard de Chardin, were driven by science to see human evolution to Christ as the omega point.[95]

There is in Osborn's use of the phrase 'the ascent of man' an open-endedness which leaves room for wondering whether Irenaeus might also be suggesting that the whole of humanity is making increasing and collective progress towards God through history. The idea of 'the ascent of man' is in itself ambiguous because although it could either denote individual human beings, each at their own point in history, ascending to God, more commonly it is taken to mean the whole human race making increasing progress through time, in a theological context, towards God.

There is no suggestion by Irenaeus of a human evolution to an omega point; rather, 'between men and God the process of accustoming moves towards a goal which is never fully achieved in time and space.'[96] Schillebeeckx was not only too keenly aware of the horrors inflicted by humanity on humanity to entertain a belief in progress, but he also argued against what he called 'spiritual Darwinism'. He

---

of him and his actions directly. We can only have a degree of understanding of God's ways of working in a mediated manner.

92. Schillebeeckx, *Jesus*, 3 [19].

93. Osborn, *Irenaeus of Lyons*, 80–1.

94. The phrase, 'God's pedagogy of salvation', is one that Schillebeeckx uses in *Jesus*, 526 [564].

95. Eric Osborn, 'Irenaeus of Lyons', in *The First Christian Theologians*, ed. G. R. Evans (Oxford: Blackwell, 2004), 123.

96. Osborn, *Irenaeus of Lyons*, 82.

speaks forcefully against a view that 'history per se mean[s] progress',[97] and calls such a belief to be of 'unChristian character'. He argues that 'spiritual Darwinism' ignores the fact of contingency:

> Unaware of the unChristian character of this belief in progress, at least some theological eschatologies (present and future) have taken over this spiritual Darwinism and its progressive and teleological conception of history. In this perspective, the disappearance of particular historical cultural forms is simply the other side of a progressive development. People again misunderstand contingency, especially the fact that historical forms, seen at the deepest level, disappear because they are mortal and contingent and not because they are on the other side of an evolutionary course of history.[98]

Schillebeeckx combines, on the one hand, an acute awareness of humanity's ability to get things wrong, even disastrously wrong, with, on the other hand, a 'grace-optimism' grounded in his faith in the absolute saving presence of God the Creator.[99] The tone of trust and hope in God that infuses his work is one with that of Irenaeus.

The result of growing in closeness to God is itself a process of salvation or well-being. Time, change and growth are intrinsic elements of human life and, for the Christian, closeness grows with his/her effort and commitment to change things for the better as (s)he grows in Christ and the Spirit. Schillebeeckx writes, '[The] gospel vision requires of Christians an unconditional concern [lived out in action] for every [person], above all for [people] in a pinch, personally or structurally. This demands of them an effort and commitment which has an eye for better structures as well as for the particular human person.'[100] Behr writes, 'It is man, and the *becoming* fully human in communion with God in Christ, that is the centre of the divine economy and of Irenaeus' theology.'[101] This same statement is true of Schillebeeckx. He explicitly argues that becoming fully human in Christ is central to Christianity:

---

97. Schillebeeckx, *GAU*, 97.
98. Ibid.
99. Mary Catherine Hilkert writes, 'the spirituality that [underlies Schillebeeckx's] theological project clearly reflects the "grace-optimism" which he claimed made Chenu "a Thomist through and through". The fundamental hope that has sustained and empowered Schillebeeckx's theological vision is not a naïve optimism that could be sustained apart from a profound belief in grace – the presence of God among us'. "Grace-Optimism": The Spirituality at the Heart of Schillebeeckx's Theology', *Spirituality Today*, 43, 3 (1991): 220–39 (220–1) (henceforth *Grace-Optimism*).
100. Schillebeeckx, *IR*, 93 [106].
101. Behr, *Asceticism and Anthropology in Irenaeus and Clement*, 43 (italics added).

[The] criterion of 'humanizing' is not a reduction of true Christianity; in modern times it is, in fact, the first prerequisite of the human possibility and credibility of the Christian faith. In the entire Bible, the coming of the kingdom of God is the coming of God as salvation by and for human beings. Jesus Christ is the great symbol of this and no other God: 'image of the invisible God' (Col. 1.15).[102]

He emphasizes that Jesus, who reveals God, simultaneously reveals what it is to be fully human:

For Christians Jesus (a) is therefore the decisive and definitive revelation of God and (b) precisely through this at the same time shows us what and how we human beings can, need to and really may be. ... To repeat what the church father Irenaeus said: (a) human salvation lies in the living God and (b) God's honour lies in the happiness, liberation and salvation or wholeness of humanity. In the man Jesus the revelation of the divine and the disclosure of the true, good and really happy humanity coincide in one and the same person.[103]

Striking in this passage is how the humanity of Jesus is not emphasized in such a way as to devalue or relativize the divinity of Jesus. On the contrary, the fullness of humanity is because of the fullness of his divinity. The two exist in direct proportion to each other. Humanity is God's most direct way of being for us.

The interplay of the glory of God and the human glory manifested in Jesus is unique. He is the Son of God and simultaneously his humanity is in common with every human being, through all time. Schillebeeckx takes directly from Irenaeus the idea of God's glory as the human being whose fullness of life is to see God. Irenaeus expresses the link between God's glory, the human being fully alive and the human being's full life as consisting of the sight of God, in these words, '*Gloria Dei, vivens homo; vita autem hominis, visio Dei*'.[104] Translated fairly closely this maxim reads, 'God's glory is a human being that is alive; the aliveness of a human being is in seeing God'[105] and it begs the question of what Irenaeus means by 'to live' or 'to be alive'. More loosely, Philip Kennedy gives the English text as 'God's glory or honour lies in the happiness and prosperity of humankind, which in turn, seeks its happiness and honour in God'.[106] In this translation, which approximates to Schillebeeckx's own, there is an interpretative expansion of what '*vivens*' may mean. It is understood (from the context of Irenaeus' writing) to mean happiness, prosperity and well-being, all vernacular terms for salvation. As such, it might be deliberately interpreting Irenaeus' maxim as linked with Jn 10.10, 'I have come

102. Schillebeeckx, *IR*, 93 [105–6].
103. Schillebeeckx, *JWC*, 17.
104. Irenaeus, *AH*, IV. xxxiv.7 (Harvey's edition, 219).
105. Own translation.
106. Kennedy, *Schillebeeckx*, 93.

that they may have life and have it to overflowing', being an echo of the scriptural text in the tradition.[107] This salvation or well-being comes from sighting or seeing God: the *visio Dei* on earth, either in Jesus on earth, or in his followers through time, and also in heaven.[108]

Schillebeeckx several times echoes and explicitly quotes Irenaeus' statement that God's glory lies in the salvation of humanity. Progress towards God is another way of expressing the increasing closeness to God that brings with it a 'true, good and happy mode of life',[109] that is, salvation. There is no template of the form the *Gloria Dei* takes in the *vivens homo* because, owing to humanity's temporal character, it can only be discovered and experienced by people living and working through time in relationship with God. Just as Balthasar wrote that 'in Irenaeus human nature is seen all along as embedded in … becoming'[110] so Schillebeeckx refers to the fact that humanity is always on the way, always in a process of becoming or reaching what God has destined for it:

> Our situation never allows us to define in positive terms what this [full life and happiness] will ultimately imply for human salvation, given the spiritual openness and the human 'self-transcendence' still to be realized in history and, moreover, in view of the absolute freedom of God as the 'God of men', a God whose glory lies in human happiness.[111]

Balthasar tells of Irenaeus demonstrating that 'it is in this [truly human] creature [Jesus] that God has chosen to reveal himself. The whole of salvation history will be written in man himself'.[112] He then identifies in Irenaeus the fact that an openness in obedience to God has a twofold effect, namely, it enables the person to become more truly human like Christ which in turn glorifies God: 'And whoever remains in [God's] love and devotion and gratitude will increasingly receive greater glory from him by being formed in the likeness of him who died for him.'[113] In obediently opening him/herself to God the human being 'glorifies the artist [God] and the artist glorifies himself in his work'.[114]

Schillebeeckx also describes how the revelation of the divine and the disclosure of true, good and really happy humanity coincide in Jesus. Drawing directly from Irenaeus' idea of God's pedagogy of salvation, Schillebeeckx writes,

---

107. Own translation of Jn 10.10. It is commonly translated as 'I came that they may have life and have it abundantly'. *Perisson* of the Greek is more, even than 'abundantly'. It denotes there being so much (of something) that it overflows.
108. Cf. Poulsom, *Dialectics*, 148–9.
109. Schillebeeckx, *Jesus*, 3 [19].
110. Balthasar, *The Glory of the Lord*, 66.
111. Schillebeeckx, *Christ*, 788 [792].
112. Balthasar, *The Glory of the Lord*, 74.
113. Ibid., 75.
114. Ibid., 74.

God's pedagogy of salvation via nature and history reached supreme concentration in Jesus Christ: he is at once paradigm and imitation, the primal image in which the tarnished imago Dei, man, is restored. The progressive pedagogic process of man's liberation triggered by natural and historical events reaches its zenith in Jesus Christ.[115]

It is through Jesus that human beings are shown 'what and how we human beings can, need to and really must be'.[116]

To be fully human

What, in summary, do Irenaeus and Schillebeeckx say about the human being in the light of Christian faith in the Creator? Human beings as creatures are dependent on God for the gift of life. They are free to acknowledge this dependence and are invited to respond to God in gratitude for life and all it offers. They express this gratitude by reciprocating God's love in a return of giving, both in prayer and action for others. Christians work with God and sanctify the creation when they build a better world in accordance with God's kingdom. In direct proportion to an awareness of dependence on God develops a sense of corresponding freedom to become fully human as oneself, *sequela Jesu*. The deepest meaning for human beings is to be found in God as he is revealed in Jesus.

Human beings are temporal beings, embedded in time and becoming, related to God by what they are and by what they become. They are made for cooperation with and progress towards God. There is an inseparable link between God's creative action, holding people in existence, and his saving action in which he reveals himself and makes it possible for people to draw closer to him and participate more fully in his life. Entering more deeply into relationship with God is both a mystical and a practical business expressed in showing God's love to fellow human beings. The salvation from God that people experience is happiness and well-being and is to God's greater glory.

The human being in whom God's glory was most fully seen is Jesus. His friends, disciples and followers saw the glory of God in human form and saw what it is to be fully human. In responding to God, followers of Jesus become the Body of Christ and the face of Christ in the world today. This allows others to see and to meet Christ in Jesus' followers and the lives they lead. Jesus' followers are called to be the *visio Dei*.

Balthasar's third point of articulation: The threefold order of salvation in the Incarnate Word of God

Minns points out that one of the major tasks that faced Irenaeus in his refutation of the arguments of the Gnostics was to demonstrate that the Old and the New

---

115. Schillebeeckx, *Jesus*, 526 [564].
116. Schillebeeckx, *JWC*, 17.

Testaments 'do not reveal each a different God, but only different stages of the relationship between the one and only God and his creation'.[117] This demonstration by Irenaeus turns into an entire theology of history 'built upon the belief that it is the God-given destiny of humankind to grow to perfection by gradual stages, and that God guides the development in a loving, infinitely patient, ever-vigilant, and non-coercive manner'.[118] The three stages in which God achieves his plan for the whole of his creation are: Adam up to the Incarnation (recounted in the Old Testament scriptures); the Incarnation (recounted in the New Testament texts); and from the Incarnation to the end-time (lived out in the Church).

Preparation for the coming of Jesus: From Adam to the Incarnation

Balthasar writes about Irenaeus' idea of the growth and development of humankind in preparation for the arrival of Jesus. He says that 'The economy of salvation is the training of man by God to encounter the God-man.'[119] He refers to the different stages of salvation history and the ways in which humankind is prepared for the *visio Dei*. He stresses the importance of the Old Testament period when he writes, 'The process of accustoming takes place in the whole order of salvation, especially in the Old Testament, which is a preliminary adaptation (*praeaptatio*), a preliminary formation (*praeformatio*), a preliminary training (*praemeditatio, prosmeletan*) of mankind for the coming of Christ.'[120] Everything in the Old Testament is 'to prepare the people's faith for the unfettered freedom of Christ'.[121] Then, with Christ, 'the Church with its timeless newness will make its entry'.[122] The Church 'is the mature product of salvation history and its final form at the end of the ages'[123] and the Lord 'continues to fulfil the New Covenant in the Church until the end foretold by the law'.[124]

The Incarnation: Jesus of Nazareth

Everything within the whole creation narrative, past, present and future, homes in on one central figure, Jesus. Although Schillebeeckx does not make a separate, methodical study of the texts of the Old Testament as the first stage of salvation history, he sees and analyses them through the prism of the New Testament texts, above all in the first book of his trilogy, *Jesus*. In this study of Jesus, in which he sets out to write down 'a piece of reflective thinking about Jesus of Nazareth, whom the churches of Christ, to which [he] belong[s], confess as final salvation',[125] his specific

---

117. Minns, *Irenaeus*, 56.
118. Ibid.
119. Balthasar, *The Glory of the Lord*, 81.
120. Ibid., 80.
121. Ibid., 83.
122. Ibid., 86.
123. Ibid., 87.
124. Ibid., 88–9.
125. Schillebeeckx, *Jesus*, 15 [33].

concern is 'with the same regard for faith and for human reason, ... to look for what a christological belief in Jesus of Nazareth can intelligibly signify to people today'.[126] Schillebeeckx, like Irenaeus, sees the Old Testament scriptures as indispensable to an understanding in faith of Jesus. He makes constant reference to the historical contexts and literary traditions of the Old Testament which formed and informed Jesus himself and other Jews contemporary with him. Those Jews who, in Irenaean terms, had allowed themselves to be guided by God's pedagogy and to live by it recognized and 'found salvation, explicitly qualified as "from God", in Jesus of Nazareth, whom they came to describe ... as "the Christ, son of God, our Lord"'.[127] In the historical span covered by the Old Testament texts, there is a progression in Israel's expectations and aspirations which enabled Jesus' disciples and followers to recognize and acknowledge their experience of salvation in him as salvation with God as its source.[128] Schillebeeckx refers to and explores 'the religious and cultural expectations, aspirations and ideologies present in [Jesus'] environment, with its own established key concepts'[129] which are inscribed in the Old Testament. He devotes a section to existing Jewish models of end-time saviour figures[130] and deals in depth, for example, with national, dynastic and prophetic, sapiential 'Davidic messianism'.[131] Tracking down the experience of encountering Jesus incarnate is the subject of the first book of Schillebeeckx's great trilogy, *Jesus*. The second and third volumes, *Christ* and *Church*,[132] explore the experience of generations of believers in the third stage of the economy of salvation, the time from the Incarnation to the end-time.

From the Incarnation to the end-time: Church, the human story of God

The three historical stages of Irenaeus' economy of salvation are demarcated by the different people through whom God educates humanity and 'accustoms them to his glory' in each stage. They are the Prophets, Jesus, God's Son on earth and the Spirit-filled members of his church. Poulsom draws attention to another Irenaean perspective in understanding the second and third stages of Irenaeus' economy of salvation. In the light of the *Gloria Dei* axiom and its context, he suggests that Irenaeus also interprets the stages of the economy in terms of 'ways

---

126. Ibid., 16 [33].
127. Ibid., 3 [19].
128. Ibid., 193 [219].
129. Ibid., 34 [51].
130. Ibid., 404–13 [441–9].
131. Ibid., 414–22 [450–9].
132. The original Dutch titles of Schillebeeckx's trilogy are: (1) *Jezus, het verhaal van een levende* [*Jesus, the Story of the Living One*] and, because of the double entendre of the Dutch, *The Story of One Alive* entitled for the English translation, *Jesus: An Experiment in Christology*; (2) *Gerechtigheid en liefde, Genade en bevrijding* [*Justice and Love, Grace and Liberation*] rendered as *Christ: The Christian Experience in the Modern World*; (3) *Mensen als verhaal van God*, [*Human Beings as God's Story*] entitled *Church: The Human Story of God*.

of seeing God'.[133] The phrase *visio Dei* is conventionally understood to mean the face-to-face beatific vision of God in heaven. Poulsom, however, writes that Canlis points out that 'Irenaeus, like many writers of his period, speaks of human life as a participation in God's life and therefore is speaking [in the maxim] not merely of [heavenly] beatitude, but also of sanctification [on earth] and, indeed, creation.'[134] Over and above ontological dependence on God for biological life, human beings, in their response to God the Creator, go further forward into participation in his life and glory.[135] Participation in God's life brings sanctification, and sanctification brings some glimpse or sight of the glory of God.[136] In view of the fact that 'Irenaeus insists upon our incapacity to bear the full weight of the glory of God, although he is equally insistent that that is what we are intended to do,'[137] Poulsom asks, 'Is there, then, a human life in which this splendour of God can clearly be seen?'[138] That life is the life of Jesus. By reason of its full bearing of the splendour of God it is the most fully human life. Jesus in the glory of his humanity was experienced as 'decisive and definitive salvation from God'.[139] It is by following Jesus, writes Poulsom, that 'our participation in the Son … is our participation in the divine, and thus our "becoming human".'[140] He concludes by describing how the vision of God is to be found this side of eternity, 'The fullness of human life is, indeed, found in the face-to-face beatific vision of God; it is to be found, too, in and on the face of Jesus who is called the Christ; it is also intended to be found in and on the faces of those who follow Jesus in the church.'[141] For Schillebeeckx the glory of God is human beings alive in their sight of God.

Of the sight or glimpse of himself that God bestows, Canlis quotes Irenaeus saying, 'for one and the same Lord … confers gifts upon men, that is, his own presence'. She goes on to say that this is the whole purpose of creation, namely, friendship with God: 'this is the thrust of creation, the purpose towards which it

---

133. Poulsom, *Dialectics*, 148.

134. Ibid., 147.

135. Participation in God's life came to be known as deification. The term 'deification' for human participation in God's life and glory was never used by Irenaeus himself although he provides later writers (e.g. Athanasius) with the content of their doctrine of deification. Norman Russell, *The Doctrine of Deification in the Greek Patristic Tradition* (Oxford: Oxford University Press, 2006), 105.

136. Poulsom says of this linking of God's creation and humanity's sanctification and beatitude (happiness because they see something of God), 'on the basis of this idea of participation, a seamless philosophical theology can be advocated, in which creation, sanctification and beatitude are linked without being confused, distinguished without being separated'. *Dialectics*, 148.

137. Canlis, 'Being Made Human', 450.

138. Poulsom, *Dialectics*, 148.

139. Schillebeeckx, *IR*, 10.022.

140. Ibid.

141. Ibid., 148–9.

bends: God sharing himself with humanity, and humanity's being able to receive him. "Now these things did indeed make man glorious, by supplying what was wanting to him, namely the friendship of God".[142]

Schillebeeckx interprets this friendship between God and humanity as one enjoyed and its purpose is to work together to establish God's kingdom on earth. The building of God's kingdom, like the sanctification of human beings, is embedded in time, now and in the future. Schillebeeckx explains that God's 'lordship' or rule and the kingdom of God are two aspects of what the New Testament encapsulates in the single concept *basileia tou Theou*.[143]

God's 'lordship' refers to 'the here-and-now character of his rule; the kingdom of God refers to the final state of bliss which forms the basis of his saving action. Thus present and future are essentially interrelated.'[144] Schillebeeckx also stresses the fact that this kingdom coming 'means that God looks to us humans to implement his "rule" in our world'.[145] Schillebeeckx expresses in workmanlike terms what Irenaeus conveys more poetically with his image of God moulding human clay, and human clay keeping itself responsive to God. The linking of creation and salvation, of growth into full humanity and God's glory, and, in Jesus, his perfect humanity and God's glory, is common to both Irenaeus and Schillebeeckx.

---

142. Canlis, 'Being Made Human', 444, quoting Irenaeus, AH IV.16.4.
143. Schillebeeckx, *Jesus*, 121 [141].
144. Ibid., 121 [141].
145. Ibid., 121–2 [142].

Part II

QUESTIONS OF CONTINUITY AND CHANGE

Chapter 3

QUESTIONS OF CONTINUITY AND CHANGE

There is a major debate about continuity and change in theological circles. In general, it is a debate about the continuing purity of truth in expressions of dogma and theology that are made in a world that changes. When there are strong, even radical, currents of change in politics, culture and society, what happens to church dogma? Does it stand rocklike, unmoved by the currents of change, or are even the solid rocks of dogma shaped and changed by the passing currents? Do existing statements of faith remain valid while new expressions are formed? With regard to Schillebeeckx, does his theology accommodate itself to modernity at the expense of the truth of the Church's dogma? Does it remain anchored in the dogmatic tradition of the Church? What is Schillebeeckx's understanding of tradition? What about his method or methods of working? Does he change them? Crucially, is there a confusion of his method with the substance of his theology? How did the method of his Christology emerge? These are the questions that this chapter examines.

The issue of change and continuity is a central constituent of Schillebeeckx studies and has three aspects: change and continuity in the historical contexts throughout which Schillebeeckx lived; Schillebeeckx's engagement in the debate about continuity and change in the formulation of church dogma; and, thirdly, continuity and change in Schillebeeckx's own method/s in his theology.

Aspects of continuity and change

Continuity and change: Historical contexts

Schillebeeckx's life (1914–2009) spanned ninety-five years. Politically he lived through two world wars, the Russian and Chinese revolutions and the emergence of international terrorism. During his lifetime horses were replaced by cars, tanks (as opposed to the horse-drawn gun carriages of the First World War) and motor-driven agricultural machinery; air travel became commonplace; and space rockets enabled astronauts to land on the moon. In medicine, antibiotics, the structure of DNA, sophisticated imaging devices and keyhole surgery were discovered and invented. The mobile telephone was invented in 1984 and, in 1991, the World

Wide Web came into use. The degree of political, cultural and societal change was, and continues to be, astonishing. These rapidly changing contexts are the ones in which individuals, institutions and nations find themselves. The way they react will be found somewhere on a spectrum between proactivity and reactivity. People may resist change but the fact of the contingencies of temporal, historical life is unalterable.

Just as things did not stand still in the spheres of politics, technology and culture during Schillebeeckx's lifetime, things also did not stand still in Christian theology and Catholic theology in particular. For churches, for their members and theologians, change is of special interest and challenge. How do they keep hold of their faith in God, revealed most fully in the one person, Jesus, while, at the same time, expressing and applying the identity of this meaning in different, sometimes radically different, historical and cultural contexts? Can there be continuity and at the same time change? What remains the same and what changes? As Schillebeeckx puts it, the quest is for 'a proclamation which will, on the one hand, remain faithful to the word of God and will, on the other hand, allow that word to ring out in a way which does not by-pass the reality of this life'.[1] Erik Borgman, in his biography of Edward Schillebeeckx, writes:

> Here biography is understood as a description of the history of a thinker in the context which surrounds and permeates him or her, and at the same time as a description of the surrounding history in the light of the history of this one thinker.[2]

Borgman's study covers the years 1914–65.[3] He speaks of a dialectic between a theologian and his changing context, stressing that 'people of stature are interwoven with their own time and context,' and he suggests that 'they show their greatness precisely in the way in which they deal with their context, not in their independence from it.'[4] In taking a contextual approach to theology and history of theology, Borgman is concerned to depict the tradition of faith and theology in the writings of Schillebeeckx and, at the same time, to analyse and clarify what he calls any 'shifts and fractures'. In other words, he is determining and explaining the continuity and change in the *oeuvre* of Schillebeeckx contextually. He writes that Schillebeeckx's theological texts 'are analysed, the shifts in them are determined and explained, the fractures are interpreted, and the continuity which perhaps lies behind them is traced'.[5]

1. Schillebeeckx, *GFoM*, 1.
2. Borgman, *Edward Schillebeeckx*, 8.
3. Erik Borgman is not writing the sequel volume to *A Theologian in His History*, an undertaking he is leaving to others (conversation 29 August 2014).
4. Borgman, *Edward Schillebeeckx*, 9. In a footnote to this remark, Borgman acknowledges his indebtedness to the contextual approach to theology and the history of theology developed by the dogmatics section in the Nijmegen theological faculty in the 1980s.
5. Ibid., 8.

Similarly, Philip Kennedy writes that Schillebeeckx's 'work could never be regarded as an objectified body of theological doctrine enunciated independently of historical change. On the contrary, it is marked by a cohesion between his theological teaching and personal history.'[6] Kennedy uses the expression 'biographically determined theology' in making an eminently Schillebeeckian point: nothing we human beings think, say or do can be divorced from our contexts.

The three main historico-theological backdrops of the Catholic Church during Schillebeeckx's lifetime were modernism, Neo-Thomism and the Second Vatican Council. 'Modernism' was the term applied by the opponents of the Catholic scholars and thinkers who wished to 'open Catholic philosophy, theology and Biblical studies to contemporary thought or at least to enter into dialogue with critical history, modern Biblical studies and new philosophical currents'.[7] The exact views of different Modernists remain under review,[8] but the fear was that those who held such views were reducing the supreme value and content of common statements of faith. Pius X, in the last year of whose pontificate (1903–14) Schillebeeckx was born, took measures aimed at reinforcing the theological stability of the church. In 1907 he condemned modernism (although as O'Collins and Farrugia note, he did so in a way that failed to make careful distinctions[9]) through the decree *Lamentabili* and the encyclical *Pascendi*. He reinforced a curriculum of neo-scholasticism[10] for courses in theology for priests in training.

Between the two world wars neo-scholasticism, which was predominantly neo-Thomistic, continued to be the system of education for those in training for the Catholic priesthood. Karen Kilby, in writing about Karl Rahner, describes neo-scholasticism as follows:

> Neo-scholasticism was both a satisfying and a frustrating intellectual system – and both for the same reasons. It was a highly structured, self-enclosed system, one which had turned its back on the modern world and all the intellectual difficulties it raises. It offered a world which was orderly and in which everything had its place. Certain questions were open for debate and disagreement and differing opinion, but these were definite, circumscribed questions, contained within a much larger whole where everything was worked out and all the important matters already resolved.[11]

---

6. Kennedy, *Deus Humanissimus*, 29.
7. McGinn, *Thomas Aquinas's Summa Theologiae*, 178.
8. Ibid., 179.
9. Gerald O'Collins S.J. and Edward G. Farrugia, S.J., *A Concise Dictionary of Theology* (London: HarperCollins, 1991), 145.
10. The term 'neo-scholasticism' is not being used synonymously with the term 'neo-Thomism' but as consisting predominantly of the content and method of neo-Thomism.
11. Karen Kilby, *The SPCK Introduction to Karl Rahner* (London: SPCK, 2007), xvii.

Kilby goes on to point out that much of Rahner's work, particularly before the 1960s and the Second Vatican Council, 'can be understood as an effort to open up this neo-Scholasticism'.[12] Rahner was not alone in wanting to open up and reconstruct the standard neo-scholastic curriculum. Hans Urs von Balthasar, who entered the Society of Jesus in 1929, found neo-scholasticism to be a straitjacket. He writes,

> My entire period of study in the Society of Jesus was a grim struggle with the dreariness of theology, with what man had made of the glory of revelation … I could have lashed out with the fury of a Samson. I felt like tearing down, with Samson's own strength, the whole temple burying myself beneath the rubble.[13]

Balthasar, in fact, later cooperated with Rahner to compose a plan for the reform of Catholic theology.[14] Schillebeeckx, who joined the Dominican order in 1934, and studied theology in the Dominican *studium* at Leuven from 1939, also found the way that theology was taught frustrating. The problem was not Aquinas' thought nor his approach to theology, both of which deeply and permanently influenced Schillebeeckx. Rather, it was 'the identification of theology with the exposition of concepts that are not related to their historical contexts and to contemporary human experiences'.[15]

These three theologians, more or less contemporaneous, who lived in different countries and did not have any contact with each other during their theological formation, nevertheless each found Thomist theology as framed by Catholic theologians of the sixteenth and seventeenth centuries dreary and dissatisfying. This was for two main reasons: as twentieth-century men, they were approaching theology from a changed context from their sixteenth- and seventeenth-century predecessors, and, secondly, as young theologians they felt compelled to articulate the truths of their faith in relation to their own experiences. It is worth noting at this point that Pope Leo XIII's own move to make neo-Thomism the official teaching of Catholicism as laid out in the encyclical *Aeterni Patris* in 1879 was itself a response to the changing context of his own time, namely, nineteenth-century modernity. Bernard McGinn points out that Pope Leo XIII, despite the condemnation of slavery in his social encyclicals, his opening of the Vatican archives to research and his outreach to some forms of democratic government, nevertheless wanted to intellectualize 'the combat with modernity … He would not come to terms with the modern values; rather he would restore in the world an objective and immutable order, with the church as its most effective guardian.'[16]

---

12. Ibid.

13. Fergus Kerr, *Twentieth Century Catholic Theologians: From Neoscholasticism to Nuptial Mysticism* (Oxford: Blackwell, 2007), 122.

14. Ibid.

15. Ibid.

16. McGinn, *Thomas Aquinas's Summa Theologiae*, 168.

Continuity and change: The formulation, interpretation and reinterpretation of Church dogma

In a discussion about change and continuity in church dogma and the articulation of beliefs, it is helpful to start with a principle stated by Thomas Aquinas and to which Philip Kennedy draws attention. Aquinas expresses the principle in these words, '*actus fidentis non terminatur ad enuntiabile sed ad rem*'.[17] [The act of a believer does not terminate at a statement [of faith] but at the reality.] The distinction between the *rem*, the reality, and the *enuntiabile*, the statement about reality, is crucial. In a survey of six articles that Schillebeeckx wrote in 1945, Kennedy highlights this Thomist principle as being part of his 'conceptual grids' which always remained operative in his subsequent works.[18] Kennedy writes that 'in his discourses on what guarantees that a reinterpretation of faith conforms to primordial Christian faith proclamations', Schillebeeckx clung to this principle. In other words, 'one believes in God, not in statements about God'.[19]

Much of the tension, and strength of feeling, in debates about whether or not, and how, there should be reformulations of dogma arises first because it can be difficult to know the point at which the distinction between the *rem* and an *enuntiabile* lies. Words have to be used even to name the fact of an unchanging *rem*. There is a borderland in which the *rem* stops and the *enuntiabile* starts. Secondly, ontologically speaking, what is it that goes on between God (who is unchanging) and our statements about him (which change)? What crosses the borderland, that is, the distinction between human beings and God? It is the activity of faith, initiated by God, given by him as a gift and made their own by human beings in their open response to God. The latter is Aquinas' *actus fidentis*. The role of faith is sometimes sidelined in debates about how to express its truths.

Where is the distinction between the rem and the enuntiabile?

To use an image, there is a borderland in which the *rem* is manifested in the creation yet remains distinct from it, and in which *enuntiabilia* are stammeringly articulated. One way of conveying this distinction might be to say that within this borderland we name the *rem*. Another way might be to say that within this borderland the naming of the *rem* becomes and grows into an *enuntiabile*. Either way, this borderland is not a no man's land because nothing or nowhere in the creation is unowned by God. God is absolutely present in his creative action and his self-revelation. To borrow from philosophy, the borderland could be described as the place where the 'veil of perception' lies.[20] If the idea of the veil of perception is applied to Aquinas' maxim, I would suggest that it falls between the reality of God (the *rem*) manifested in his creation and sense perception-cum-concepts, rather than falling between sense perception and concepts.

---

17. St Thomas Aquinas, *Summa Theologiae*, II-II, q. 1, a. 2, ad 2.
18. Kennedy, *Schillebeeckx*, 57–60.
19. Ibid., 58.
20. https://plato.stanford.edu/entries/perception-problem, section 3.1.3.

Consistent with this positioning of the veil of perception is Schillebeeckx's understanding of what makes human knowledge possible. In writing about the concept of truth he distances himself from Maréchal's, and the Maréchalian, corrective to scholastic conceptualism. Although Maréchal and De Petter both criticize the conceptualism of neo-scholasticism and also agree on two basic points, there is a critical difference between their fundamental positions.[21] They agree that 'human concepts do not in themselves apprehend reality in itself, but only grasp individual objects as a part of totality', and they agree that there is 'a non-conceptual basis for the validity of conceptual knowledge'.[22] Their difference, however, is that 'Maréchal locates the non-conceptual element of knowledge in the dynamism of the human intellect, whereas De Petter places the emphasis on the dynamic element of the *contents* of knowledge that have reference to the infinite'.[23] Borgman, in his account of De Petter, writes that De Petter's argument was against a particular epistemological notion that had a large following in Traditional Thomism, namely, that the 'thought of entities is brought into being through the abstract concepts of metaphysics'.[24] De Petter called this notion 'conceptualistic' because it claimed that 'it was the metaphysical concepts which brought reality together into a totality'.[25] In De Petter's view, as Borgman explains, 'metaphysical concepts explicated an experience implicitly present in the knowledge of reality' something 'which made it possible to ask whether the traditional Thomist concepts expressed this experience adequately'. De Petter developed the theory of what he called an 'implicit intuition of totality'.[26] According to this understanding, knowledge does not presuppose just a known object and a knowing subject. Rather, the knower and the known form part of a whole that binds them together. For De Petter 'philosophizing in terms of "implicit intuition" connected Catholic thought directly with human experience'.[27] De Petter sought to combine metaphysics, as in Aquinas, with phenomenologies such as Husserl's.

In 1962 Schillebeeckx writes that Maréchal, in providing a solution to the problem of scholastic conceptualism, based 'the reality and validity of our knowledge of God not on these [scholastic] concepts in themselves, but [precisely] on a non-intellectual, dynamic element – the dynamism of the human spirit towards the infinite'.[28] He says that one of the things that is 'unsatisfactory about Maréchal's solution is that … the validity of knowledge is based on an extra-intellectual element',[29] that is, one that supposes to cross from the thought and

21. De Petter had, when a student of theology, written a thesis on the epistemology of Maréchal.
22. Fiorenza, 'The New Theology and Transcendental Thomism', 197–232 (202).
23. Ibid.
24. Borgman, *Edward Schillebeeckx*, 41.
25. This account of De Petter is taken from Erik Borgman, *Edward Schillebeeckx*, 41–2.
26. De Petter's main sources for his phenomenologies were Husserl and Merleau-Ponty; Borgman, *Edward Schillebeeckx*, 41, and Kennedy, *Schillebeeckx*, 40.
27. Borgman, *Edward Schillebeeckx*, 42.
28. Schillebeeckx, *R&T*, 197.
29. Ibid.

linguistic conditions of the created to somewhere beyond. Schillebeeckx holds that the two do not, and cannot, exist separately. He sees experience as shaped by our concepts and our concepts as shaped by our experience. Knowledge cannot happen if it lacks either one. He neither jettisons the conceptual nor promotes the experiential at the expense of the conceptual. In accordance with his habitual thought pattern of relational dialectic, he sees human knowledge as an intertwining or two-way crossover of the conceptual and the experiential. He writes, 'Experience and conceptual thought thus together constitute our single knowledge of reality.'[30] For this reason I would suggest that for Schillebeeckx the veil of perception falls decisively between the *rem* and the *enuntiabile*.

In summary so far: in practice the point at which the distinction between the *rem* and the *enuntiabile* lies is not always obvious. The *rem* (God) has to be named. When does the naming of the *rem* morph into describing? Among the names of God in the Old Testament are, for example, Yahweh or Lord, and God is often described as Spirit. In the New Testament God is named and described as Son as well as Spirit. Is 'The Holy Trinity, Father, Son and Holy Spirit' a naming of the *rem* or an *enuntiabile* about God? It is easy to see how confusion can arise. For Schillebeeckx an awareness of the Thomist distinction between the *rem* and an *enuntiabile* is crucial to an understanding of questions about the formulation of dogma.

The rem, the enuntiabile and the actus fidentis

In theology, articulations of belief, doctrine and dogma are made because they attempt to describe or define something. The thing, or reality, that doctrine names and attempts to say something about, is: what/whom we call God, the attributes of God and what God reveals of himself to humanity, supremely in the person of Jesus. The *rem* has to have a name, yet it is distinct from the *enuntiabilia*, statements that believers make about the object or *rem* of their faith. Unlike the unchanging *rem* of faith, *enuntiabilia* change.

Where, then, does the distinction between reality and the statement of faith leave statements about God? In different periods of history (patristic, medieval and modern, for example), statements and ways of talking about God and his revelation in Jesus, do, in fact, change and they have been presented in different terms according to the linguistic and cultural thought forms of the day. Does that invalidate earlier expressions or forbid fresh attempts? At stake, in seeking new ways of expressing the Christian faith, is whether that faith is made recognizable as belief in the gospel of Jesus confessed as the Christ or whether the truths of that faith are being falsified or eroded.[31] Can new expressions of Christian faith

---

30. Ibid., 199.

31. Schillebeeckx argues that categories of thought and speech change to such an extent that, in order to talk about God in a meaningful way, our 'language about God must grow and change with the development of our existential experience'. See Schillebeeckx, *GFoM*, 44 [72-3].

be both distinct from the old expressions and, at the same time, be in continuity with them?

In answering this question it is necessary to look at the third element at work in Aquinas' statement, namely, faith, or the act of the believer. There can be no statements of belief about God without faith.

Faith as the parameter and underlying dynamic in Schillebeeckx's understanding of continuity and change in statements of dogma

Faith for Schillebeeckx is the sine qua non of theology. It is 'an inner demand of theology'.[32] He says that theology begins with reflection and that the reflection that is inherent in the life of faith can take two forms. The first is 'the spontaneous, undeliberate reflection on faith which all Christians pursue' and the second is when that spontaneous reflection is extended to 'a deliberate, methodical, and systematic reflection, [which] is precisely theology'.[33] Faith is the magnetic field and parameter of theology, its essential and distinguishing dynamic. Schillebeeckx makes the distinction between theology and the study of Christianity in this way:

> It is possible to study Christianity scientifically outside this faith, and even to study its dogmatic content (as, for example, Buddhism is studied in comparative religion), but in that case we shall be concerned with a purely 'humane' activity, and not with theology proper, which is concerned with pronouncements about the supernatural reality as this is in itself.[34]

Faith is 'concerned with pronouncements'. Schillebeeckx wrote these words in 1958 and, in the same article, already alluded to the development of dogma. He says that in the post-apostolic church it was the task of theology 'increasingly to illuminate' the revelation expressed under divine guarantee in Scripture. In fact, it is the task of theology to study all the writers who testify to the faith throughout the course of time 'from the fathers of the church down to those of the present day, without neglecting a single period, since God has never failed to keep his end up'.[35]

It is a point on which he disagrees with Bultmann, about whose understanding of hermeneutics he writes,

> The criterion for an authentic interpretation of the kerygma is therefore in Bultmann's opinion, to be found in man himself, in his present understanding of himself as preunderstanding. In other words, the hermeneutical principle is

---

32. Schillebeeckx, *R&T*, 71.
33. Ibid., 73.
34. Ibid., 74.
35. Ibid., 79.

not contained in faith, but in human preunderstanding which, however, submits itself to the correction of the word of God.[36]

The fact that Schillebeeckx firmly sets hermeneutics within faith is a vital point to bear in mind. This is because when he comes to consider the 'truly human condition', under the heading of God's rule of humanity, he is not jettisoning the mystical or metaphysical aspects of theology.[37] The human being is contained within the embrace of the Creator and only knows God – and how he or she might become fully human in relationship with God – because of faith.

Schillebeeckx goes on to say that 'theology speaks a universally intelligible language – its principles are the universal hermeneutical principles of all human understanding – but theology does not deduce its intelligibility from these universal principles'.[38] For Schillebeeckx it is faith that gives theological understanding (expressed in *enuntiabilia*) intelligibility. He writes, 'the theological use of hermeneutics implies a *dogmatic* problem – dogmatic theology, faith, [which] does not come exclusively within the sphere of *general* hermeneutics'.[39] He goes on to state that hermeneutics and dogmatics are not identical, yet they are inseparably linked. 'Without faith, there is no understanding of faith, but without understanding there is also no faith.'[40] The nuances of the word 'faith' are already evident.

---

36. Schillebeeckx, *GFoM*, 10 [15]. Schillebeeckx points out that as a consequence of the view that 'the hermeneutical principle is not contained in faith',

> several people have already maintained that a separate theology faculty is an absurdity and that theology should be a branch of the faculty of 'philosophy and literature' because, in its interpretation of [statements of] faith, theology recognizes no other scientific law than that of the exegesis and the interpretation of texts in general (applied in this case to the Bible, confessional texts and so on). (Ibid., 10–11 [15])

More colourfully, Heinz Zahrnt writes of Bultmann that he 'fails to do justice to the cosmic scope of … revelation, its relationship not only to the existential life of the individual, but also to the destiny of the whole world … All that is left of the whole long process is a single point … God's great drama has become An "existentialist private performance"'. Heinz Zahrnt, *The Question of God*, trans. R. A. Wilson (New York: Harcourt, Brace & World, 1969), 243–4, quoting Rudolf Bohren. Zahrnt, in turn, is quoted by Nicholas Lash, *Change in Focus: A Study of Doctrinal Change and Continuity* (London: Sheed and Ward, 1973), 144.

37. Edward Schillebeeckx, *Jesus*, 142 of original translation, preferred here. The new translation (122) renders 'truly human condition' as 'true humanity'.

38. Schillebeeckx, *GFoM*, 11 [16].

39. Ibid.

40. Ibid.

But what is faith?[41] In contemporary north-western culture, Davies writes that 'in much day-to-day discourse, and in much that is written, "faith" is what a person has when (s)he believes in the existence of God'.[42] As such it tends to have a one-dimensional, somewhat cerebral connotation: it consists of assent to formulations of belief. Certainly, in common contemporary understanding, faith is sometimes thought of as a 'thing', perhaps somewhat randomly distributed by God, which enables a person to believe. A person either has it or does not have it. This understanding might suggest a God who verges on the deistic. Davies, in contrast to a distorted and reductionist concept of faith of this kind, tells how Aquinas understands faith. He says that 'faith is a divinely given disposition', 'the virtue of wanting and attaining God, the ultimate good, as he has revealed himself to us in the person of Christ'.[43] God is the source of faith and this gift that he offers asks for a response. From the moment of God's revealing of himself to human beings, words are used by them to formulate inner thoughts and then to speak these thoughts aloud to each other.

Schillebeeckx expresses it this way: 'Believing is receiving what could not be thought out by men.'[44] Human beings could not have invented what comes with faith. Christian faith '*causes* us to think. ... Thinking in faith is always thinking afterwards, reflecting about what has been heard'.[45] Those with Christian faith, and especially the theologians among them, think, and they attempt to put into words something of the mystery which God reveals of himself to humanity. 'The God of Salvation is made the subject of a conversation between men.'[46] Truth is brought to light only within human intersubjectivity and this dialogue is only possible by the power of the Holy Spirit. This conversation is held by theologians 'in a context enriched by the meditation on the faith of the early Christians, constantly listening and interpreting the words for themselves in their own

---

41. One answer is the one that Peter gave when Jesus asked him, 'Who do you say that I am?' Peter said, 'You are the Messiah, the Son of the living God' (Mt. 16.16). More recent is the full and carefully worded definition of faith decreed at Vatican I in the Dogmatic Constitution on the Catholic Faith:

> This faith, which is the beginning of human salvation, the Catholic Church professes to be a supernatural virtue, by means of which, with the grace of God inspiring and assisting us, we believe to be true what he has revealed, not because we believe its intrinsic truth by the natural light of reason, but because of the authority of God himself who makes the revelation and can neither deceive nor be deceived. (Ch. 3, *On Faith*, 24 April 1870; downloaded from www.ewtn.com/library/COUNCILS, 10 February 2016)

42. Davies, *The Thought of Thomas Aquinas*, 274.
43. Ibid.
44. Schillebeeckx, *UF*, 42 [47].
45. Ibid.
46. Schillebeeckx, *GFoM*, 3 [006].

hearts'.⁴⁷ Schillebeeckx, in more technical and, at the same time, mystical terms, refers to 'the structure of the act of faith'. He writes that it 'contains a correlation between the saving mystery of Christ and the basic intentionality or orientation of the act of faith which is inwardly determined by the mystery of Christ'.⁴⁸ On the part of a believer, faith is a response. Schillebeeckx emphasizes that faith is not 'a neutral, previously given structure, which can afterwards be directed towards the saving mystery of Christ. If faith is basically correctly orientated, it is inwardly determined by the mystery of Christ.'⁴⁹

Above all, whatever goes on between God and a person, and God and the church as the community of believers, is dynamic, not static. For Schillebeeckx faith is, as it were, the umbilical cord of new/second birth that connects God's human creatures to the Creator. It is the conduit through which God's invitation to get to know him flows one way, and through which a person's response flows back to God the other way. From the side of God (so to speak), his Spirit is at work to enable human beings to respond in faith. From the human side, their work, in the dynamic of faith, is to listen, articulate, converse and meditate on the texts and teachings that are handed to them by the tradition while at the same time asking the questions that arise from their own context. This dynamic of faith is an essential element, operating through time and in changing historical contexts, which underpins all attempts to articulate, to interpret and to rearticulate the content of faith. We can say all sorts of things about faith but we cannot physically touch or grasp faith with our fingers any more than we are able to touch or grasp existence, whatever it is from God that keeps us breathing. The mystery of faith is the connection between the truth that we are trying to articulate and our articulation of that truth by means of the material creation.

We cannot access the true mystery of faith independently of language and experience. It is faith, living and dynamic, that makes possible the fundamental unity and equality of the relation between differing articulations of the evangelical message and changing historical situations.⁵⁰ This fundamental unity and equality is what Schillebeeckx means by the phrase 'the identity of [the datum of] faith'. The identity of a human being, which is the reality of a person, is a good analogy for the identity of faith. A human being is alive in a genetically stable but waxing and waning body (body in the widest sense, to include all physical and mental functions), which is constantly conditioned by his/her environment and interactions with it. In this way the identity or sameness of a person involves

---

47. Ibid.
48. Ibid., 42 [47].
49. Ibid., 54 [60].
50. See Edward Schillebeeckx, *Essays: Ongoing Theological Quests*, trans. Marcelle Manley (except ch. 2, trans. Edward Fitzgerald and Peter Tomlinson), The Collected Works of Edward Schillebeeckx 11 (London: Bloomsbury, 2014), 62.

change.[51] Likewise, Schillebeeckx's phrase 'the identity of faith' refers to the corresponding relation between the unchanging offer and gift of faith from God and the changing expressions, articulated and lived out, in the response of myriad individuals who accept that gift each in their historical context.

It is not surprising that the propositions of faith are sometimes confused with what it is that they are referring to. The word 'faith' is used equivocally to express a range of meanings. The meanings denote things which, when working together, form the stepping stones, as it were, of friendship between God and human beings. It is used to mean any of the following singly or in combination: faith is a gift of God; faith is (always) an initiative of God's who prompts and invites through his Spirit; in human beings faith is a response, or disposition of being open to God and wanting to get to know him; faith is the means by which believers come to work out and express truths about God; faith is those truths professed; it is a belief in, or set of beliefs about, God as revealed; the word 'faith' is often used as a collective singular noun to mean the articles of faith, for example, the creeds that a Christian professes.

For Schillebeeckx an essential element of faith is, of course, its expression in articles of belief although faith is not *merely* an assent to beliefs. More than that, he wrote that understanding faith as a requirement to assent to formulations of belief *framed in the past* can cause serious tension in those who do, in fact, believe. He states that there is a serious tension when 'a message of God to men expressed and interpreted in a specific historical situation of the past becomes the norm for, and the test of, *our* Christian faith today – a faith that is experienced in a totally different historical situation'.[52] Nicholas Lash makes the same point more strongly. He writes,

> If doctrines ... which, in one cultural context, appropriately expressed or protected the central affirmations of Christian belief, are simply carried over, 'untranslated', into a different context, then they become not merely useless, but harmful. In the new context they do not, and cannot, express the same meaning as they originally did.[53]

---

51. Cf. Martin Poulsom who says that the personal identity of a human being is a good example of continuity within change. He uses it in his discussion of what Schillebeeckx calls 'the evangelical identity of meaning' which is 'only to be found at the level of a *corresponding relation between the original message* (tradition) and the constantly changing situation, then and now'. It does not refer to corresponding terms but to corresponding relations between such terms. Martin G. Poulsom, 'New Resonances in Classic Motifs: Finding Schillebeeckx's Theology in Translation', Review of *The Collected Works of Edward Schillebeeckx* (11 vols, London: Bloomsbury T&T Clark, 2014) *Louvain Studies* 38 (2014): 370–81 (henceforth *New Resonances*).

52. Schillebeeckx, *GFoM*, 3.

53. Nicholas Lash, *Change in Focus: A Study of Doctrinal Change and Continuity* (London: Sheed and Ward, 1973), 147.

Part of Schillebeeckx's life work as a theologian was to unravel the confusion between the *rem* and the *enuntiabile* and to make a reformulation ('stammeringly' as he might have put it) about the person of Jesus.[54]

Disentangling the rem from the enuntiabile

Schillebeeckx, in his writings before and after Vatican II, is intent on disentangling the confusion of the reality of the mystery of God (the *rem*) with statements about it (the *enuntiabilia*). As early as 1952, he works at unravelling the confusion, teasing out the distinction. He writes, for example, that during the interpretative phase, from the end of the apostolic church until now 'nothing new has been added to the *content of* faith, but its hidden wealth has been more sharply defined since the closing of revelation with the death of the last apostle'.[55] What exactly, the reader might ask, is meant here by 'the content of faith'? Is it *whom* you believe in (God and Jesus), or is it a core, definitive statement of belief about God and Jesus? In accordance with what Schillebeeckx writes elsewhere, it has to be the former. In an article of 1958 titled 'What Is Theology?' Schillebeeckx expands on Aquinas' understanding of the distinction between the *rem* and the *enuntiabilis*. He writes,

> According to Aquinas, the object of faith is not in the first place a number of truths, but the Veritas prima [salutaris] – the single, saving Truth par excellence. But this Veritas prima, as it is known to us in faith (and, it should be added, as it is manifested in a history of salvation), is, as it were, made plural in various judgements of faith. These, however, form a single organic whole, in which some cardinal points act as joints by means of which the whole functions as a harmoniously connected entity.[56]

Ten years later, in 1968, Schillebeeckx refers to an 'older solution' to the problem of how continuity of faith is ensured through changes in the articulation of faith. He calls this solution 'The Kernel and its mode of expression'. This older solution claimed a distinction between the 'essential dogmatic affirmation' and its 'modes of expression'.[57] This view held, for example, that the definitions of Chalcedon on

---

54. Schillebeeckx more than once refers to the efforts of Christians and theologians to express something of the truth of God and Jesus as a 'stammering', for example, 'From the life of Jesus, Christians learn to give stammering utterance to the content of what "God" is and the content of what "man" is.' Schillebeeckx, *IR*, 115 [132]. It is a word (balbutio) and idea that he adopts from Aquinas, cf., for example, Aquinas *ST*, 1a 4, 1 ad 1: *balbutiendo, ut possumus, excelsa Dei resonamus*, 'stammering, we echo the heights of God as best we can' (translation taken from Lubor Velecky, *Aquinas' Five Arguments in the Summa Theologiae* 1a 2, 3 (Kampen: Pharos, 1994), 17.

55. Schillebeeckx, *R&T*, 43 [63].
56. Ibid., 95–6 [146].
57. Schillebeeckx, *GFoM*, 7.

the divinity and humanity of Jesus, and the definitions of the Council of Trent on the Eucharistic presence of Christ, were 'essential dogmatic affirmations'. The 'modes of expression' were the ways in which subsequent generations interpreted these 'essential dogmatic statements'. Poulsom points out that there are theologians who still use a version of 'The Kernel and its mode of expression' today in that they talk about a dialectical interplay between tradition and interpretation, and sometimes an interplay between tradition and situation. He says that whichever way they talk about it, they give the very strong impression that the tradition element of the dialectic does not change, and by it they tend to mean something like the Chalcedonian definition of Christology.[58] This means that an *enuntiabile* of tradition is being treated as though it were itself part of the unchanging *rem*. Schillebeeckx comes to the conclusion, however, that there cannot, in fact, be a '*dogmatic* essence' in the sense of an *expression* of doctrine that is an 'unchangeable element of faith' because what might be termed the 'essence' is always concealed *in* a historical mode of expression.[59] Poulsom considers that this view of Schillebeeckx's, which is Thomist, is often misunderstood and that those theologians who work according to 'The Kernel and its mode of expression' model, and their critics, seem to think that this is what Schillebeeckx is doing too.[60] These theologians correlate tradition and interpretation (and are therefore called correlational theologians) but in a crucially different way from how Schillebeeckx relates them. Schillebeeckx maintains that the

> fundamental identity of meaning between successive eras in Christian interpretation of tradition does not refer to corresponding terms, for instance between the biblical situation and ours (which would permit us to invoke Jesus' cleansing of the Temple as a direct biblical justification for an Amsterdam squat), but to corresponding relations between such terms (message and situation then and now).[61]

This is one reason why Poulsom is reluctant in his work to call Schillebeeckx a correlational theologian because the dialectical interplay in the 'Kernel and its mode of expression' method, namely, between the pole of unchanging tradition and the pole of changing interpretation, is seen as the defining method of correlational theology (by both its proponents and opponents).[62]

---

58. Poulsom, conversation 25 June 2016.
59. Schillebeeckx, *GFoM*, 8 [12].
60. Poulsom, conversation, 25 June 2016.
61. Schillebeeckx, *Essays*, 62.
62. Poulsom, *Dialectics*, 107: 'Relational dialectic helps to distinguish the correlational method used in Schillebeeckx's philosophical theology from that used by the majority of correlational theologians,' 109:

> The correlation [Schillebeeckx] uses finds its identity of meaning '*on the level of the corresponding relation between the original message (tradition) and the always different situation*, both in the past and in the present', quoting Edward Schillebeeckx, 'The Role of History in the New Paradigm', in *Paradigm Change*

The thing about which theology makes a statement (and it can never do this fully) Schillebeeckx names in various ways. He calls the object of theology 'reality'; for example, he writes, 'the [theological] interpreter ... goes beyond the texts and their meaning and enquires about the *reality* to which the texts intentionally or unintentionally bear witness'.[63] He refers to the object of theology as the 'matter' (beyond a text).[64] He uses the expression 'a real datum of faith' when discussing the Tridentine theologians' language of transubstantiation and writes, 'In truth, this [Aristotelian language of substance and accident] only means that those theologians were genuinely able to *understand* the real datum of faith in that interpretation, that it was capable of being grasped by them in those terms'.[65] Whether he calls the *rem* 'reality', the 'matter' or 'the real datum of faith' (to name some of the ways he refers to the mystery of God who gives himself in self-revelation), he refers to the attempts to say something about the mystery of God as 'interpretations'. There is no '*nuda vox Dei*, a word from God without alloy coming down to us, as it were, vertically in a pure divine statement' because God's word is given to us within the interpretative response to it.[66]

At a conference in 1983, in a discussion of models (in the sense of thought categories) that lie behind theological statements, Schillebeeckx crystallized the distinction between the *rem* and the *enuntiabile*. He avers that 'thinking-in-models is important because it enables us to make a conscious distinction between the *substance of faith* and the model in which the faith is put into words'.[67] He mentions two examples of models, the Anselmian, Germanic-feudal 'model of a legal order', used to shed light on Christian soteriology, and the 'two-natures model' in Christology.[68] On expressions of faith he writes,

> The expressions of faith in the Bible and church's traditions depend on context and culture; they are localized and particular, while they nonetheless keep referring to the universal message of the gospel. The point at issue is the historical identity of what is permanent, precisely in what is transitory because of its contingent character.[69]

> in *Theology: A Symposium for the Future*, ed. Hans Küng and David Tracy, trans. Margaret Köhl (Edinburgh: T&T Clark, 1989), 307–19 (313) (henceforth *Role of History*). There is 'a fundamental unity and equality', but this is to be found not between the terms, but in 'the corresponding relations between the terms'. ... Schillebeeckx ... calls his approach dialectical, speaking of the 'Dialectical Relation between Tradition and Situation', as well as that between theory and praxis. (Poulsom quoting Schillebeeckx, ibid.)

63. Ibid., 22 [33].
64. Ibid., 12 [18]. 'Matter' may be considered a close translation of the Latin *rem*.
65. Ibid., 7 [11].
66. Schillebeeckx, *GFoM*, 3 [5].
67. Schillebeeckx, *Role of History*, 309. Italics added.
68. Ibid., 308 and 309.
69. Ibid., 311–12.

Schillebeeckx and tradition

Philip Endean, in a review of Eric Borgman's biography of Edward Schillebeeckx, sketches in some background to pre-Vatican II theology. He refers to the theological stance of Rahner, Congar and Schillebeeckx in wanting to engage with modernity in the years before the Council as 'progressive'.[70] He writes of them, '[they] were not able to justify their progressive stance by claiming to replace tradition with a modern alternative' so they had to resort to the technique of *ressourcement*.[71] Schillebeeckx's aim was never to replace tradition but, rather, to add to it. Far from disowning tradition Schillebeeckx argues forcefully that a fundamental insight of hermeneutics is that 'man is, because of his historicity, *in a tradition*'.[72] Human beings are temporal and cannot delete the fact that both collectively, including in their institutions, and individually, they have pasts. According to Schillebeeckx, what is said or done within a past interval of time makes it possible for people, from their present existential experiences, to give a certain objectivity to their understanding of their past, provided that they are aware of and use their prejudgements correctly. The past provides us with a series of understandings which form a tradition, a chain of understandings in continuity with each other, yet differently expressed. Schillebeeckx writes,

> It is therefore preferable to speak of the development of tradition rather than the development of dogma. What has been handed down to us, for example, in connection with the Eucharist is not simply the *Eucharist* but also – and above all – the reality itself of the celebration of the Eucharist, the meaning and content of which are expressed in conceptual terms in the doctrine.[73]

Lash, writing about the sensitivity to historical problems of '*la nouvelle théologie*' after the Second World War, reinforces the fact that Schillebeeckx 'prefers to call his subject [i.e. his historical theological investigation] the development of tradition rather than the development of dogma, so as to relate the dynamic handing on of revelation to the entire reality'.[74]

---

70. Philip Endean, Review of 'Edward Schillebeeckx, a Theologian in His History, Volume One: A Catholic Theology of Culture (1914–1965)', *TLS* (23 July 2004): 26.

71. Ibid. In order not to be condemned as Modernists, theologians who resorted to *ressourcement* practised new methods on historical sources; for example, they examined the writings of Aquinas as embedded in time and place and analysed how Aquinas harnessed writers from outside Christianity, such as ancient Greek and Islamic philosophers, in order to elucidate Christian understanding and teaching. '*Ressourcement* looked to the past for norms of practices or mind-sets to be used in changing, correcting or at least qualifying the direction things were moving in the present.' John W. O'Malley, *What Happened at Vatican II* (Cambridge, MA: Belknap Press of Harvard University Press, 2010), 42.

72. Schillebeeckx, *GFoM*, III, 18 [27].

73. Schillebeeckx, *R&T*, 55 [83].

74. Lash, *Change in Focus*, 135, quoting Mark Schoof, *Breakthrough: The Beginnings of the New Catholic Theology*, trans. N. D. Smith (Dublin: Gilland Macmillan, 1970), 217.

For Schillebeeckx the chain of understandings that make up the continuity of tradition is an essential source of contemporary understanding and creativity, to be 're-activated'.[75] The image of a person in a rowing boat on a river, to illustrate that we go forward into an unknown future while looking back on the past, is apt.[76] The river represents time, the terrain on either bank once passed represents history. The rower is making his or her way purposefully along the river (through time) but cannot see what lies ahead (the future) because, owing to the nature of rowing, their back is turned to it. As the rower progresses along the river (through time), they constantly refocus the cognitive lens through which they see and comprehend the stretch of the river through which they have already rowed (their past). The changing distance, perspectives and light cause their perception of the increasing stretch of river to change as more features come into view and give a fuller picture of the landscape. The riverscape remains the same but the rower's understanding of it changes. The stretch of river passed along provides a series of landmarks which punctuate the journey.

What about the Christological landmarks in the tradition of the Church? In his concern with Christology, Schillebeeckx's focus is centred around, and springs from, the two pre-eminent Christological dogmatic landmarks of the Church's history, namely, the primordial texts of the New Testament and the dogma of Chalcedon. Both sets of texts are part of tradition. The Bible surpasses all other texts as the sacred, foundational, canonical texts. In 1958 Schillebeeckx explained that, even within the Bible, as well as in later theology, many different *enuntiabilia* are made about the *rem*:

> Light can be thrown on the same datum [rem] from many different sides and it can be approached from various directions, with the result that different and complementary, but correct views [enuntiabilia] of the same question are always possible. Typical of this are the synoptic, the johannine, and the pauline views of the figure of Christ …, the later Alexandrian and Antiochian christologies, and finally the thomist and scotist views. The difference in value between the biblical and the theological views is, of course that all the elements of the various biblical christologies are correct, whereas this cannot be claimed a priori in the case of the various theological views of the figure of Christ.[77]

How, at the end of his formal university career in 1983, did Schillebeeckx explain the combination of continuity and change in the expression of dogma? The theme of his farewell lecture at Nijmegen was the theological interpretation of faith. In it

---

75. 'It belongs to man's very being to be within a tradition while re-activating it, and there is a living tradition only if, in the light of the present that is oriented towards the future, what has already found expression is reinterpreted towards the future.' Schillebeeckx, *GFoM*, III, 18 [27].

76. I once heard this image attributed, in a lecture by Professor H. D. F. Kitto, to an ancient Greek but have never been able to find a source for it. The elaboration is added.

77. Schillebeeckx, *R&T*, 101–2 [155–6].

he describes a dialectical relation between what he calls the 'twin poles' of tradition and situation.[78] This is how he describes the 'pole' of tradition: he affirms that the 'substance of faith [is] embedded in the Jewish and Judaeo-Hellenistic culture of the Bible (and in the various cultures of the church's tradition in the past)'.[79] He then describes the 'pole' of situation for Christians as being the contemporary situation, not as something neutral or which demands accommodation but as a situation that needs the 'substance of faith' applied to it. He writes that '[the second pole is] that same substance [of faith] that we need to apply to our contemporary situation, hence a contemporary piece of "Christian tradition"'.[80] In these remarks faith is the central and vital dynamic. The action of the Holy Spirit and the act of the believer work together, in the dynamic of faith, to produce *enuntiabilia*. In the published version of his farewell lecture Schillebeeckx gives a chart to show how the 'evangelical identity of meaning' lies neither 'at the level of the Bible and past religious tradition *as such*, [… nor] does it lie at the level of the situation, then and now, *as such*'.[81] Rather, it is to be found 'at the level of a *corresponding relation between the original message* (tradition) *and the constantly changing situation, then and now*'.[82] What the chart does not in itself indicate is the role of faith in the different corresponding relations.

Making statements or *enuntiabilia* of faith, in the power of the Holy Spirit, is what Schillebeeckx calls 'to actualise faith'. He writes,

> Actualised faith … mean[s] representing the Christian religious and experiential tradition intelligibly and vibrantly in other, historically altered situations and other experiential and thought categories. That requires critically yet continuously relating past Christian tradition and our contemporary socio-historical and existential situation to the concrete praxis of present-day Christians, in such a way that the actualisation does not impair the liberating disclosure of the truth of the Gospel tradition – in other words while preserving orthodoxy.[83]

To summarize so far, Schillebeeckx, from the earliest days of his theological studies, was aware of the Thomist distinction between the *rem* and the *enuntiabilia* of faith, the former unchanging, the latter changing. He also understands the dynamic of faith as having and providing an underlying identity, the 'identity of faith', that guarantees the truth of articulations of the faith in differing historical contexts. Thirdly, Schillebeeckx shows how the evangelical identity of meaning is wrought and to be found in a corresponding relation between tradition and situation.

---

78. Schillebeeckx, *Essays*, 54.
79. Ibid., 59.
80. Ibid.
81. Ibid., 62.
82. Ibid.
83. Ibid., 60.

Continuity and change in Schillebeeckx's method

Methods used in theology

In this section the word 'method' is deliberately used rather than the word 'methodology'. 'Methodology' is taken to mean the science of method, and, in a theological context, to mean the study of the suitability of techniques or methods used in theology. The question of change in the methods which Schillebeeckx used is examined, rather than change in any study he might have made of method. The term 'method' covers a number of things. It can refer to a theologian's philosophical presuppositions, the different sorts of sources/data (s)he uses (e.g. biblical, liturgical, philosophical, magisterial). It can refer to the literary genre of writing according to the period in history and the aim of the theologian, so, for example, in arguing against Gnosticism, Irenaeus' method is polemical refutation; for thirteenth-century university teaching, Aquinas' method is disputation; the teachings of Trent are propositional and Chenu's method is historical (both in that he establishes the details of Aquinas' career and explains the development and activity of religious thought in history).[84] Method can also refer to the tools a theologian uses such as those employed in biblical criticism (textual, form or redaction criticism) and hermeneutics. Method can refer to an habitual way of thinking in the construction of an argument. St Paul, for example, in interpreting the Christ event, has a strong tendency in Romans to present his arguments in typological pairs, where the Old Testament 'type' foreshadows the New Testament 'antitype' and the pairs of types are both parallel and antithetical. There is no synthesis because one of the pair supersedes the other (grace supersedes Law, Christ supersedes Adam and freedom in the Spirit supersedes slavery to sin);[85] Schleiermacher thinks in a correlational way, Barth in a dialectical way.[86] Method can refer to a theologian's starting point, namely, whether (s)he starts by thinking and talking about God in God's transcendence or in God's immanence. Method covers whether a theologian's aim is to treat all major doctrines systematically in a coherent whole or it may be thematic in which case a theologian sets out to tackle a particular problem of overriding concern to him/her, or to work eclectically, according to the demands or needs of his or her audience.

---

84. Edward Schillebeeckx, *In Memory of Marie Dominique (Marcel) Chenu O.P. (7 January 1895–11 February 1990)* in *HT* 90.

85. Rom. 6.14; 5.14-19; 8.2 (Own analysis.)

86. Reference to the dialectical theology of Barth by Daniel W. Hardy, 'Karl Barth', in *The Modern Theologians: An Introduction to Christian Theology since 1918*, ed. David F. Ford with Rachel Muers (Oxford: Blackwell, 2006), 21–42 (23). Schillebeeckx's dialectic has been identified by Poulsom as relational (in distinction from Barthian, Rahnerian and Lonergonian forms).

The evolution in Schillebeeckx's theological method

Despite the multiple forms that method may take, there is a consensus that Schillebeeckx changed his theological method in the 1960s. Although, as William L. Portier remarks, Schillebeeckx 'rarely addresses the methodological question that so exercises contemporary theology', it is useful, first of all, to look at what Schillebeeckx himself says.[87] The words he uses to describe the process of change in his theological method are 'evolution' and a 'continual reorientation'. In conversation with Francesco Strazzari (in 1993) he said, 'there has been evolution in my theological reflection' and, when he named the two biblical texts that sustained him throughout his career,[88] he referred to his 'continual attempt to reorientate [himself] in the unexpected directions in which the Spirit of God breathes'.[89] The components of the threefold change which Schillebeeckx made in his theological method in the 1960s are generally agreed: a switch of major focus from Church dogmatics to the Bible as his source material; the use of historical criticism in his study of the Bible; and an engagement with hermeneutics vis-à-vis the Bible and Church dogmatics.

He says that he began his theological career by commenting on the *sacra doctrina* in St Thomas.[90] *Sacra doctrina* and the Bible are different sources for theology but they are not disconnected from each other. Frank Bauerschmidt's description of the content of *sacra doctrina* shows it also to be more than mere doctrinal statements:

> Thomas sees the content of sacra doctrina as encompassing the somewhat vague knowledge of God that everyone has by intuition, the clearer knowledge of God that philosophers have by argumentation, and the knowledge of God had through revelation, which outstrips the previous two in both clarity and extent, and which is transmitted to us through scripture.[91]

For Schillebeeckx, also, *sacra doctrina* was not simply dogmatics in the sense of a system of dogma laid down by the Church and which, on long mooring

---

87. Portier, 'Interpretation and Method', 22.

88. Edward Schillebeeckx, 'Always be prepared to make a defence to anyone who calls you to account for the hope that is in you' (1 Pet. 3.15b) and 'Do not quench the Spirit, do not despise prophecies, but test everything; hold fast what is good' (1 Thess. 5.19-21), *HT*, 81-2.

89. Schillebeeckx, *HT*, 41 and 81.

90. The sentence that follows Schillebeeckx's clear statement (that he began by commenting on what you might call *sacra doctrina* in St Thomas) is a confusing one: 'It is not the sacred doctrine of the church, but Holy Scripture, which includes not only the Bible but also patristics and the whole Christian tradition' (*HT*, 41). The English comes via the original French or German in which Schillebeeckx conversed with Strazzari which was then translated into Italian from which it was finally translated into English by John Bowden. It seems that there was some scrambling along the way.

91. Bauerschmidt, *Thomas Aquinas*, 47.

cables, appears to float free from Holy Scripture and the Christian tradition of theology. He says in conversation with Strazzari, *sacra doctrina* 'is not the sacred doctrine of the church [disconnected], but Holy Scripture, which includes not only the Bible but also patristics and the whole Christian tradition'. He goes on to specify,

> There are two currents in St. Thomas: one accepts the use of sacred doctrine with reference to theology, the other argues that theology begins with the Bible and that the Bible is the foundation of all theology. Theology is the Bible, which expands in history. In the first phase of my theological reflection I followed the method of sacred doctrine.[92]

Sacra doctrina and Scripture are the two currents in the one mighty river of theology and Schillebeeckx moved from one to the other practising *ressourcement* in both.

In the first half of the twentieth century one way of exploring the prevailing Thomism had been by means of *ressourcement*, a theological method of enquiry which involved 'going back to a study of the historical circumstances that gave rise to particular doctrines'.[93] As Kennedy explains, 'Rather than attempting to understand Aquinas simply by reading his texts *in vacuo*, the *ressourcement* method examined his texts *in situ*, that is, with attention to the historical setting in which they were produced.'[94] Marie-Dominique Chenu (1895–1990) used this method to show that Aquinas was not 'the author of a timeless speculative system, but an example of how the Christian faith achieves theological expression in diverse ages and historical contexts'.[95] While Dominicans, in the practice of *ressourcement*, had concentrated on the historical texts of the early medieval period, the Jesuits (whose use of the approach had been labelled 'the New Theology' by Garrigou-Lagrange) had mainly concentrated on patristic Christian writings.[96] Schillebeeckx's first major exercise in *ressourcement* was in his monograph *De Sacramentele Heilseconomie*, published in 1952, which the subtitle described as a 'theological reflection on St. Thomas's teaching on sacraments in the light of tradition and the current sacramental problematic'.[97] His method in his *ressourcement* at this stage was 'to relate classical Christian doctrines to contemporary problems and understandings'.[98] In the 1960s Schillebeeckx as a theologian who, like Aquinas, was seeking the intelligibility of faith decided to go one step further back in his *ressourcement* of Christian writings and to interpret the earliest and canonical Christian texts, namely the

---

92. Schillebeeckx, *HT*, 41.
93. Kennedy, *Schillebeeckx*, 40.
94. Ibid.
95. McGinn, *Thomas Aquinas's Summa Theologiae*, 189.
96. Ibid., 188.
97. Kennedy, *Schillebeeckx*, 61.
98. Ibid.

New Testament. This was a move which was in tune with Aquinas' argument that theology begins with the Bible and that the Bible is the foundation of all theology. As Chenu had written of Aquinas, 'The very pith of his work was scriptural and his theology had its root in the Gospel movement of his day, just as it did the [theological] renaissance movement of which it was one of the effects', so the same could be said of Schillebeeckx.[99] The switch of main source material was one part of the change which Schillebeeckx made in his method.

Schillebeeckx speaks of his entry into a hermeneutical phase, as well as other factors that influenced his theology, when he writes,

> In the 1960s, along with the arrival of the human sciences, there appeared criticism of society, of culture, of ideology and also of theology as a theological discipline. I followed this trend. So I entered a hermeneutical phase, which in fact developed side by side with the critical phase.[100]

Schillebeeckx's following of the hermeneutical trend, however, did not start as a bolt out of the blue. He points out that people (himself included) had been talking 'of the evolution of dogmas, then of the evolution of the Christian tradition and finally of hermeneutics'.[101] He says that the hermeneutical 'thesis', that 'we cannot grasp the biblical text directly "in itself", as though we, as readers or believers, *transcended time* … although commonly held to have originated with Bultmann and the theologians who followed him, … is one of the essential elements of Catholic theology'.[102] He gives a full example of the Catholic development of dogma in the Chalcedonian definition of Christology:

> The Catholic sense of dogma – for example the Christological dogma of Chalcedon – implies, after all, that the biblical view of Christ has been reinterpreted in the light of the Church's experience and the secular and social situation in the fifth century and, what is more, in such a way that this new interpretation really expresses the same datum of faith that is promised to us in the Bible and no other – the same datum in a reinterpretative testimony.[103]

In his conversation with Strazarri, Schillebeeckx names a third phase in which he engaged with a new method, namely, the one in which he tackled structuralism. Other than stating that it was a phase, Schillebeeckx does not expatiate on it. He summarizes the whole topic of his method by saying that his theological method 'is based on human and Christian experience, communal and personal, which he applies to tradition'.[104]

---

99. McGinn, *Thomas Aquinas's Summa Theologiae*, 190.
100. Schillebeeckx, *HT*, 41.
101. Ibid.
102. Schillebeeckx, writing about the 'Hermeneutical Circle', *GFoM*, 3–4.
103. Schillebeeckx, *GFoM*, 4.
104. Schillebeeckx, *HT*, 41.

Much better known, perhaps, than his remarks to Strazzari in 1993 is Schillebeeckx's statement, published in 1974, that he realized 'some time ago', that is, some while before 1974, that he needed to make a clear break with the '"implicit intuition" of the totality of meaning maintained by classical philosophy like that of De Petter, Lavelle and certain French philosophers'.[105] Kennedy argues that this shift in Schillebeeckx's philosophical presuppositions does not entail a disconnection with what went before. He argues that Schillebeeckx, in attempting to 'link two movements in human history: proto-Christianity and the European Enlightenment, ... has not in any way or at any time abandoned the most basic metaphysical and epistemological fundamentals which have informed his theology since the beginning of his career'.[106] As Kathleen Anne McManus writes, 'It would seem that Schillebeeckx's fundamental continuities are due to the permanence of his phenomenological roots.'[107]

A confusion between method and substance

A process of transference, however, is sometimes at work. The fact that there was a break in Schillebeeckx's method is sometimes transferred onto the content or substance of his theology, as though it, too, became fundamentally different. When this happens, Schillebeeckx's pre-1960s theology is thought to have no connection with his post-1960s theology. He becomes, as it were, a different theologian from what he had been in the 1960s. Even when the perception is not of such a radical change, it is nevertheless the case that many think of his theology, in a similar way to his theological method, as falling into a 'before' and an 'after' the Second Vatican Council. So, for example, when Jennifer Cooper first undertook her research on Schillebeeckx's theological anthropology, she assumed that she would focus her attention on his later theology. She 'fully expected to read through his early works fairly speedily and move quickly on'.[108] Instead she discovered that his earlier theology is significant and rewarding. She writes that

> the earlier period of Schillebeeckx's own theology is sometimes misinterpreted or too quickly dismissed. [His] later work is widely regarded as marking

---

105. Philip Kennedy, 'Continuity Underlying Discontinuity: Schillebeeckx's Philosophical Background', *New Blackfriars* 70 (1989): 264–77 (264–5). This statement is made by Schillebeeckx in *Jesus*, 580 [618] (henceforth *Continuity and Discontinuity*).
106. Ibid., 265.
107. Kathleen Anne McManus, *Unbroken Communion: The Place and Meaning of Suffering in the Theology of Edward Schillebeeckx* (Lanham, MD: Rowman and Littlefield, 2003), 14 (henceforth *Unbroken Communion*).
108. Jennifer Cooper, *Humanity in the Mystery of God: The Theological Anthropology of Edward Schillebeeckx* (T&T Clark Studies in Systematic Theology, London: T&T Clark, 2011), x.

a substantive rupture with his earlier output but I am convinced that the continuities in his thought are far more significant.[109]

In contrast, John Bowden, in his *Portrait* of Edward Schillebeeckx, sees the turn to biblical criticism in the 1960s as marking not only changes in method but also a radical change in his theology. He writes that the student rebellions in 1968 'made him aware of the importance of the approach of the sociologists of the Frankfurt School with their critical theory' and that 'travelling through the Americas in 1967 had given him first-hand contact with the Latin American theologians of liberation'.[110] Bowden's proposal is that Schillebeeckx's changes in method of doing theology, together with the influences of the intellectual and social currents of the 1960s, wiped the slate clean of Schillebeeckx's earlier Christology. He draws a stark contrast between the thinking of Schillebeeckx before and after his writing of *Jesus* in 1974, on which he had worked for nine years. He writes,

> We may certainly see *Jesus* as a watershed. The distinction between Schillebeeckx the Catholic theologian of the church and Schillebeeckx the theologian of the world and the kingdom of God, which brings him into conflict with the church … is a real one, and there is no doubt that for our time the latter concern is incomparably more interesting and, of course, more relevant.[111]

Bowden's image of a watershed suggests that just as a ridge of mountains separates two river systems, so there is no connection between the theology and, in particular, the Christology of Schillebeeckx pre and post his writing of *Jesus*. There are two points of confusion in this view. First, it confuses theological method with theological substance. Schillebeeckx preserves the meaning of Chalcedon but interprets and expresses the same truth of it in divergent terms. Secondly, Bowden suggests that Schillebeeckx dichotomizes the Church and the world and so implies that the two are in opposition. In fact, in Schillebeeckx's theology, the Church is of essential importance, not because it itself is salvation but because it is a sacrament of the salvation that God brings about in the world. Schillebeeckx writes, 'Churches are the places where salvation from God is thematized or put into words, confessed explicitly, proclaimed prophetically and celebrated liturgically.'[112] The Church exists not for its own sake but for the sake of God and humankind in all the world.

Aloysius Rego, in turn, refers to a 'theological turnabout' that occurred after 1966. He says that 'from 1966 Schillebeeckx's theology underwent a major change initiated by his confrontation with modernity and, in particular, with

---

109. Ibid., xi.
110. Ibid., 34.
111. John Bowden, *Edward Schillebeeckx: Portrait of a Theologian* (London: SCM Press, 1983), 9.
112. Schillebeeckx, *Church*, 13 [13].

the phenomenon of secularisation'.¹¹³ A turnabout is nothing less than a sudden and complete change. It is the case that Schillebeeckx added hermeneutics to his repertoire of theological method, but nothing that he wrote from 1966 contradicted his previous theology. Schillebeeckx's post-1966 theology was built on his earlier theology. Rosino Gibellini, for his part, talks of two periods in Schillebeeckx's theology, but he frames them in terms of a change of method (from scholastic Thomism to the 'new hermeneutics'). He does not confuse method with substance and clearly states that 'the method [hermeneutics] is intrinsically legitimate and does not lead to a radicalization of the substance of his theology'.¹¹⁴

A different assessment is made by Tracey Rowland who considers that during the papacy of John Paul II (1978–2005) there was a 'self-secularizing accommodation to modernity' by some theologians, evident in the interpretation of, in particular, the conciliar constitution *Gaudium et Spes*. The context of Rowland's remark suggests that with the 'self-secularizing accommodation to modernity' came also an abandoning of Christocentricity. Rowland names Schillebeeckx (and refers to 'others associated with the *Concilium* journal') as a theologian in whose theological publications this 'accommodation to modernity' is to be found, and therefore, by implication, that there is a failure to be Christocentric.¹¹⁵ But Schillebeeckx draws from Aquinas, and avers that 'theology is *essentially* Christological with regard to its method, but theocentric with regard to its subject'.¹¹⁶ Keenly aware also of the need to be true to Chalcedon and to focus both on the divinity of Jesus and on his humanity, he writes,

> We are ever inclined to pass cursorily over the human life of Christ, to overlook his existence as a man and consider only his existence as God. But it is as man that the Son is the mediator of grace; he is mediator in his humanity, according to the ways of humanity.¹¹⁷

The crux of the Incarnation is that the Divine is manifested in the human. It is through the human disposition, the words and deeds of Jesus that human beings are given the fullest revelation of God. In Jesus the divine and human are unitary,

---

113. Aloysius Rego, *Suffering and Salvation: The Salvific Meaning of Suffering in the Later Theology of Edward Schillebeeckx*, Louvain Theological and Pastoral Monographs, 33 (Louvain: Peeters Press, 2006), 34.

114. Rosino Gibellini, in the Introduction 'Honest to the World: The Frontier Theology of Edward Schillebeeckx' in *HT*, ix–x.

115. Tracy Rowland, 'Christ, Culture and the New Evangelisation', in *The New Evangelisation: Faith, People, Context and Practice*, ed. Paul Grogan and Kirsteen Kim (London: Bloomsbury, 2015), 47.

116. Schillebeeckx, *R&T*, 91, with reference to *ST* I, q. 1, a. 7. (Italics added.)

117. Edward Schillebeeckx, *Christ the Sacrament of the Encounter with God*, trans. Paul Barrett and N. D. Smith, revised by Mark Schoof and Laurence Bright, The Collected Works of Edward Schillebeeckx 1 (London: Bloomsbury, 2014), 30 (henceforth *CSEG*).

but they are the two aspects of him that we are able only to speak of one at a time. In the late 1960s, in order to do theological justice to the humanity of Jesus, Schillebeeckx embarked on the oldest method of theology, namely, searching the scriptures. He used two tools of which Roman Catholic biblical scholars had only relatively recently become keenly aware: the science of hermeneutics and historical–biblical criticism. As a consequence, his Christology includes an intensive study of how the first followers of Jesus Christ experienced God himself working his divine salvation in the person of Jesus of Nazareth and of why they confessed him to be the Christ, Son of God. Jesus' disciples, then and now, identify the source of his full humanity to be his relationship and unity with God the Father. They learnt that Jesus Christ is the way for human beings, in their turn, to live fully human lives in the world through relationship with God.

The need for change in order to maintain continuity

In various countries, the 1960s–1970s were a period of cultural revolution,[118] and were experienced and perceived as such, provoking different reactions. One element of this cultural revolution was a new-found freedom to question traditional values, social conventions and those in authority who were seen to be the guardians of the status quo. Schillebeeckx found that the traditional articulation of the mystery of the humanity and divinity of Jesus had become obscure to many people. When he was travelling in North America in the late 1960s he was repeatedly asked, 'Is Christ really God?'[119] This question was not prompted by scepticism but because the enquirers wanted to have their faith in Jesus, the Christ, illuminated and strengthened. The aim at the Council of Chalcedon had been to 'prevent a reduction of Jesus in our human history'.[120] As Schillebeeckx writes, 'The Fathers of that Council were not directly concerned with abstract metaphysics – this was, purely by chance, the referential framework – but rather had an all-embracing existential problem in mind: can and may a *man*, however exalted he may be, claim our unconditional surrender without at the same time forcing us into a depersonalizing form of idolatry?'[121] The categories of Greek philosophy, used at Chalcedon to define Jesus in specialized terms of 'person' and 'natures', could make it seem to contemporary people that they were either being asked somehow to think of Jesus in two parts, one divine and one human in a dichotomized Christology, or to assent to an impossible equation, namely, that a (particular) human being equals God. This would seem to be in contradiction to

---

118. The most dramatic social revolution in Europe took place in France in May 1968. See: Julian Jackson, *A Certain Idea of France: The Life of Charles de Gaulle* (London: Allen Lane, 2018), chapter 28, 'Revolution, 1968', 709–37.

119. Kennedy, Schillebeeckx, 101, quoting Schillebeeckx in 'Catholic Life in the United States', *Worship* 42 (1968): 134–49 (137).

120. Schillebeeckx, UF, 44.

121. Ibid.

Christian faith that understands a human being to be a creature and therefore not the Creator who is God. The conclusion that Schillebeeckx reaches is,

> It is clear that Christian revelation in its traditional form [as expressed in traditional articulations] has ceased to provide any valid answer to the questions about God asked by the majority of people today, nor would it appear to be making any contribution to modern man's real understanding of himself in the world and in human history. ... The situation requires us to speak of God in a way quite different from the way in which we have spoken of him in the past. If we fail to do this, we ourselves shall perhaps still be able to experience God in outmoded forms, but clearly our own witness of and discussion of God will be met by most people with head-shaking disbelief as mumbo-jumbo.[122]

This statement is not recommending an 'accommodation to modernity'; rather, it urges that language be found to express and convey the unchanging truth (in this case, the divinity and humanity of the one person, Jesus Christ) in such a way that conveys the unchanging meaning and content of the faith.

At the same time as observing that in the 1960s–1970s 'it is often said that we live in a period of radical intellectual and cultural transformation',[123] Schillebeeckx also cautions that 'we are well advised to situate this transformation more accurately and especially to qualify it, for every cultural revolution (even if it involves our entire philosophy and all experience) is still in some respects relative'.[124] This remark applies to Schillebeeckx's own theology. He described the process of change in his theological method as an evolution and a continual reorientation. His teaching and writing began as a commentary on the *sacra doctrina* of St Thomas, the metaphysical tenets of whose theology (and creation theology in particular) undergird his entire theological project. Philosophically, Schillebeeckx describes himself as having made a 'clear break' with the 'implicit intuition' of the totality of meaning maintained by De Petter and others, although this break did not entail abandoning the basic metaphysical and epistemological fundamentals of his theology. In the 1940s, after the Second World War, at *Le Saulchoir* and in Paris, the historical dimension was opened to Schillebeeckx, above all by Chenu's use of *ressourcement*. In the 1960s he entered a hermeneutical phase which involved an exhaustive scientific and hermeneutical study of the texts of the New Testament. At every stage, in Paris, Leuven and, later, in Nijmegen and on visits to America, he had his ear to the ground in that he was picking up numerous intellectual currents and, in a Thomist manner, using them to serve theology in the task of convincing people of the meaning and centrality of Christ to true human living. Through all these phases of Schillebeeckx's theology, what was the continuity and what were the changes?

---

122. Schillebeeckx, *GFoM*, 31.
123. Schillebeeckx, *Jesus*, 539 [576].
124. Ibid.

Chapter 4

CONTINUITY AND CHANGE IN SCHILLEBEECKX'S CHRISTOLOGY: THE EARLIER CHRISTOLOGY

In this and the next chapter the aim is to examine the way in which Schillebeeckx links creation and Christ in his work, and how the link between them has changed, developed and broken with past versions of that link in his work. The linking of creation and Christ is a structural element of the Church's Christology as delineated in a number of New Testament texts, but it is an element which has lain dormant and been somewhat overshadowed by a more soteriological emphasis in Christology (as, for example, in Anselm's theory of atonement). Schillebeeckx, through his *ressourcement* or recovery of the sources of faith in the Thomist tradition, positions his Christology within the matrix of creation faith. The study below starts with *Christ the Sacrament of the Encounter with God*, published in Dutch in 1959, and follows through to his Christological trilogy, *Jesus* (1974), *Christ* (1977) and *Church* (1989) and later publications. The purpose is to identify the key elements or component threads of his Christology (the substance), as well as noting various features and aspects of methods which have a bearing on substance, and to gauge what is continuous and what is discontinuous within his Christology. At the same time this exploration shows how Schillebeeckx's Christology fits in with the dogmatic tradition of the Church.

In considering the question of continuity and change in Schillebeeckx's Christology, the threefold model of change of the *Annales* school of French historiography is used rather than a twofold Kuhnian model. A model of change which allows for continuity at the same time as allowing for change, and which takes into account varying rates of change in the different elements of his theology, fits Schillebeeckx's theology better than the twofold model.

Models of change

The twofold Kuhnian model

In 1962 Thomas Kuhn, a physicist and historian of science, published his book *The Structure of Scientific Revolutions*.[1] In it he examines how radically new hypotheses

---

1. Thomas S. Kuhn, *The Structure of Scientific Revolutions*, 50th Anniversary Edition (Chicago: University of Chicago Press, 2012).

and theories emerge. A prime example that Kuhn gives of a radically new hypothesis replacing a previous one is Copernicus' heliocentric theory of our planetary system which replaced a geocentric understanding. Such a revolutionary break with the past is from (a) (geocentric) to (b) (heliocentric), that is, it is a twofold change from one explanatory model or paradigm to another radically different explanatory model, hence the word 'Revolutions' in the title of Kuhn's book.[2] The point of the book, however, is to explore the structure of such a revolution in scientific understanding. Such changes in ways of understanding do not happen overnight, but they emerge in a protracted and complex dialectical process of new evidence challenging existing theories.[3] The result of such a process is the replacement of a formerly accepted model by a radically different, new one. Kuhn names such a replacement a 'paradigm change', often referred to as a 'paradigm shift'. With the expression 'paradigm shift' goes a connotation of something as apparently sudden in cause, incidence and outcome as a tectonic plate shift at the epicentre of an earthquake, even though the pressure that will cause the shift has been building up for a long time before it actually happens. This means that if the phrase 'paradigm shift' is transferred from the natural sciences to the humanities, the basic structure of change being modelled is twofold, and tends to suggest a sudden rupture with what has gone before.

The threefold Annales *school model*[4]

In 1983 Schillebeeckx was invited to participate in a symposium, the theme of which was *Paradigm Change in Theology*. It was convened by Hans Küng and David Tracy to discuss whether a unifying pattern or paradigm could be found in Christian theology in a postmodern era, post-Auschwitz and post-Hiroshima, when new natural and humane sciences, democratically pluralistic societies and liberation movements of every kind were emerging.[5] In his preparatory paper

---

2. Copernicus' treatise *De revolutionibus orbium caelestium* (c. 1543) is often cited as marking the beginning of the scientific revolution. The different meanings of the word *revolution* are intriguing. In Copernicus' title it refers to the slow, majestic and apparently unchanging pattern of revolutions or orbits of the celestial bodies. On the other hand, his heliocentric theory provoked a revolution in the sense of a decisive overthrow of one way of modelling the planetary system by another.

3. A less well-known example of such a paradigm change is Lavoisier's theory of combustion, namely, that combustion is due not to a concentration of phlogiston but to the absorption of oxygen. Kuhn writes, 'That theory was the keystone for a reformulation of chemistry so vast that it is usually called the chemical revolution' (Kuhn, *The Structure of Scientific Revolutions*, 56).

4. Compare *Jesus*, 539 [576]–544 [582] in which Schillebeeckx discusses the '"Conjunctural" Hermeneutic Horizon and A-Synchronous Rhythm in the Complex Transformation of a Culture'.

5. The book of the symposium papers was published in 1989. Hans Küng, 'Introduction', in *Paradigm Change in Theology: A Symposium for the Future*, ed. Hans Küng and David Tracy, trans. Margaret Kohl (Edinburgh: T&T Clark, 1989), xv–xvi (xv).

for the symposium, *Paradigm Change in Theology*, Küng applied Kuhn's theory of paradigm change to a résumé of Christian dogma through the centuries.[6] Schillebeeckx, however, had reservations about using the Kuhnian model for theology. In his paper for the symposium he proposes, as an alternative to the twofold Kuhnian model, the *Annales* analysis of historical–cultural change that is offered by French cultural critics which 'can provide theology with more light on the matter than Kuhn'.[7]

Schillebeeckx had written about the French historical–critical *Annales* model of change, nine years earlier in *Jesus*.[8] Their analysis of culture as a whole can be applied to 'sub-vectors and cultural vectors, including human thinking'[9] and hence to religious thought and expression. The French analysis identifies change of three types as ephemeral, conjunctural and structural. There is 'factual' or 'ephemeral' short-term history 'with its brief duration and fast rhythm: everyday events come and go'; in addition there is ' "conjunctural" history, which is more expansive, has a more profound impact and is more comprehensive, but proceeds at a much slower tempo – in other words, a cultural conjuncture lasts a long time'; lastly, there is a 'structural history with a timespan of many centuries, verging on the zero point between motion and immobility, albeit not a-historical',[10] and so, although almost identical with stagnation, it nevertheless moves.[11]

Poulsom describes the multiple imagery that Schillebeeckx uses in speaking about ephemeral, conjunctural and structural change.[12] Schillebeeckx's first image is of three planes which he describes in this way: 'Each historical process occurs on at least three planes, but they do not run parallel: they encompass and interpenetrate one another, and together constitute the history of mankind.'[13] Poulsom proposes that in depicting the three planes as encompassing or (in the 1974 translation) as enfolding one another, there is a suggestion of the complementary image of the intertwining cords of a rope. He goes on to describe two other images that Schillebeeckx uses in fairly quick succession, that of 'concentric orbs about a slow-moving axis' and 'a turning but stationary top, around which everything revolves, fast or not so fast', before returning to the image of planes.[14] Poulsom goes on to

---

6. Ibid., 15–18.

7. Edward Schillebeeckx, 'The Role of History in What Is Called the New Paradigm', in *Paradigm Change in Theology: A Symposium for the Future*, ed. Hans Küng and David Tracy, trans. Margaret Köhl (Edinburgh: T&T Clark, 1989), 307–19 (309).

8. Schillebeeckx, *Jesus*, 539 [576]. The French cultural critics that Schillebeeckx cites are Braudel (1969), F. Furet (1971) and P. Chaunu (1970).

9. Ibid.

10. Ibid., 539–40 [577].

11. Schillebeeckx, *Role of History*, 309.

12. Poulsom, *Dialectics*, 103.

13. Schillebeeckx, *Jesus*, 539 [577].

14. Poulsom, *Dialectics*, 103.

compare Schillebeeckx's use of imagery in his account of history in *Jesus* with that of his account in 'The Role of History'. He finds that in the latter Schillebeeckx

> seems not to use any clear imagery at all. There are suggestions of the image of a tree, when he says that conjunctural history 'branches out further, penetrates deeper'; and of a river, when he says, of structural history, that it 'passes very slowly' and that its duration 'is almost identical with stagnation, and yet it moves', but these are extremely light touches, using metaphors rather than models.[15]

The value of a model of cultural history which includes three aspects is that the model includes three planes of change and thus allows for a more adequate expression of the complexities of history than a two-plane Kuhnian model can.[16] While, therefore, there may be ephemeral change, the model takes into account conjunctural and structural continuity, and while there may be conjunctural change, the model takes into account structural continuity. A second strength of the three-plane model is that it allows for the three strands of history or cultural expression to move asynchronously. There is not what might be called a 'homogeneous evolution', but rather in place of evolutionary and developmental models of doctrinal history 'a more episodic view of history [emerges] which pays close attention to the problem of transposing meanings and values from one cultural context to another'.[17] Schillebeeckx is not saying that in human thinking there are eternally valid concepts (not even at the structural level) because every concept is a linguistic expression of truth and all language is conditioned by time and place. Rather, Schillebeeckx is able to make the case, in 1974, that 'continuity and discontinuity can be compatible as long as the interaction between them uses a three-term, rather than a two-term, structure'.[18]

When Poulsom applies the *Annales* model to Schillebeeckx's thinking and writing he speaks in terms of *change* at the ephemeral and conjunctural levels and of *development* at the structural level. He writes that 'a relational dialectic of continuity and change, in which the two are not opposed but mutually co-constitutive … can be applied to Schillebeeckx's own development'.[19] Of the ephemeral level, he says, 'as time has gone by, particular ephemeral aspects of his thought have come and gone, without disturbing the overall development taking

---

15. Ibid.

16. In his symposium paper on paradigm change in theology, Schillebeeckx wrote, 'In my view the *Annales*-school of French historiography can provide theology with more light on this matter than Kuhn.' He says that conjunctural history 'shows a resemblance to what at this congress is called "paradigm" '. Schillebeeckx, 'The Rôle of History', 309-10.

17. Lash, *Change in Focus*, 144.

18. Poulsom, 'New Resonances in Classic Motifs: Finding Schillebeeckx's Theology in Translation' (Book essay on *The Collected Works of Edward Schillebeeckx*), *Louvain Studies* 38:9 (2014): 370-81 (374).

19. Poulsom, *Dialectics*, 104.

place within a particular conjunctural stage'.[20] Of the conjunctural plane he writes, 'There have also been changes of framework, what might be called paradigm shifts. These have, however, been conjunctural changes – important, yes, but not ultimate.'[21] He then distinguishes between *change* and *development* at the structural level: 'The structural aspects of Schillebeeckx's philosophical theology – creation among them – have *developed* slowly through these changes, finding expression in the various conjunctural eras in distinct and related ways.'[22] The distinction here between change, meaning development, and break or rupture, is crucial. The structural may be confused with the *rem* (the reality about which statements are made) or, more probably, with 'The Kernel' in terms of the old solution of the kernel and its mode of expression.[23] There is change in the sense of development at the structural level but no break or rupture. It is this structural level that is in continuity throughout Schillebeeckx's theological career. In accordance with the idea of three sectors of change, Schillebeeckx avers, in 1994, that 'sometimes structural continuity can *only* come about through conjunctural discontinuity'.[24]

Continuity and change in Schillebeeckx's theology

In the analysis of continuity and change in Schillebeeckx's Christology which follows, the threefold *Annales* model and its terminology are used. 'Ephemeral' history 'with its brief duration and fast rhythm' of everyday events coming and going is not the focus of attention. Rather, the focus is on the other two planes of the *Annales* model: the 'conjunctural' and the 'structural'. As mentioned above, the conjunctural elements are 'more expansive, [have] a more profound impact and [are] more comprehensive, but [proceed] at a much slower tempo – in other words [last] a long time' compared with ephemeral history.[25] The structural element has a 'timespan of many centuries, verging on the zero point between motion and immobility, albeit not a-historical'.[26] In what follows, the expression 'paradigm shift', which is more appropriately used in a twofold model of change, is not used to designate a change at the conjunctural level in Schillebeeckx's Christology. In this way, potential confusion between Schillebeeckx's thinking in terms of the threefold *Annales* model as opposed to the thinking of those who use the Kuhnian twofold model will more easily be avoided. It will also serve to emphasize that changes which in Schillebeeckx's analysis are called conjunctural do not work exactly like

---

20. Ibid.
21. Ibid.
22. Ibid. Italics added.
23. Cf. Schillebeeckx, *GFoM*, 6–7. 'The Kernel': a primary, authoritative statement of doctrine, treated as the sole source for any further re-expressions of the content of that doctrine.
24. Poulsom, 'New Resonances', 374.
25. Schillebeeckx, *Jesus*, 539–40 [577].
26. Ibid., 540 [577].

his interlocutors' paradigms owing to the different conceptual frameworks of the two models of change.

Schillebeeckx's earlier Christology

In his book *Christ the Sacrament of the Encounter with God*, first published in Dutch in 1959, Kathleen McManus describes Schillebeeckx as 'still operating out of an old paradigm, starting with the doctrinal formulas of Chalcedon and transposing them into the realm of common human experience and language'.[27] This is true, yet at this stage, Schillebeeckx is clearly linking creation with Christ. In the introduction to an article of 1957, which summarizes the themes of *Christ the Sacrament of the Encounter with God*, Schillebeeckx sketches some of the theological parameters of his sacramental theology.[28] He pinpoints two elements of his creation theology, namely, epistemological and causal, which are compressed into one sentence: 'By his created powers man can reach God only through the medium of his creation as its First Cause.'[29] He draws together the transcendence and immanence of God as Creator, in the same article, when he writes that God is 'the Creator who by his power guides the historical course of all nations in creative transcendence [and is] the one who takes part in the vicissitudes of history and who stands on the side of Israel'.[30] Despite this somewhat philosophical and general way of talking about God, Schillebeeckx depicts God the Creator's wholehearted involvement with humanity. His premise is that 'Religion … is a dialogue between God and man',[31] a dialogue that is continued sacramentally. The history of the dialogue of God's covenant with Israel is told in the Old Testament. It is a turbulent story of a 'dialectical situation' marked by struggle between 'God's constant fidelity and the ever-recurring infidelity of his people'.[32] Schillebeeckx likens this dialectical struggle to wrestling: 'God wrestles with human freedom in his desire to save

---

27. Kathleen McManus, 'Suffering in the Theology of Edward Schillebeeckx', *Theological Studies* 60 (1999): 476–91 (480, note 5) (henceforth *Suffering*).

28. The article predates the Dutch version of *Christ the Sacrament of the Encounter with God* by two years (details below).

29. Edward Schillebeeckx, 'The Sacraments: An Encounter with God', in *Christianity Divided: Protestant and Roman Catholic Theological Issues*, ed. Daniel J. Callahan, Heiko A. Oberman and Daniel O'Hanlon, trans. John L. Boyle (New York: Sheed and Ward, 1961), 245–75 (245) (henceforth *SEG*). This article is listed as published in 1957, in the *Bibliography 1936–1996 of Edward Schillebeeckx*, compiled by Ted Schoof and Jan van de Westlaken, the extended and corrected version of the bibliography published in the book with the same title (Baarn: Nelissen, 1996): 57/23 'Sakramente als Organe der Gottbegegnung', in *Fragen der Theologie heute*, ed. J. Feiner, J. Trütsch and F. Böckle (Einsiedeln, 1957), 379–401.

30. Schillebeeckx, *SEG*, 246.

31. Ibid., 245.

32. Ibid., 247.

mankind.'³³ In this image Schillebeeckx has slipped in another key element of his creation faith, namely, that God's constant presence in his creative 'wrestling' with human beings in their freedom is 'a desire to save mankind'. Creation and salvation are linked. Schillebeeckx in turn links creation with Christ, who is encountered in the sacraments, by demonstrating that in Jesus God fulfils his creative purpose because Jesus embodies both God's invitation to humanity and also the perfect human response to that invitation.

Schillebeeckx, therefore, sets his sacramental theology in the context of creation faith. The problem that Schillebeeckx addresses in *Christ the Sacrament of the Encounter with God* is described by John Bowden as follows: 'Traditional theology … does not always bring out sufficiently well the distinction between mere physical presence of natural objects and the unique character of conscious human reality and human experience' or, expressed differently, the problem is that a true understanding of the sacraments is endangered if they are seen as an 'impersonal cause-effect relationship, leading to the impression that receiving grace in them is largely a passive affair'.³⁴ Kathleen McManus refers to the then prevailing understanding of the sacramental dynamic as 'mechanistic'. She summarizes Schillebeeckx's achievement in this work by saying that 'this truly ground-breaking study shattered the prevailing mechanistic understanding of grace and sacraments and established the human basis of Christ's mediation of God'.³⁵ In observing that Schillebeeckx established the human basis of Christ's mediation of God, McManus touches on an element that was to develop and to find full expression in his later Christology, namely, the significance of the humanity of Jesus.

Three structural components of Schillebeeckx's thinking evident from the 1950s

From an examination of his earlier work, three structural components of Schillebeeckx's thinking, as opposed to structural dogmatic elements of his Christology, are evident. The first, as shown above, is the way in which he places the study of Jesus Christ in the context of creation faith.

The second structural component is to earth humanity's contact with God in experience. In the wake of post-Tridentine and neo-Thomist conceptualism

---

33. Ibid. Cf. Benedict XVI's reading of Gen. 32.24-32, Jacob's struggle with the Angel: 'For the believer the episode of the struggle at the Jabbok thus becomes a paradigm in which the people of Israel speak of their own origins and outline the features of a particular relationship between God and humanity' (http://w2.vatican.va/content/benedict-xvi/en/audiences/2011/documents/hf_ben-xvi_aud_20110525.html). Also cf. Jacob Epstein's sculpture of Jacob wrestling with the Angel in Tate Britain.

34. John Bowden, *Edward Schillebeeckx, Portrait of a Theologian* (London: SCM Press, 1983), 41.

35. McManus, *Suffering*, 480, note 5.

Schillebeeckx is, in fact, rehabilitating experience. In the case of his study of the sacraments he draws on existentialism as a conjunctural model or tool to overcome a mechanistic approach to the sacraments and to bring out the encounter-aspect of the sacraments with the idea that the sacraments are a personal experience of grace-filled encounter with Christ. Kennedy observes that, as a corrective to seeing the sacraments as impersonal cause–effect relationships, in *Christ the Sacrament of the Encounter with God* 'Schillebeeckx employs, to considerable effect, the existentialist notion of personal encounter as a way of expounding the meaning and significance of sacraments regarded in themselves as an economy of salvation'.[36] Or, as is being suggested here, Schillebeeckx borrows from existentialism in order to convey the deeper, structural component of his thinking that human beings come to know God in and through their experiences. Existentialism emphasizes the existence of the individual person as a free and responsible subject who, theoretically and to some extent at least, in practice, determines his/her own development by the decisions (s)he makes in order to arrive at an authenticity of existence.[37] Schillebeeckx draws on this notion to counter a supposition of passivity on the part of the recipient of the sacraments, which precludes the element of experience and the ensuing development of authenticity. The notion of existentialism is also partly an ingredient of a hermeneutical way of textual interpretation which Schillebeeckx was to embrace in the 1960s. The experiences of those who read a text are as relevant as the experience of those who wrote the text. In his later biblically based, hermeneutical Christology, his emphasis on the experiential is in order to invite and provoke a direct response to Christ as he is discovered in the New Testament.

The third structural component of Schillebeeckx's thinking in *Christ the Sacrament of the Encounter with God* is that he proposes the human basis of Christ's mediation of God. Pertinent to understanding more of the context in which Schillebeeckx was writing about sacramental grace is the significant theological backdrop of the extrinsicism versus intrinsicism debate concerning grace, in twentieth-century Roman Catholic theology.[38] Although Schillebeeckx does not mention the debate, in *Christ the Sacrament of the Encounter with God* he is finding a middle way between extrinsicism and intrinsicism. He is seeking and choosing a middle ground, in this case a structural positioning

---

36. Kennedy, *Schillebeeckx*, 62.

37. The modern philosophical view of existentialism would understand the individual human being, possessing free will, as standing in an absurd and meaningless world. This was obviously not Schillebeeckx's stance. Nor did he see the 'individual as the sole judge of his/her own actions, with human freedom understood precisely as the freedom to choose'. Philip Stokes, *100 Essential Thinkers* (London: Arcturus, 2006), 212.

38. Andrew Dean Swafford discusses the two poles of *extrinsicism* and *intrinsicism* in the Nature-Grace debate in *Nature and Grace: A New Approach to Thomistic Ressourcement* (Cambridge: James Clarke, 2015), 6–8 and Francis Fiorenza describes de Lubac's argument against extrinsicism, 203.

for his subsequent theology and Christology. In the light of his creation faith, Schillebeeckx understands the danger of extrinsicism which treats the ontological distinction between creation and God to mean a separation of God from the world, so that the dispensation of sacramental grace becomes an impersonal bestowal, as it were from on high, on a passive recipient. At the same time, he sees the opposite danger of intrinsicism which is to think of God's closeness to the creation in such a way that the distinction between creation and Creator is blurred and nature and grace are collapsed together in a form of pantheism.[39] Extrinsicism and intrinsicism are aspects of the transcendence-immanence question and in his Christology Schillebeeckx focuses on the relational dialectic between the two. Uniquely in Jesus the covenantal dynamic of the divine and the human is given expression.

In this first major book, a sense that human beings encounter the transcendent God sacramentally in the human and risen Christ lies behind Schillebeeckx's emphasis on the 'human basis of Christ's mediation of God'.[40] Schillebeeckx writes,

> Mutual human availability is possible only in and through man's bodiliness … This makes it clear that on the side of Christ the man it is the Resurrection which makes it possible for him precisely as man to influence us by grace. This is of capital importance. For we are ever inclined to pass cursorily over the human life of Christ, to overlook his existence as man and consider only his existence as God. But it is as man that the Son is the mediator of grace; he is mediator in his humanity, according to the ways of humanity.[41]

A sacramental understanding midway between extrinsicism and intrinsicism emphasizes, on the one hand, that the transcendent God offers his grace abundantly and, on the other hand, that Jesus on earth instituted sacraments, above all the Eucharist, so that by the most basic of earth's elements (water, bread, wine, oil) he can be encountered mediating God's grace. The passage quoted is of key importance because, as well as a structural positioning midway between extrinsicism and intrinsicism, it indicates what was alluded to and could be described as the main task of Schillebeeckx's later Christology, namely to correct a tendency to 'pass cursorily over the human life of Christ'[42] and thus to prevent a lopsidedness in interpreting the definition of Chalcedon let alone any intimation

---

39. Among his apophatic statements about creation, Schillebeeckx avers that creation faith is not pantheistic: 'Christian creation faith also distinguishes itself from pantheistic conceptions; for if God's presence were to mean that everything else outside God were in some way to be explained as an illusion or as part of an actual definition of God, then God would not seem to have sufficient active presence to bring autonomous, non-godly beings into existence.' *GAU*, 93.
40. McManus, *Suffering*, 480, note 5.
41. Schillebeeckx, *CSEG*, 30.
42. Ibid.

of Docetism. In what comes next, elements of structural *dogmatic content* evident in Schillebeeckx's earlier Christology are identified.

Schillebeeckx's linking of creation to Christ in Christ: The Sacrament of the Encounter with God

Schillebeeckx understands the sacraments themselves as a key part of God's economy of salvation, which is his saving plan for humanity revealed through creation and carried out in Christ Jesus.[43] In exploring the sacraments understood in this way, Schillebeeckx begins at the beginning with creation and with Augustine's three great phases of the Church's coming into being: humanity pre-Israel; God's relationship with Israel culminating in the life, death and resurrection of Jesus; and thirdly, the interpersonal relationship with Christ of members of the church who experience Jesus' saving activity sacramentally.[44] In the second phase, God's relationship with Israel, there is an 'existential two-way struggle between God who calls and man who resists, [and] God's calling seems to fail; Israel was not faithful until God himself raised up a man Jesus, in whom was concentrated the entirety of mankind's vocation to faithfulness'.[45] It is in these words that John Bowden, either consciously or unconsciously, anticipates the maxim that Schillebeeckx was to formulate in his later writing, namely, that 'Christology is concentrated creation', because Jesus is the person in whom God's creative purposes are concentrated and perfected. In 'The Sacraments: An Encounter with God', Schillebeeckx, in a passage that is overtly Christological, explains how the 'entirety of mankind's vocation to faithfulness' is concentrated in Jesus. Not only does Schillebeeckx emphasize the interplay of the relationship between God and Jesus, he also expresses with luminous clarity the highest fulfilment of humanity in its response to God:

> In a single person both elements are fulfilled: the invitation and the reply of perfect fidelity, and in such a way that both the invitation and the response constitute the completed revelation of God. The man Jesus is not only the one sent by the Holy Trinity, he is also the one called to be the representative of all humanity. He is not only the visible embodiment of God's wooing of man, but also the representation and highest fulfilment of the human response of love to God's courtship. Jesus, the free man, who in his humanity reveals to us the divine invitation of love, is at the same time, as man, the person who in the name of all of us and as our representative accepts this invitation.[46]

---

43. Cf. Eph. 3.9, 11: 'The plan of the mystery hidden for ages in God who created all things ... the eternal purpose that he has carried out in Christ Jesus our Lord.'
44. Schillebeeckx, *CSEG*, 5 [5].
45. Bowden, *Edward Schillebeeckx, Portrait of a Theologian*, 42.
46. Schillebeeckx, *SEG*, 247. Bowden quotes this passage in his *Portrait* on page 42.

This is an extraordinary passage Christologically. It is Irenaean, Augustinian, Chalcedonian and contemporary all at once. In what may sound like a variation on the theme of Irenaean recapitulation, Schillebeeckx here calls Christ the 'representative' of all humanity. It is Augustinian in interpreting Jesus as the culmination of God's relationship with Israel in what Augustine defines as the church's second phase of coming into being. It is Chalcedonian in that it attributes to Jesus full divinity ('Jesus is the one sent by the Holy Trinity') and full humanity ('the man Jesus', 'Jesus the free man', 'who in his humanity'). The passage is also contemporary in that it speaks of God and humanity in terms of relationship, without using any Irenaean or Chalcedonian special terms. With regard to the definitions of Chalcedon, it has both an Alexandrian and an Antiochene bent. Jesus is referred to as the one who is 'sent by the Holy Trinity', by which it is clear that he is a member of the Holy Trinity, the Second Person, fully divine. In a more Antiochene leaning, Schillebeeckx refers, in the same breath, to Christ as 'the free man, who in his humanity reveals to us the divine invitation of love, [who] is at the same time, as man, the person who in the name of all of us' accepts God's invitation.[47] Later, in dialogue with Ansfried Hulsbosch, Schillebeeckx will reappraise whether there is a better way to express the full divinity and full humanity of Jesus.[48] In this passage, however, although Schillebeeckx does not use the word 'concentrated', he nevertheless anticipates and expresses the idea of a concentration in Jesus of all that is entailed in creation, supremely God's invitation to human beings and the human response of love to God.

Already, at this early stage in his writing, there are two identifiable structural dogmatic elements of Schillebeeckx's Christology. From the earliest days of his theological schooling he learnt these structural elements of the Church's dogma both during his childhood and his Dominican training in preparation for ordination as a priest. It is likely that even as a schoolboy, with the Jesuits at Turnhout, he and his peers were thoroughly rehearsed in the Chalcedonian definition of Christ as one person with two natures.[49] During the time of his theological studies he read and studied in depth the patristic writings, and those of Augustine and Thomas Aquinas. The first structural element identified is the unity of divine-in-human in Jesus; the second is the idea of Jesus as representative of humanity.

---

47. Bowden, *Edward Schillebeeckx, Portrait of a Theologian*, 42.

48. See pp. 113–14.

49. Referring to his schooling with the Jesuits, Schillebeeckx said, 'I am bound to say that we fifteen-year-old boys knew more about [God as the Trinity and Jesus at the centre] then than first-year theology students now at Nijmegen University. The catechism was drummed into our heads at school in those days.' Edward Schillebeeckx, *God Is New Each Moment*, in conversation with Huub Oosterhus and Piet Hoogeveen, trans. David Smith (London: Continuum, 2004), 6 (henceforth *GNEM*).

The first structural element in Schillebeeckx's Christology: The unity of divine-in-human in Jesus[50]

The unity of divine-in-human in Jesus is the most fundamental of all the structural dogmatic elements of Schillebeeckx's Christology.[51] In Jesus the mystery of the divine Word is embodied in human flesh and in human flesh the mystery of what it means to be human is revealed by Jesus. Just as in his sacramental theology Schillebeeckx treads a path between extrinsicism and intrinsicism, so in his Christology he treads a path between the Alexandrian and the Antiochene emphases. He always confessed the Nicene Creed and adhered without reservation to the reality that is expressed in the dogma or *enuntiabile* of Chalcedon. Despite its length, the following passage is worth quoting in full to see how he wrote, in 1959, about the Chalcedonian definition, describing a unity of the divine-in-human in Jesus:

> The dogmatic definition of Chalcedon, according to which Christ is 'one person in two natures', implies that one and the same person, the Son of God, also took on a visible human form. Even in his humanity Christ is the Son of God. The second person of the most Holy Trinity is personally man; and this man is personally God. Therefore Christ is God in a human way, and man in a divine way. As a man he acts out his divine life in and according to his human existence. Everything he does as man is an act of the Son of God, a divine act in human form; an interpretation and transposition of a divine activity into a human activity. His human love is the human embodiment of redeeming love of God.[52]

In 1983 Huub Oosterhuis and Piet Hoogeveen questioned Schillebeeckx on how the figure of Jesus should be approached theologically.[53] Schillebeeckx told them that at Leuven, from 1947 to 1958, when he was teaching theology to Dominican students and also acting as their spiritual director, he taught Christology in 'real dogmatic' terms, and took 'Jesus as God' as his point of departure, an Alexandrian approach. In complementarity to the doctrinal aspects of Christology, however, he took a different approach in his spirituality lectures, namely, 'the man Jesus'. When he contemplated the man Jesus, Schillebeeckx 'tried to find a connection with Thomas Aquinas' disputed term *persona humana divinae naturae* – "a human person of divine nature"'.[54] These statements of Schillebeeckx show how

---

50. By way of a prefatory remark, the section which follows is intended to show why the expression 'the unity of divine-in-human' in Jesus is used rather than the more common 'divine and human' of Jesus.

51. The difference between this 'structural dogmatic element' of Christology and the *rem* or underlying reality of Christology is that the latter is the Creator's most intimate and concrete involvement in humanity, in the person of Jesus, whereas the structural dogmatic element is an attempt to express the unity of divine-in-human in God's incarnation in Jesus.

52. Schillebeeckx, *CSEG*, 10.

53. Schillebeeckx, *GNEM*, 20.

54. Ibid.

at Leuven he was already complementing the traditional doctrinal language of his Christology with a search for ways of understanding Christ as 'someone in whom human nature is assumed in such a way as *to be the person* of the Son of God' and, vitally, what the meaning of the person of the Son of God, Jesus, is for human beings.[55] With the help of Aquinas, Schillebeeckx was already saying that it is in 'the man Jesus [that] what God really means for us is made clear to us'.[56] There was a symbiosis between the theology of his doctrinal and of his spirituality lectures, a symbiosis between the Alexandrian and the Antiochene emphases for Christology. The Second Person of the Trinity, the Word or full expression of God, became flesh in the body of Jesus; he, in his particular historical context, was fully and perfectly human. In the light of Christian creation faith, the perfect humanity of the divine Jesus reveals both something of God's transcendence and, at the same time, his intimate involvement with men's and women's longings and strivings for the fullness of humanity in themselves.

A change at the conjunctural level: The way of expressing the divine-in-human in Jesus

An article by Schillebeeckx in a 1966 issue of the Dutch theological journal, *Tijdschrift voor Theologie*, which was devoted to Christology, provides evidence of Schillebeeckx's continuing insistence on the necessity to adhere to the Chalcedonian statement of hypostasis in Christology (that both a divine and a human nature exist in the person of Christ). This insistence was in contrast to Piet Schoonenberg who had queried in the same edition of the journal 'whether the Chalcedonian definition needed to be retained for the purposes of specifying the authenticity of Christian belief and the uniqueness of Christ'.[57] Schillebeeckx's response was to say that 'it is necessary to retain the notion of hypostasis in Christology', thereby holding what is expressed in the Chalcedonian definition as a structural element of his theology, as it is of the Church's dogma. At the same time, however, he made a conjunctural change in the way that he expressed the hypostatic union. Kennedy attributes the change in the way that Schillebeeckx expresses the divine and the human in Jesus in large part to the influence of Ansfried Hulsbosch. What Hulsbosch wrote in his article, entitled 'Jesus Christ, known as man, professed as Son of God', in the same issue of *Tijdschrift voor Theologie*, struck a deep and lasting chord in Schillebeeckx.

The burden of Hulsbosch's argument is that it is unacceptable to 'dichotomize the person of Jesus Christ into two components: one divine, the other human, one a transcendent divinity, the other a historical humanity', which, he suggested, could be argued to be a form of dualism.[58] Schillebeeckx, in his adherence to

---

55. Kennedy, *Schillebeeckx*, 104.
56. Schillebeeckx, *GNEM*, 20.
57. This account of the 1966 issue of *Tijdeschrift voor Theologie* devoted to Christology is drawn from Philip Kennedy, *Schillebeeckx*, pp. 105–6.
58. Ibid., 105.

the truth expressed by the Chalcedonian statement, tells his readers that from as far back as 1953 he had opposed the theological formulae 'Christ is God and man' and 'the man Jesus is God', which are two ways of expressing the hypostatic union.[59] Instead he preferred to speak of 'Jesus the Christ, who is Son of God *in humanity*' and to speak of 'hypostatic *unity*' as opposed to 'hypostatic union'.[60] In the light of Hulsbosch's argument, however, might the way, or the kind of way, in which Schillebeeckx had written about Jesus in 1957, as in the passage quoted on page 110 strike him as splitting Jesus into two: on the one hand describing him as 'the one sent by the Holy Trinity' and, on the other hand, naming him 'the representative of all humanity'? Hulsbosch was seeking a way to express Chalcedon's dogma of the unity of divine and human in Jesus intact, by means of a more hermeneutical *enuntiabile*. Kennedy points out that 'the noteworthy facet of Schillebeeckx's response to Hulsbosch is that he lauded the latter's inclination to supersede a dualistic Christology'.[61] He also notes that 'twenty-two years after dissecting Hulsbosch's article, Schillebeeckx is still to be found speaking of Jesus' historical way of living that enables him to be confessed as the Christ'.[62]

In the light of Hulsbosch's insights in the 1966 Christological debate in *Tijdschrift voor Theologie*, Schillebeeckx's stance shows him holding fast to the reality that the Chalcedonian definition expresses and, at the same time, shows him reinterpreting the reality of the divine-in-human of Jesus in the light of his discussions with theologian colleagues. This was a change at the conjunctural level. Earlier it had been the notion of existentialism that was the vehicle of a conjunctural change in the way Schillebeeckx unfolded the meaning of the sacraments: receiving grace in the sacraments was not a passive affair but an active experience of encounter with Christ mediating God's grace. It was in response to Hulsbosch's critique of the language used to express the truth of Chalcedon that Schillebeeckx engaged in a conjunctural change by speaking of Jesus in a non-dualistic way: in the words of Hulsbosch's title, 'Jesus Christ, known as man, professed as Son of God'.

Germane to the development of Schillebeeckx's Christology at the time of the 1966 issue of *Tijdschrift voor Theologie* devoted to Christology is the fact that, in the same year, he made his first journey to North America where he experienced the questioning already mentioned: 'Is Christ really God?'[63] Those questioners were perplexed by the contradiction suggested by a statement in stark terms that a human being is God. Schillebeeckx works with the structural warp threads of the

---

59. Schillebeeckx describes the Councils of Nicea, Ephesus, Constantinople and Chalcedon as intending 'to safeguard the basic "first-order" creed (decisive Salvation in Jesus given by God)' in the 'conjunctural framework' of patristic thought (*Jesus*, 526–7 [564–5]). Schillebeeckx in his turn intends to safeguard the 'second-order' affirmations of Chalcedon in the conjunctural framework of post-enlightenment thought.

60. Ibid., 106.

61. Kennedy, *Schillebeeckx*, 106.

62. Ibid.

63. Ibid., 101.

New Testament and Chalcedonian Christologies, weaving them with additional conjunctural weft threads, so as to come up with a different way of expressing the same truth (or *rem*) of the unity of divine-in-human in Jesus. In doing this, he uses different forms of expression, meaningfully to convey to his readers the truth of Chalcedon. As Kennedy points out, 'he preferred to speak ... of Jesus the Christ, who is Son of God *in humanity*'.[64] The year 1966 was also the year in which he entered 'a hermeneutical phase', teaching hermeneutics at Radboud University Nijmegen.[65]

The second structural element in Schillebeeckx's Christology: Jesus is representative

The idea of representation by Jesus which Schillebeeckx propounds is another structural element of his Christology. It is redolent of Irenaeus' ideas of recapitulation but only redolent and not equivalent. Eric Osborn writes about the complexity of Irenaeus' theological concept of recapitulation. He says that at least eleven ideas are combined in different permutations in Irenaeus' use of the concept and lists unification, repetition and redemption, to name a few.[66] Despite areas of overlap between the ideas of recapitulation and representativeness, Schillebeeckx's idea of Jesus as representative does not match exactly any of the ideas listed by Osborn.

A change at the conjunctural level: A twofold understanding of Jesus as representative

Schillebeeckx interprets the way in which God's purpose is summed up or represented in Jesus Christ in a new conjunctural model. The perspective from which Schillebeeckx considers Jesus is not so much an Ephesian one, focusing on what he will represent or recapitulate in the consummation of God's divine plans at the 'fullness of time',[67] nor is it to see him primarily in a Pauline way, as the Second Adam who made good the damage of Adam's sin.[68] Instead, Schillebeeckx draws

---

64. Ibid., 106.
65. Schillebeeckx, *HT*, 41.
66. Osborn, *Irenaeus of* Lyons, 97–8. The full list of ideas that Osborn identifies in Irenaeus' concept of recapitulation is: unification, repetition, redemption, perfection, inauguration and consummation, totality, the triumph of *Christus Victor*, ontology, epistemology and ethics.
67. Eph. 1.9-10: '[God] has made known to us the mystery of his will, according to his good pleasure that he set forth in Christ, as a plan for the fullness of time, to gather up all things in him, things in heaven and things on earth.'
68. Rom. 5.18: 'Just as one man's trespass led to condemnation for all, so one man's act of righteousness leads to justification and life for all.'

attention to how Jesus' humanity is representative both of God and of humanity, simultaneously in the present and across time, as it were in two directions. Sent from God, Jesus of Nazareth reveals God in bodily humanity, expressing in concrete, earthly practice God's divine love for human beings. Born and living in human flesh, Jesus, at the same time, embodies and represents the fullest human response to God's love. Such a response to God is expressed in profound and intimate relationship with God, which overflows with life and makes for joy. In Jesus the meeting ground of God and humanity is found.

At the conjunctural level, this twofold understanding of Jesus' representativeness is a break from a notion of representation that is implicit in a mechanistic sacramental theology against which Schillebeeckx was arguing in *Christ the Sacrament of the Encounter with God*. The notion of representation in a mechanistic sacramental theology, in which humanity tends to be seen (in its relation to God) as the passive recipient of grace, is one-sided because it concentrates almost exclusively on Jesus as a representative of God. In a twofold understanding of Jesus as representative, Jesus is not only Son of God, he also represents what human relationship with God entails.

Schillebeeckx's two-way understanding of the representativeness of Jesus is another example of the relational dialectic that characterizes his thinking. It contains the core theme in his Christology, both in his writing on the sacraments in the 1950s and in his Christological trilogy. The theme is that of understanding Jesus as 'concentrated creation': that Jesus is the visible embodiment of God's whole purpose in creation, namely, to woo humankind, to reveal his unwavering, saving love of humanity and to invite human beings to love him faithfully in return.[69] Jesus embodies God in his covenant with humanity, on God's side, an unshakeable alliance of unconditional love made with Abraham, sustained in history and given concentrated and human expression in Jesus' life, death and resurrection. The life of Jesus is one of absolute saving presence in the midst of humanity, both while he was on earth and sacramentally in his resurrection. In the accounts of the Last Supper, the impending spilling of Jesus' blood is charged with meaning: it is the blood of God's love, his covenant supremely expressed in Jesus. Jesus as the 'representation and highest fulfilment of the human response of love to God in a fidelity that knows no bounds – which does not shrink even from the death of the Cross'[70] represents in himself what God longs for from his human creatures, that they freely choose to share ever more deeply in his life and love. Schillebeeckx summarizes this idea of Jesus' twofold representation in these words:

> In [Jesus] there was a visible realization of both sides of faith in the Covenant. In the dialogue between God and man, so often breaking down, there was found at last a perfect human respondent: in the same person there was achieved the

---

69. Cf. Bowden, *Edward Schillebeeckx, Portrait of a Theologian*, 42.
70. Schillebeeckx, *SEG*, 247.

perfection both of the divine invitation and of the human response in faith from the man who by his resurrection is the Christ.[71]

That Jesus perfectly embodies God the Creator's invitation, in love, to humanity and at the same time gives the perfect human loving response to his Father is the bedrock of Schillebeeckx's proposition: 'Christology is concentrated creation'. In Jesus, God's purpose in creation is revealed in his humanity and, at the same time, what it means for humanity to be truly human is revealed in his divinity. Jesus, in his divinity, is unique but God's invitation to human creatures is not only to share God's gift of life by their mere existence but also to become sharers in the Creator's divine life.

Excursus: Talking about the divinity and humanity of Jesus

At this point it is helpful to note the logical impossibility of talking directly about two things at the same time. The divinity and the humanity of Jesus are of equal importance; neither must be diminished yet a theologian can only talk about them one at a time because the mystery of the unity of divine-in-human in Jesus eludes simple, human verbal expression. So, on the one hand, Jesus may, for example, be spoken of as Christ in whom all things in heaven and on earth are to be recapitulated (from the Ephesian perspective of his divinity)[72] and, on the other hand, as Jesus, the representative of humanity, who embodies the highest fulfilment of the human response of love to God's courtship (from the perspective of his humanity). To talk of Jesus as the divine Christ is not necessarily to ignore the humanity of Christ (let alone to deny it) and to talk of Jesus as the representative of humanity is not necessarily to ignore the divinity of Jesus (let alone to deny it). Rather, to talk of either, and to explore the implications of either, might be precisely intended as a way of speaking about each as having equal importance. Each speaks from the perspective of creation faith. To use the image of a compass, as early as 1957 and even as far back as 1947, rooted, as he was, in the theology of Chalcedon, Schillebeeckx takes his bearings from Chalcedon in order to arrive at a balanced interpretation of both the humanity and the divinity of Jesus. In 1972 he writes vehemently about the need for the divinity and the humanity of Jesus Christ to be held together and for one not to eclipse the other:

> I believe in Jesus as the Son of God and I do not want to leave you in any uncertainty. ... At the same time, I believe in what Chalcedon wanted to preserve when the great Council said: One and the same person, i.e. Jesus of Nazareth, is truly man and truly God. ... But precisely as a Christian I must also point to the threatening danger of an exclusive and wholesale divinization of the man

---

71. Schillebeeckx, *CSEG*, 9 [12–13].
72. Eph. 1.10.

Jesus. Such a divinization ... distorts the fundamental direction of the revelation which ... has shown us who he is and how he acts.[73]

Talking about humanity, Jesus' and our own, is not a diversion but it is central to theology. Schillebeeckx's later focus on anthropology, in the light of the humanity of Jesus Christ, was not a deviation from Christocentricity but rather an intensified focus on what the humanity of Jesus Christ means for humanity in its relation to God our Creator and in its place in the creation. In Jesus of Nazareth, human beings are given the fullest revelation of both God and humanity. In Jesus the two are combined in an interrelationship. As Schillebeeckx writes,

> It is not a matter of fitting together two models or concepts – 'human being' and 'divine being' – so as to arrive at a conceivable (or inconceivable) 'amalgam' of God-man, at the perhaps abstractly conceivable model of 'God made man', for which Jesus of Nazareth might have been a historical occasion. Turning to Jesus to find salvation in him means approaching him in a state of not knowing, or rather of 'open knowledge' of the true meaning of humanity and divinity alike, maybe to learn from him the true nature via their interrelationship as manifested in Jesus.[74]

Returning to the way in which Schillebeeckx addresses the problem of a mechanistic understanding of the sacraments, he works from the standpoint of '*intersubjectivity* or *existential personal encounter*'.[75] He writes, 'He [Jesus] is the consummate [i.e. highest and supreme] actualisation of the communion of love of man with God.'[76] His own communion with God is an extension of God's invitation (both while he lived on earth and now as the raised Christ) for all to hear. God the Creator longs for and invites human beings, who are his works of art (marred only when they sin), to enter into life with him in Christ Jesus. Elsewhere in *The Sacraments: An Encounter with God* Schillebeeckx summarizes God's invitation and Jesus' response, both through the medium of the humanity of Jesus, in these words:

> God desired not only to be God for us, he wanted to be God for us in a *human* way. For the first time we can fully grasp what sanctifying grace means; how it reveals, on the one hand, God's boundless desire for a personal communion with us, for the man Jesus who longs to befriend is precisely revelation of God. On the other hand, it also reveals how profoundly meant our response to that divine love ought to be, for the man Jesus whose devoted childlike intimacy with his Father remaining faithful even unto death is also a vicarious realization of our

---

73. Schillebeeckx, *GAU*, 43.
74. Schillebeeckx, *Jesus*, 566–7 [604].
75. Schillebeeckx, *SEG*, 245 (original italics).
76. Ibid., 263.

devotion, the highest realization of religious intimacy with the living God which man has ever undertaken.[77]

In Jesus is found an embodiment, a summary, a representation of what it means most fully to be human, and an invitation from God to join him in that response.

Multivocality in New Testament Christology

Bowden points out that Schillebeeckx identifies four New Testament Christologies in *Jesus*. They are: Jesus seen as the eschatological prophet resulting in a *parousia* or *maranatha* Christology; Jesus seen as the wonder worker; Wisdom Christology (Jesus could either be identified with divine Wisdom or be seen as having been sent by it); and Jesus seen as 'the crucified one whom God had raised from the dead, an approach in which great stress came to be laid on the resurrection'.[78] In noting these four New Testament Christologies identified by Schillebeeckx, Bowden does not make any analysis about subsequent continuity or change with regard to them. The fact, however, that there are different Christologies raises two questions. The first is a point about multivocality in theology. In the case of the New Testament there are multiple witnesses and the authors of the scriptural texts do not all say the same thing. As Schillebeeckx writes in *Jesus*, 'Study of modern exegesis helps us to recognize diverse early Christian credal strands, each of which perpetuates certain facets of Jesus' life on earth'.[79] For Schillebeeckx the different credal strands, and the chain of understandings that make up the continuity of tradition, are essential sources of contemporary understanding and creativity, to be reactivated.[80] The second question raised by the fact of four New Testament Christologies (and variations in subsequent Christologies) is, what is the identity of Christology? According to the threefold *Annales* model, each Christology in itself may, and possibly does, contain structural, conjunctural and even ephemeral elements which are at times asynchronous. All three elements change, including the structural element even if only very slowly. By analogy with what Schillebeeckx writes about the evangelical identity of meaning, what can be discovered about the Christological identity of meaning?

The Christological identity of meaning

While the 'evangelical identity of meaning' is about the gospel as a whole, Christology is a subdivision of the gospel, with its own identity of meaning, just as there might be, say, a Trinitarian identity of meaning. The Christological identity of meaning shares a common structure with the identity of meaning of the gospel

---

77. Ibid., 250.
78. Bowden, *Edward Schillebeeckx, Portrait of a Theologian*, 70.
79. Schillebeeckx, *Jesus*, 370 [404].
80. Cf. Schillebeeckx, *GFoM*, vol. III, 18 [27].

as a whole. The idea of proportional relations applies here, too, to illustrate the Christological identity of meaning.[81] To transpose Schillebeeckx's words about the evangelical identity of meaning, the Christological identity of meaning does not lie at the level of Christological doctrines or statements *as such* but neither does it lie at the level of the situation, then and now. It is to be found at the level of a corresponding relation between articulations of Christology and the socio-historical situations in which they are made. Just as it can be said that it is the grace of faith that prompts evangelical interpretations and makes them possible, it is specifically the grace of experiencing God's saving action in and through Jesus Christ that prompts Christological interpretations and makes them possible. The *actus Salvatoris* gives rise to Christologies in different eras. Saving action, in the widest possible sense, denotes the gift of fullness of life in God, achievable in Jesus Christ, which brings liberation from all that is stunting, oppressive and alienating. What is here called the Christological identity of meaning, Schillebeeckx calls 'the constant unitive factor' of Christology. He writes,

> A (modern) christological interpretation of Jesus cannot proceed from the kerygma (or dogma) about Jesus, and even less from a so-called 'purely historical' Jesus of Nazareth, even though a historico-critical approach, informed by an intention of faith, remains the only proper starting point. Since all these attempts have proved unsatisfactory, what is left in the way of a constant unitive factor? I would say (and that is saying quite a lot): the Christian movement itself! In other words, a *Christian oneness of experience* which does *indeed derive its unity from the one figure of Jesus*, while remaining pluriform in its verbal expression or articulation.[82]

He goes on to say, 'The constant factor ... is that particular groups of people find their ultimate salvation imparted by God in Jesus of Nazareth.'[83] Without the experience of salvation in Jesus the Christ, there would be no articulation of Christologies. All *enuntiabilia* about the *rem* can only be made, after all, in the context of faith, because they are all faith statements. The acknowledgement of faith in Jesus by his disciples and followers in his lifetime was the original, inchoate Christology, brought about by the salvific, life-giving effects of his words and deeds while he was among them on earth. In the time from Jesus' death and resurrection to the gelling of the New Testament canon, the four Christologies identified by Schillebeeckx emerged.[84] In patristic times the experience of being saved by Christ was expressed in terms of having been released by Christ from being in thrall to the

---

81. For Schillebeeckx's explanation of the 'evangelical identity of meaning', and the idea of proportional relations, see *Essays*, p. 62.
82. Schillebeeckx, *Jesus*, 38 [56].
83. Ibid.
84. Ibid., 369–401 [403–39].

devil in a theology of *Christus Victor*.[85] By the time of Chalcedon the full force of the need to clarify, so far as was possible, the mystery of the person of Jesus Christ, who and what he is in himself, had made itself felt. The definitions of Chalcedon (451) reaffirmed 'the definitions of Nicaea [I, 325] and Constantinople [I, 381] asserting them to be a sufficient account of the orthodox faith about the Person of Christ'.[86] Structural elements hardly change but nevertheless do; the Christological identity of meaning, or what Schillebeeckx calls the 'constant unitive factor', however, consists in an identity of effect, namely, the experience of an aliveness in the Spirit of Jesus the Christ which brings about a salvific release from whatever it is that inhibits true flourishing. The oppression of human beings takes different forms according to changing historical–cultural contexts, but in being empowered to be released from oppression and the bondage of sin, Christians meet the same Christ whose power is constantly at work. As Schillebeeckx writes, 'Memories of particular words and actions of Jesus are thus handed down because these earliest congregations had somehow found salvation in Jesus. Acknowledgement of salvation in Jesus was the matrix of all traditions about him.'[87] Openness to God is the path to God's saving action which is the other side of the coin of his absolute creative presence.

---

85. See Gustav Aulén, *Christus Victor: An Historical Study of the Three Main Types of the Idea of the Atonement* (London: SPCK, 1978), 4–7; and Colin Gunton, *The Actuality of Atonement: A Study of Metaphor, Rationality and the Christian Tradition* (London: T&T Clark, 2008), 54–5.

86. *Oxford Dictionary of the Christian Church*, ed. F. L. Cross and E. A. Livingstone (Oxford: Oxford University Press, 1997), 315.

87. Schillebeeckx, *Jesus*, 63 [83].

Chapter 5

CONTINUITY AND CHANGE IN SCHILLEBEECKX'S LATER CHRISTOLOGY: SUFFERING AND SIN

Three dominant elements emerge in Schillebeeckx's later Christology. They form interwoven strands which are inextricably connected with each other. They are: a focus on suffering; speaking about God in terms of the praxis of the kingdom of God; and an exploration of what the humanity of Jesus Christ means for human beings. Many scholars see these three strands as brand new elements which give Schillebeeckx's later theology and Christology their distinguishing character. In what follows, each of these strands is examined and dogmatic elements within them are identified and analysed according to the *Annales* model of change. The subject of Chapter 5 is suffering and sin and Chapter 6 focuses on the praxis of the kingdom of God and the humanity of Jesus Christ. It is found that these strands, suffering, the praxis of the kingdom of God and the interpretation of the humanity of Jesus, consist of elements both of continuity and of change.

The timing of Schillebeeckx's major focus on suffering, the connection between sin and suffering, and the place of original sin in Schillebeeckx's theology are considered. Jesus is salvation from God, setting people free from both sin and suffering, not by crucifixion interpreted as a propitiatory sacrifice but by the praxis of the reign of God. Creation faith believes human beings are entrusted by God with the task of no less than 'the transformation of the world, the development of a better and more tolerable human society, and a new earth', bringing in the kingdom of God *sequela Jesu*.[1] Schillebeeckx adopted 'Critical Theory's understanding of itself as the self-consciousness of an emancipative, critical praxis, to define theology as "the critical self-consciousness of Christian praxis in the world and the church" '.[2] In Schillebeeckx's work the definitive salvation of the kingdom of God is eschatological, unable fully to be realized until God's destiny for creation is fulfilled at the end of history. In considering the meaning of the humanity of Jesus, he says that what God is like 'is even more concentrated and compressed in Jesus than anywhere else both in what he conceals and what he discloses'.[3]

---

1. Schillebeeckx, *GAU*, 96.
2. Kennedy, *Schillebeeckx*, 50, quoting Schillebeeckx, *UF*, 135 [154].
3. Schillebeeckx, *GAU*, 31.

Suffering

Eric Borgman tells how, when Schillebeeckx was about fifteen (1929 or 1930), 'he was quite convinced that he wanted to become a Jesuit. He had become interested in Hinduism and Buddhism and, like his brother, wanted to go to India to study these religions.'[4] In the autobiography of the Jesuit William Wallace (1864–1922) he had read how Wallace did not see his Christian faith as clashing with 'the religious heart of the collection of rites and customs which Westerners had baptized as "Hinduism" but he understood his Catholic faith as the "fulfilment and perfection" of this religion'.[5] Borgman proposes that Wallace's view influenced Schillebeeckx in the way that, later on, he looked at modern Western culture. Schillebeeckx did not regard the maelstrom of the pluralistic currents of the 1960s and 1970s in Europe as an enemy to be clashed with. In his own description of the evolution of his theological reflection, he says, 'In the 1960s, along with the arrival of the human sciences, there appeared criticism of society, of culture, of ideology and also of theology as a theological discipline. I followed this trend.'[6] During the vigorous pluralism of the 1960s and 1970s in the Western world, in the context of the phenomenon often known as secularization, there was a palpable crisis of faith. Steven M. Rodenborn describes how, although historical progress was not presumed inevitable in the wake of two world wars, 'historical advancement was [nevertheless] envisioned as attainable' which would render religion redundant:

> With the unprecedented prosperity of the 1950s and 1960s ... a renewed enthusiasm determined by the ongoing economic and material productivity of the sciences, as well as a progressive optimism in the possibility of socio-political transformation illustrated by the well-known student movements of 1968, reinvigorated confidence in the possibility of historical progress and a better future. ... What was now predicted by [the] proponents [of this theory of secularization], though, was the dissolution of religion.[7]

In a review of Peter Berger's book *The Many Altars of Modernity*, David Martin refers to Berger's analysis in the 1960s, which states that 'as societies become more modern, they become less religious', as 'a key element in the most vigorously contested theory in the sociology of religion: secularisation'.[8] In the 1960s zeitgeist of North America and Europe, the new theory and perception of secularization

---

4. Borgman, *Edward Schillebeeckx*, 30.
5. Ibid., 31.
6. Schillebeeckx, *HT*, 41.
7. Steven M. Rodenborn, *Hope in Action: Subversive Eschatology in The Theology of Edward Schillebeeckx and Johann Baptist Metz* (Minneapolis, MN: Fortress Press, 2014), 8–9.
8. David Martin, 'Everything Old Is New Again', *The Tablet* (1 November 2014), 20. Berger, in fact, 'believed that he made a serious mistake, in common with most people who worked in the field [of sociology of religion] in the 1950s and 1960s, in holding that modernity necessarily leads to a decline in religion'. Christopher Lewis, 'Secularisation: An

fuelled religious uncertainty and a lack of confidence which many Christians experienced as they struggled with former ways of expressing the content of their faith and the manner of living it out.

It was within this context of pluralism and of perceived secularization that Schillebeeckx chose suffering as a common ground, shared by all human beings, Christians and non-Christians alike, from which he could point to God and show the meaning of Jesus. In the way that William Wallace had identified expressions of the desire for God and what God wills for human beings in Hinduism, Schillebeeckx chose the common human abhorrence of suffering, and its opposite, namely, the human longing for wholeness and well-being, as a way of talking about God and Jesus. As Kennedy writes,

> Schillebeeckx searched for a human experience that could serve as a universally accessible and intelligible basis for explaining the meaning of Christian faith to audiences that might not share traditional Christian concepts and assumptions. The experience he came upon was suffering.[9]

Schillebeeckx's decision to use suffering or negativity (as he also calls it) as a common human experience from which to talk about God, and his exegetical researches in the New Testament which shone the spotlight on God's response to suffering in and through the life of Jesus, combined to lead to his major focus on suffering and the praxis of the reign of God. Some scholars aver that Schillebeeckx's later, major focus on suffering is, in fact, the starting point of his Christology.[10] John P. Galvin, for example, writes,

> Schillebeeckx's Christology begins with a problem, not a formula or theory. His quest for a common starting point common to all human life and therefore accessible to all leads him to concentrate on the universal experience of evil, the bitter awareness that the history of the human race is one of suffering.[11]

Given that Galvin neither makes mention of any earlier Christology, nor an evolution in his Christology, but simply talks about what is, in fact, Schillebeeckx's later Christology, it seems that Galvin might well be said to be interpreting him as

---

Outmoded Concept?', in *A Religious Atheist? Critical Essays on the Work of Lloyd Geering*, ed. Raymand Pelly and Peter Stuart (Dunedin: Otago, 2006), 73.

9. Kennedy, *Schillebeeckx*, 8.

10. To propose that suffering is the starting point of Schillebeeckx's Christology is either to imply a rupture with any Christology dating from before the mid-1960s, or simply to deal with his later Christology as though it were a self-contained unit on its own, an unhistorical approach.

11. John P. Galvin, 'The Story of Jesus as the Story of God', in *The Praxis of the Reign of God: An Introduction to The Theology of Edward Schillebeeckx*, ed. Mary Catherine Hilkert and Robert J. Schreiter (New York: Fordham University Press, 2002), 81.

a theologian who uses the hermeneutics of rupture before and after Vatican II, and to whom, therefore, a twofold, Kuhnian model would apply. The extent to which a concern with suffering can be argued to be coeval with Schillebeeckx's Christology is explored below.

The contingency of the moment at which Schillebeeckx drew the whole question of suffering into the centre of his theological thinking is of interest in itself. Kennedy writes that Schillebeeckx became 'much more aware … of pervasive human suffering in contemporary societies' in the years from 1966 onwards.[12] He observes,

> A major oversight, indeed questionable trait, of Schillebeeckx's early theology, written as it was in the immediate trail of WW II, is that it did not explore intently the theological ramifications of human suffering. Adorno and other Western Marxists were much more forthright in drawing attention to the portentous significance of suffering, especially as it is encapsulated in the symbol of Auschwitz.[13]

In defence of Schillebeeckx, there are two factors, one contextual, the other motivational. There is also Kathleen Anne McManus's thesis that 'suffering operates as a formative factor throughout the whole of Schillebeeckx's theological development'.[14] First, the changing circumstances and contexts of Schillebeeckx's life are relevant to the explanation of the timing of his major focus on human suffering. While he pursued his own philosophical studies at the Dominican House in Ghent and while he studied and taught theology at the *studium generale* in Leuven until 1957, Schillebeeckx led a more or less cloistered life. When he became professor of Dogmatics and the History of Theology at the University of Nijmegen in 1958, he emerged from the cloister and came into contact with a much wider range of people. As a professor at a Catholic university, partly funded by the state, he was no longer responsible for the spiritual formation of a large group of Dominican friars. Instead, he taught mainly postgraduates and was able to devote more time to research and to accepting invitations to speak in public. The speaking engagements brought Schillebeeckx into direct contact with Christians all over the Netherlands who voiced their questions and concerns. He became known both to the wider public and to the Dutch bishops with whom he worked as they prepared for the Second Vatican Council.[15]

Secondly, if one takes an overview of his oeuvre, it can be argued that the overriding motive in Schillebeeckx's writing in the 1940s and 1950s propelled him into his later preoccupation with human suffering in his theology and Christology. His later idea about the universality of the negative experience of human suffering

---

12. Kennedy, *Schillebeeckx*, 51.
13. Ibid.
14. McManus, *Unbroken Communion*, 2.
15. See Kennedy, *Schillebeeckx*, 25.

as common ground in a pluralist society on which to engage in dialogue about God revealed in Jesus is in continuity with his earlier preoccupation in post-war Flanders (1945–6) and in Paris (1946–7) with how to find a way of speaking about God in dialogue with the atheists and existentialists whose work he studied in France.[16] In 1945, for the first time, Schillebeeckx addressed a wider public as a theologian at a time when existentialist nihilism was recognized by many people as an adequate expression of how they felt about life after the horrors of the war.[17] Borgman describes how, in response to what Flemish Catholic youth were saying, Schillebeeckx 'directly grapples with existentialism as an expression of feelings about life, with the desire for spiritual orientation, shattered idealism and the will to accept life which was expressed by the texts of the young Catholics'.[18] His engagement with atheism and existentialism in the 1940s paved the way for his later incorporation of suffering into his theology as an experience common to all human beings.

McManus, in her extended study of the place and meaning of suffering in the theology of Schillebeeckx, observes that 'amidst many streams of influence his theological project is consistently shaped by suffering as mystery and challenge'.[19] Rego points out that she shows that there is continuity between Schillebeeckx's early Thomistic theology and his later hermeneutical theology. Of her analysis he writes, 'the early thomistic influences, which speak of suffering in terms of human solidarity in "original sin" and "original justice", are now translated into the language of "negative experience of contrast" and solidarity in a "political mysticism"'.[20] McManus makes the case that the roots of the way in which Schillebeeckx later speaks of suffering as *negative experience* and of the seeking of good in situations where good is absent, as *negative contrast experiences*, are firmly lodged in Thomist soil. Despite the overwhelmingly concrete and present reality of suffering, both Aquinas and Schillebeeckx 'emphasize the absolute goodness of a nevertheless mysterious God and … insist that we speculate about evil from this base'.[21] It is in her examination of 'how Aquinas's definition of evil as privation bears itself out in his analysis of pain and sorrow' that elements of 'contrast and contingency [are found which are] most pertinent in relation to

---

16. Schillebeeckx made a close study of Sartre's *L'être et le néant: Essai d'ontologie et phénoménlogique* under the supervision of Louis Lavelle (Kennedy, *Schillebeeckx*, 81) and also remarked, 'In the métro and on the train one often sees shop workers and semi-intellectuals gobbling up *Les Mouches* or *Huis Clos* [existentialist novels by Jean-Paul Sartre], and to all appearances existentialism is the centre of interest in the salons of Paris' (Borgman, *Edward Schillebeeckx*, 113).

17. See Borgman, *Edward Schillebeeckx*, 69.

18. Ibid., 71.

19. McManus, *Unbroken Communion*, 2.

20. Aloysius Rego, *Suffering and Salvation: The Salvific Meaning of Suffering in the Later Theology of Edward Schillebeeckx* (Louvain: Peeters Press, 2006), 9.

21. McManus, *Unbroken Communion*, 49.

Schillebeeckx's development of negative contrast experience vis-à-vis suffering'.[22] She writes,

> Speaking of the contrariety of pain and pleasure, Thomas notes that, even though opposite, one contrary can be the accidental cause of the other. That is, from sorrow at the absence of something good or loved, one seeks it more eagerly. Here is an important root of what Schillebeeckx will come to speak of as negative contrast experience.[23]

Both Aquinas and Schillebeeckx share a concept of God's original plan for humanity in terms of what Aquinas calls 'original justice'. As McManus points out, 'While Thomas finds this image in the past, Schillebeeckx finds it in the promised future.'[24] Aquinas' construct of 'original justice' looks back to the Genesis account of paradise in Eden and he perceives it as something lost at a moment in time. Original sin, a main cause of suffering, is about the loss of grace when Adam and Eve disobeyed God's command. Schillebeeckx, in his interpretation, rather than looking backwards, looks forward to a state of original justice which will be accomplished when God's kingdom is fulfilled. In his understanding, original sin constantly hinders the bringing about of the kingdom of God and original justice is 'an eschatological vision, a harbinger of hope, an emblem of the salvation historically [and vitally] experienced in fragmentary ways'.[25]

Although McManus does not use the *Annales* model of change and continuity, she nevertheless describes currents of both continuity and change within Schillebeeckx's understanding of original sin and suffering as follows:

> Schillebeeckx, in his earlier writings, gives evidence of an early formation that could not help but be touched by literalist interpretations. [His] later hermeneutical development will gradually nuance his treatment of the roots of suffering in original sin while illuminating the deepest meaning of the historical truth of human experience. Yet, the core of his earliest, traditional understanding will remain the animating spirit of even his most sophisticated critical appropriations of anthropology, myth, and symbol where evil, suffering and original sin are concerned.[26]

Sin and humanly caused suffering

There is a common categorization of suffering into what has traditionally been called 'natural evil' and 'moral evil'. 'Natural evil' results from contingent events

22. Ibid.
23. Ibid., 50.
24. Ibid., 52.
25. Ibid.
26. Ibid., 55.

in nature which humanity, in the ignorance of its finitude, has not yet learnt to prevent or remedy, for example, the detection of seismic zones before they cause earthquakes or the prevention and cure of 'new' diseases. So long as human beings live, they will be finite in the contingent universe and therefore part of the human task will always be to work to minimize 'natural evil'.

'Moral evil' refers to suffering caused by harmful, that is, sinful human actions. To borrow the image of a coin, one side is sin and the other side is moral suffering. There is a direct link: if the first is avoided, so is the second. On the side of the coin representing those harmed by sin, there are, typically in Christian understanding, two categories of people who are harmed. The first is the more obvious category, namely, the people who are the direct object of someone else's sinful action, and the second category is the perpetrators of sin themselves. There is no mystery about the active cause of this kind of suffering. What is odd and incomprehensible is that human beings are so persistent in causing each other and themselves to suffer, and that is sin. 'Moral suffering' is remediable with *metanoia* and a reliance on God's help together with the mutual support of each other. If, however, in the words of Gemma Simmonds, 'human beings turn away from the root of their very existence, namely, the Creator God, they have a default mechanism of self-implosion and self-destruction'.[27] There is nothing inevitable about moral suffering. Controversial though it may be, it is even possible roughly to quantify these two different kinds of suffering if only in an unscientific way. Without in any way dismissing or underestimating the pain caused by natural suffering, it does not seem unreasonable to suggest that most suffering in this world is the result of sin committed by perpetrators. Innocent victims of the sins committed by others are never to blame for their suffering. With regard to natural suffering, God does not punish by inflicting suffering because he is absolutely against suffering. The Christian concept of God 'assigns pure positivity only to God; i.e. by nature God promotes good and opposes evil, injustice and suffering'.[28] Human beings cause themselves and each other suffering by misusing their freedom, ignoring, or ignorant of, the source of that freedom.

Schillebeeckx does not analyse suffering in this sort of way and nor is he concerned with theodicy which attempts to vindicate God in view of the existence of evil suffering in a creation that is good. Mary Catherine Hilkert writes, 'Schillebeeckx does not attempt any theoretical response to the problem of human suffering [mainly caused by sin]. Instead he explores God's own response in and through the life-story of Jesus.'[29] He does explain to 'atheistic and religiously sceptical moderns that evil and suffering do not have their source in God as

---

27. Gemma Simmonds, *Ignatian Spirituality: Blowing in the Wind*, Paper presented at the Heythrop Summer Conference, 'Let Him Easter in Us', 5 July 2018. Accessed on YouTube, 14 August 2020, under Dr Gemma Simmonds CJ Ignatian Spirituality.

28. Schillebeeckx, *GAU*, 99.

29. Mary Catherine Hilkert, '"Grace-Optimism": The Spirituality at the Heart of Schillebeeckx's Theology', *Spirituality Today*, 43, 3 (1991), 220–39, 227.

Creator'.[30] He insists that 'while accounting for an element of chance, our own contingent will can explain why the world looks as it does'.[31] The task of Jesus Christ and of human beings is to prevent, abolish and alleviate suffering. Because of the intrinsic link between sin and morally caused suffering, human subjection to the reality that the dogma of original sin expresses is identified as a structural element in Schillebeeckx's theology of suffering.

A third structural element in Schillebeeckx's Christology: Humanity is subject to original sin

Schillebeeckx agrees profoundly that there is what has been, and is, called original sin; he is also acutely aware of the horrors of human suffering. He does not, however, spell out the natural and moral categories of suffering although he does allude to these two categories of suffering when, for example, he writes, 'In the light of what is in fact the unrelieved state of suffering in nature and society, [a Christian prophetic impulse] is what is needed.'[32] Nor does he probe the link between sin and suffering so much as stress that what matters supremely is what human beings do in the face of suffering.

Excursus: Schillebeeckx's use of the terms 'evil' and 'suffering'; the hazards of using the word 'evil' in an inexact way

In exploring Schillebeeckx's treatment of suffering in terms of humanity being subject to original sin, it is helpful first to see how he uses the terms 'suffering' and 'evil' and to identify the hazards of using the word 'evil' in an inexact way. Aloysius Rego remarks, convincingly,

> It must be noted that Schillebeeckx does not clearly distinguish between 'suffering' and 'evil'. He does not delve into the metaphysics of evil. However, from the context of his writings it might be suggested that when he refers to 'evil' he means suffering which confounds critical rationality.[33]

When Schillebeeckx uses the word 'evil' it is invariably in the context of a point he is making about suffering and sin. He uses the term 'evil' as a descriptor of the human actions that wilfully cause unnecessary suffering and as a descriptor of the human pain endured in humanly caused, unnecessary suffering. His preoccupation is clearly with the nature of sinful actions that cause suffering, not with a supposed ontological thing called Evil. An example which illustrates

---

30. Kennedy, *Schillebeeckx*, 91.
31. Ibid., 92.
32. Schillebeeckx, *GAU*, 100.
33. Rego, *Suffering and Salvation*, 148–9.

the way in which he uses the term occurs in a discussion of the resurrection of Jesus. In that discussion he writes of the crucifixion, 'It was not God but men and women who put Jesus to death', in other words, the suffering that Jesus endured in his execution by crucifixion was caused by human beings, not by God nor by some 'thing' named 'Evil'.[34] Men and women took decisions and actions which culminated in the consequence of the crucifixion of Jesus. In the same context Schillebeeckx goes on to say, 'The basic experience of the first disciples after Good Friday was that evil, the cross, cannot have the last word.'[35] In this statement he uses the word 'evil' as shorthand to describe the evil decisions and actions taken by human beings which resulted in the evil suffering of the crucifixion.

The word evil may be used either adjectivally or substantively. If the word is used substantively, a reification takes place. Something named 'evil' is brought conceptually, by an act of the imagination or by assumption, into virtual being although it does not, in fact, exist. The evil property or accident of something is assumed to have a separate concrete existence as 'Evil'. Augustine argued against the idea that evil is an existing, separate thing. After a tightly reasoned analysis in the *Enchiridion*, he writes,

> This leads us to a surprising conclusion: that, since every being, in so far as it is a being, is good, if we then say that a defective thing is bad, it would seem to mean that we are saying that what is evil is good, that only what is good is ever evil and that there is no evil apart from something good. This is because every actual entity is good, omnis natura bonum est. Nothing evil exists in itself, but only as an evil aspect of some actual identity.[36]

In this way he refuted dualism, the Manichaean brand of which he had professed for nearly ten years before his conversion to Christianity. In Christian faith and theology there is, therefore, no place for evil as a thing.[37] If, however, the word is loosely used substantively there may be unconscious verbal slippage into dualism. What Rego was quoted above as saying is the case, namely, that Schillebeeckx sometimes appears to use the words 'suffering' and 'evil' interchangeably. On the other hand, Schillebeeckx does not reify evil; he is not in danger of slipping into

---

34. Schillebeeckx, *Church*, 125 [126–7].

35. Ibid., 126 [128].

36. Augustine, *Enchiridion, on Faith, Hope and Love* IV:13, trans. Albert C. Outler (Dallas, TX: Southern Methodist University, 1955), downloaded 22 September 2016. www.tertullian.org/fathers/augustine_enchiridion-02_trams.htm.

37. Schillebeeckx, however, writing about 'God's "no" to our suffering in history', warns against arguing away the pain of suffering by invoking the theoretical explanation that there is no such thing as 'Evil': 'theological distinctions of God's "positive" and "permissive" will were introduced by theologians seeking a theoretical explanation for suffering, like the Greek attempts to describe all forms of evil as a "non-being" so as not to have to fathom it – an escape route for people who could not locate evil theoretically'. *Jesus*, 154–5 [178].

dualism. His position is absolutely opposed to any form of dualism and in this respect he is Augustinian.[38]

A second reason for wariness in using the word 'evil' substantively is because such a use may, and does, sometimes appear to shift human responsibility away from human beings onto some supposed ontological power called Evil (which does not exist). In a passage in which he catalogues various reactions to the 'incomprehensible occurrence' of suffering, Schillebeeckx gives, among others, the refusal to accept responsibility. He sees the danger that to deny responsibility shifts responsibility away from human beings who, in fact, have powers of autonomy. He writes,

> [No one] can explain the reality of injustice and suffering in the way in which they disrupt and distort mankind. People curse God or try to justify him; they blame Adam or the devil, or refuse to accept any responsibility for it themselves. Any explanation of human suffering trivializes this painful experience or asks too much of human responsibility; it looks for an excuse for this incomprehensible occurrence or finally makes God a torturer intent on teaching a divine lesson.[39]

Human behaviour and actions that make people suffer unnecessarily do, in fact, explain actual and particular suffering although the uncontrollable, unforeseen consequences of such behaviour and actions are less easy to analyse and trace. The truly 'incomprehensible occurrence' is that we human beings continue to cause immeasurable suffering to each other when it is in our power to choose and strive not to do so.

In contemporary Western culture it is possibly true to say that, as a result of various insights of psychology and sociology, the knowledge that we are conditioned (which is perhaps conflated with the idea that we may be determined) often diminishes people's sense or conviction of human responsibility. At the same time, human autonomy, more often called and admired as 'independence' or as a form of self-fulfilment sometimes described as 'moving on to find oneself' (at the cost to others), is extolled, or it is often reduced to a mere 'right to choose' or 'doing things one's own way'. Unthinking selfishness and self-interest at the expense of others slip in easily. When suffering is at its direst and appears most senseless, people often resort to saying, with vehemence, 'It's evil', suggesting that there is some kind of rule of correspondence: the worse the suffering inflicted, the more incomprehensible it is that anyone could cause it; it must be due, therefore, all the more, to some supposed ontological thing called Evil. The story of Adam and Eve is humanity's story. Human beings are beguiled and fail to own their responsibility to God. Even without theories of conditioning or determinism, human beings often blind themselves to the consequences of their actions or inaction.

---

38. See, for example, *GAU*, 91–2 for Schillebeeckx's refutation of dualism.
39. Schillebeeckx, *GAU*, 149.

Schillebeeckx's use of the word 'evil' may be somewhat vague, but his conviction of the power of responsibility of human beings in their freedom and its use leaves no room for any form of determinism, fatalism, resignation or dualistic belief in evil as a thing. He writes,

> Even though man as God's creature derives all his freedom from the absolute freedom of God, he alone, with the exclusion even of God, is himself the subject of his free actions. ... It is precisely this origin [of human free action in the subjectivity of the human being] which makes me the unique, ultimate and responsible subject of all my actions.[40]

It is human beings' misuse of their freedom which is sin and it leads to an 'incomprehensible occurrence' of suffering.

Humanity, however, is not on its own in the exercise of its freedom. Christian creation faith holds an unshakeable belief in the 'absolute presence of God' which is a saving presence. As Schillebeeckx writes, 'the believer knows that God makes himself present in a saving way' and 'faith points out that the contingency of all worldly and human figures (which philosophy also knows about) is supported by the absolute saving presence of God in all that is finite'.[41] Christologically speaking, the saving presence of God has been made known most vividly in the historical person of Jesus. Those who knew Jesus on earth discovered that it was 'only by uniting ourselves to the man Jesus [that] our own personal fidelity to the covenant becomes possible. Our personal communion with God can only take place, explicitly or implicitly, by an interpersonal relationship with the man Jesus'.[42] Schillebeeckx wrote those words in 1957. He remained convinced: if humanity is to use its freedom aright in order both to avoid causing suffering and also to abolish or alleviate suffering where it already exists, there is an absolute need for God's grace (experienced by Christians as imparted in the Holy Spirit). In *God and Man* (1965), Schillebeeckx writes, 'Revelation tells us that only in and through Jesus Christ is there any possibility of bringing our lives to a definitively good end.'[43]

Human subjection to original sin is a structural element of Schillebeeckx's theology and Christology (as indicated by McManus) but the way in which he expresses the reality of it involves two changes at the conjunctural level. The first change is the rearticulation of the reality of original sin and the second is an understanding that sin is not only individual but also social and systemic.

---

40. Edward Schillebeeckx, *God and Man*, trans. Edward Fitzgerald and Peter Tomlinson (London: Sheed and Ward, 1969), 58.
41. Schillebeeckx, *Church*, 229 [231].
42. Schillebeeckx, *SEG*, 248.
43. Schillebeeckx, *G&M*, 59.

A change at the conjunctural level: The rearticulation of the reality of original sin, which does not cause the creation in and of itself to become flawed

It is significant that in a publication of 1951, Schillebeeckx's articulation of what is traditionally called original sin already constitutes a conjunctural break not so much with previously published theological statements of his own but with the Tridentine expression of the dogma. He was moving away from concepts of humanity as something static and, therefore, from a concept of original sin as a fixed, inherited state within human beings, able to be washed away by baptism.[44] Rather than treating the creation of the world as a chronological event in the early stages of which it was spoilt by humanity's sin, Schillebeeckx identifies that there are ever-continuing tensions between salvation and lack of salvation in humanity's history on earth. There is a Heraclitean sense of constant flux in his description of humans as 'being[s] in situation', a situation which is never still. He writes,

> Man is a seeking, groping being who does not follow his own course unerringly because of an infallible natural impulse. He freely chooses his own course in life and, as a being who is both free and temporal, he is naturally unstable and inconstant with the result that his freedom has to re-orientate itself again and again in a state of tension.[45]

Implicit in this description of the situation of human beings is that their errors may often be sinful. As remarked earlier, finite conditions are not in themselves spoilt by sin. Mistakes are made but mistakes are not necessarily sinful although they may sometimes be. Schillebeeckx vividly describes two fundamental tendencies at work in human behaviour and history, 'an upward, constructive movement and a downward destructive movement and these two movements are intermingled'.[46] Owing to this 'constitutional character' of humanity's being in the world, it is possible for it 'to plunge into a situation without salvation, into disaster'.[47] A 'situation without salvation' is one way of describing the reality of original sin in the world. Schillebeeckx says of it, 'Sin especially remains in the world, a malignant cancerous tumour that is constantly spreading. The old and new worlds exist side by side and intermingled, as the parable of the wheat and the tares tells

---

44. An understanding of human beings as not static, in the sense of being temporal and free, concurs with Irenaeus' understanding of a human being as a person in a state of becoming: '*homo fit*'. In more philosophical language, a person is 'neither a pure nature nor an inert thing, but [the subject of] an evolving narrative or a free and active historical event' (Kennedy, *Schillebeeckx*, 35).

45. Schillebeeckx, *W&C*, chapter 1, 9 [12]. This chapter first appeared as 'Godsdienst en wereld: het aanshijn der aarde vernieuwen' in *Het geestelijk leven van de leek* (Drakenburgh-conferenties 1951), Tilburg 1951, 7–27.

46. Ibid., 10 [13].

47. Schillebeeckx, *W&C*, 9 [12].

us.'⁴⁸ In his introduction to his book *Jesus*, Schillebeeckx concludes that although 'the possibility of overcoming various forms of human alienation through science and technology is perfectly real', there is a deeper question about 'whether there is not a more profound alienation, linked with human finitude and entanglement with nature ... whether, indeed, there is not some alienation wrought by guilt and sin'.⁴⁹ Crucially, 'humanity's self-redemption would seem to be limited after all'.⁵⁰

In an article, *Discontinuities in Christian Dogma*, published in 1994, the conjunctural discontinuity with the Tridentine definition is evident in Schillebeeckx's articulation of original sin. He writes,

> The Council of Trent solemnly declared the reality of original sin, a dogma, and that dogma tells us something quite real about [the *rem* of] our human condition. Every human being who enters this world arrives to a society that is a product, partly of a lot of good that happened in the past, partly of the accumulation of a lot of evil [actions and their consequences]. The actual society into which we are born exists, so to speak, in a state of sin. The 'sin of the world' precedes our free will. Even before we embark on a voluntary act we are already in a situation that willy-nilly prompts – but does not compel – us to sin. Because human beings are situated in a history of both salvation and doom, [the consequences of] evil [actions] affect ... all people even before they act.⁵¹

What he next writes is an articulation of the 'proneness to evil [sin] inherent in human nature [which] *precedes* exposure to a corrupting environment'.⁵² In Tridentine terms this reality is expressed by saying that Adam and Eve's original sin is passed on through human generation and inherited by all human beings as part of their make-up. In the following two sentences Schillebeeckx describes the effects of sin as somehow objectively internalized, not by physical inheritance but by the external reality of sin:

> The external situation becomes an inner state as well. We are already steeped in sinfulness, as it were; it has lodged in our inner being as a vague propensity and remains as a threat of personal sin. This is the crux of the dogma.⁵³

While Schillebeeckx holds that, despite original sin, creation is not flawed, he is no naïve optimist about conditions in the world. In a section on the bewildering mix of good actions and the consequences of evil actions in the world, he writes (in 1996),

---

48. Ibid., 10.
49. Schillebeeckx, *Jesus*, 8–9 [25].
50. Ibid., 9 [25].
51. Schillebeeckx, *Essays*, 101.
52. Gabriel Daly, 'What Is Original Sin?', *The Tablet*, 8 February 1997, 170–1 (171).
53. Schillebeeckx, *Essays*, 101.

> On the one hand it is clear that the presence of so much goodness, beauty and meaning is constantly contradicted and overshadowed by the evil [deeds] and viciousness [of the behaviour and disposition of some] around us and in us, by flagrantly obvious and covert suffering, by abuses of power and terrorism. These manifest contradictions create the impression that [what is] evil and [what is] good cancel each other out and argue each other away. That's how cynics see it! Non-cynics, on the other hand, do not see it as indicative of a society so decadent that there is nothing left to motivate people to live or to be worth dying for. Despite all their misery people remain aware of their human dignity and refuse to judge and evaluate evil [human behaviour which causes suffering] on a par with human goodness.[54]

In an article about the new Critical Theory and theological hermeneutics, originally published in *Tijdschrift voor Theologie* in 1971, Schillebeeckx talks about the formulation by Christians of faith in Christ 'through the form of a confession of original sin' because 'they were aware of their impotence themselves to bring about salvation and peace, both at the personal and the collective level'.[55] In comparing the Christian doctrine of original sin and Critical Theory he writes,

> According to both, despite everything, the present situation is wrong. In conjunction with this condemnation of the present, critical theory maintains an 'optimism of reason' with regard to the future. The optimism of reason is not denied by the doctrine of original sin, but insists that it is transcended in a pessimism that changes into an 'optimism of grace'. In other words redemption – redemption also for reason. In this way, the Christian view, ... is ultimately a correction of the over-optimism of critical theory.[56]

Hilkert avers that the source of Schillebeeckx's 'optimism of grace' or 'grace-optimism' is a profound belief in the presence of God among us. Despite the horrors that human beings inflict upon each other, and therefore the seeming absence of God, Schillebeeckx is convinced of God's presence because of what he calls 'negative contrast experiences'.[57] These experiences are caused by 'the absence of "what ought to be" which leads to dissatisfaction and action rooted in a very basic form of human hope'.[58] Christian hope is rooted in a dynamic of trust that is part of creation faith. That God entrusts the creation to human beings is a pledge of his trust in them by which he invites them to reciprocate with their trust in him.

---

54. Ibid., 155.
55. Schillebeeckx, *UF*, 129–30 [148].
56. Ibid., 130.
57. Hilkert, 'Grace-Optimism', 222.
58. Ibid.

A change at the conjunctural level: An understanding and articulation of sin as not only individual but also as social and systemic

Schillebeeckx's understanding of sin and its consequences in causing suffering widened from something which appeared confined to an individual to something that is often, at the same time, endemic in society and its institutional systems. In his last academic year at school, 1932–3, when he was intent on discerning his vocation, Schillebeeckx expressed his Christian aim as wanting to give himself 'wholly and utterly to the salvation of souls'.[59] This is not a statement intended to portray sin as an individual phenomenon but it does, perhaps, reflect a general outlook that focuses on salvation from sin for the individual without mentioning, and therefore, perhaps, without having much awareness of, systemic sin. In 1978, in marked contrast, he wrote that to work for the human happiness (i.e. salvation) that is God's glory is not simply an individual concern, 'the salvation of souls', but it is also a concern for the whole world. He writes,

> Individual action is in no way socially neutral or politically innocent, above all in modern conditions (as J.B. Metz, among others, is accustomed to say). That means that the believer's concern for God's honour is also a struggle for more justice in the world, a commitment to a new earth and an environment in which human beings can lead fuller lives. … Christian salvation is not simply the salvation of souls but the healing, making whole, wholeness of the whole person, the individual and society, in a natural world which is not abused. Thus Christian salvation also comprises ecological, social and political aspects, though it is not exhausted by these.[60]

Schillebeeckx, therefore, is keenly aware of what Herbert McCabe calls 'the interlocking complexity of evil [decisions and deeds]'[61] and how people may suffer oppression powerlessly because others exploit and dominate them. He says, 'People live in their human condition that includes a spiritual dimension, yet are trapped in a tangle of external and inner sinfulness, which alienates them from God.'[62]

In 1987 John Paul II was 'the first to use the notion [of structural sin] in an encyclical [*Sollicitudo rei socialis*], where he is careful to point out that the structures of human interconnectedness are never sinful in a literal sense'.[63] John Paul II is emphatic, both in *Sollicitudo rei socialis* and in *Reconciliatio et Paenitentia*

---

59. Borgman, *Edward Schillebeeckx*, 32.
60. Schillebeeckx, *GAU*, 100.
61. Herbert McCabe, *God Still Matters* (London: Continuum, 2005), 168.
62. Ibid., 158.
63. Downloaded from www.catholicsocialteaching.org.uk/principles/glossary:structures, 14 January 2017. The oppression of social systems was a theme adopted by novelists long before 1987, for example, John Steinbeck in *The Grapes of Wrath* tells the story of a migrant family driven from its land in Oklahoma as they make their way to California and struggle to find work under an almost feudal system of agricultural exploitation. John Steinbeck, *The Grapes of Wrath* (Harmondsworth: Penguin Books, 1967, first published 1939).

(1984), that situations of sin, or so-called social sins or structural sins, 'are rooted in personal sin, and thus always linked to the concrete acts of individuals who introduce these structures, consolidate them and make them difficult to remove. And thus they grow stronger, spread, and become the source of other sins, and so influence people's behaviour.'[64]

In saying that individual action is in no way socially neutral or politically innocent, Schillebeeckx does not mean that it is the task of Christian faith to provide specific solutions to political and economic problems. What is '"socially possible" and "politically attainable" … is the concern of politicians, certainly in a democratic society'.[65] In 1987, Schillebeeckx writes, 'I use the term … politics to denote an intensive form of social commitment (and thus not the political activity of professional politicians per se), a commitment accessible to all people.'[66] Rather it is the role of Christian faith to provide a 'prophetic impetus'.[67] In 1989 Schillebeeckx further develops the idea of sin as systemic, giving specific examples: 'In our time the Christian understanding of sin also includes the recognition of systemic disruptions of communication like sexism, racism and fascism, antisemitism, hostility to and attacks on immigrant workers, and the Western cultural and religious sense of superiority.'[68] He goes on to describe the Christian response to such systemic sin in these words, 'Christian love which is the basis of community therefore also includes the necessity to recognize the need for deep involvement in present-day work of political, cultural and social emancipation.'[69] The way that Schillebeeckx talks about this kind of involvement in this phase of his writing is 'the praxis of the reign of God', identified and discussed below as a model change at the conjunctural level. The detail of daily work for emancipation, the form it takes, will involve both conjunctural and ephemeral changes.

McManus succinctly summarizes the asynchronous structural and conjunctural planes in Schillebeeckx's treatment of sin and suffering in this way:

> Schillebeeckx's early works address the dimension of suffering and sin in very personal and even privatized terms. While his later works deal increasingly with the complex social dimensions of suffering, sin and evil, obedience remains their discernible core. No longer overtly concerned with doctrines of original justice and original sin, Schillebeeckx's thought continues to be informed by the tension of these contrasting paradigms, which sustains his roots.[70]

---

64. Ibid., *The Social Concern of the Church* (1987), paragraph 36.
65. Schillebeeckx, *GAU*, 100.
66. Schillebeeckx, *JWC*, 71–2.
67. Ibid. Cf. 'Jesus did not want to be a messianic-political leader, but this does not mean that his message and his life journey did not have political significance.' Schillebeeckx, *Church*, 124 [125].
68. Ibid., 130.
69. Ibid.
70. McManus, *Unbroken Communion*, 56.

How does the reality of original sin, and the fact of human suffering, shape Christology? The Council of Trent, in the wake of the Reformation, was concerned to define the role of Jesus Christ in the justification of humanity. Its presupposition is an Augustinian one, that the graced state of original justice which Adam and Eve enjoyed before they fell into sin was lost. The Tridentine Decree on Original Sin states that the 'sin of Adam, which in its origin is one, and being transfused into all by propagation, not by imitation, is in each one as his own'.[71] The Council states that it is 'by baptism [that] the guilt of original sin is remitted [although] in baptised persons there remains concupiscence or an incentive (to sin)'.[72] It describes all of humanity as having 'lost its innocence in the prevarication of Adam – having become unclean' and as being 'the servants of sin, and under the power of the devil and death' to such a degree that without Christ neither Gentiles nor even the Jews, 'by the very letter itself of the law of Moses' were able to be liberated.[73] There is no Tridentine reflection on the Incarnation in general. Rather, within the context of humanity's enslavement to sin, Jesus is straightforwardly defined as a propitiator. The Decree on Justification states, 'Him [Jesus] God hath proposed as a propitiator, through faith in his blood, for our sins, and not for our sins only, but for those of the whole world.'[74] Jesus' role is further defined as and narrowed down to redeemer on the cross. His release of humanity from sin is described in terms of the category of propitiating sacrifice. In the Decree on the Sacrifice of the Mass the Council states, 'Our Lord Jesus Christ ... our God and Lord [offered] Himself once on the altar of the cross unto God the Father, by means of his death, there to operate an eternal redemption.'[75]

The salient features of the Tridentine Christology are that Jesus is sent by God the Father to liberate humanity from sin; that Jesus then propitiates his Father after humanity's disobedience; and that the redemption of humanity is achieved by Jesus' death on the cross which is understood in terms of a propitiatory sacrifice. Such a Christology appears to presuppose that the Incarnation was contingent upon sin and tends to restrict Jesus' salvific function to his crucifixion understood in sacrificial terms. How, then, does the reality which the doctrine of original sin teaches and the fact of suffering shape Schillebeeckx's Christology?

---

71. The Council of Trent (1545–63), *The Canons and Decrees of the Sacred and Oecumenical Council of Trent*, trans. J. Waterworth (London: Dolman, 1848), PDF downloaded from The Council of Trent – Documenta Catholica Omnia, 20 May 2017. The Fifth Session, *The Decree Concerning Original Sin*, Paragraph 3, 22.

72. Ibid., paragraphs 5, 23 and 24.

73. Ibid., The Sixth Session, *The Decree on Justification*, chapter I, 31.

74. Ibid., chapter II, 31.

75. Ibid., The Twenty-Second Session, chapter I, 153.

A fourth structural element in Schillebeeckx's Christology: Jesus is salvation which comes from God and saves humanity from sin and suffering

Schillebeeckx avers that Jesus is salvation from God and that his salvation liberates humanity from sin and suffering. There is an irony in the fact that while Schillebeeckx is sometimes perceived as advocating a Christology 'from below', as a result of the change in his *method*, the *substance* of his Christological soteriology stands and starts firmly and structurally with God the Father and Creator who is revealed most fully in Jesus in his humanity.[76] The basis of Schillebeeckx's Christological soteriology is that God saves as Creator, in and through creation and supremely in God's humanity in Jesus. His salvific action is inseparable from his creative action.

> The obverse of the finitude of human creatures is that God is with and in us, even in our failures, our suffering and our death, just as much as he is in and with all our positive experiences and experiences of meaning. It also means that he is present in forgiveness for the sinner.[77]

Both in his earlier and his later Christology Schillebeeckx holds that Jesus is salvation from God, expressed first as the mediator of saving grace from above and subsequently as God's great act of salvation in this world, not only in his dying but in every aspect of his life, death and resurrection. God's opposition to all that is inhuman, both to sin and to the suffering it causes, is given expression in Jesus' life. God's salvation in Jesus, experienced as such by those who knew him on earth, and God's salvation in the risen Christ experienced by his followers ever since through his Holy Spirit are structural elements of Schillebeeckx's theology and Christology.

A change at the conjunctural level: Jesus is salvation from God brought about in the praxis of the kingdom of God

Schillebeeckx makes a break at the conjunctural level with his earlier Christology in the articulation of Jesus as Saviour. In *CSEG*, in a section about the actions of Jesus' life, Schillebeeckx deals first with the human actions of Jesus 'as they come from above' and then with his actions 'as coming from below'.[78] When talking of Jesus' actions as they come from above, he speaks in categories of grace, redeeming love and acts of redemption, and when talking of Jesus' actions from below he speaks in terms of Jesus as 'the supreme worshipper, the supreme realization of all religion'.[79] The idiom in which he is thinking and writing is an abstract one of

---

76. Gerald O'Collins, for example, writes, 'A Christological approach "from below", which has in various ways been developed by Kasper, Küng, Pannenberg, Schillebeeckx, Sobrino, and others, has raised the question: was Jesus (humanly) conscious of his divine identity?' Gerald O'Collins, *Christology*, 2nd edn (Oxford: Oxford University Press, 2009), 251.
77. Schillebeeckx, *GAU*, 94.
78. Schillebeeckx, *CSEG*, 12 [18].
79. Ibid.

doctrinal formulas. He sees the Incarnation in terms of a somewhat abstract, two-directional, vertical economy of salvation with a stress on Christ as the mediator between humanity and God the Father. Christ is the channel of saving grace from above and the channel of perfect praise of God from below:

> And so we must say that the incarnation in the Son itself redeems us. This mystery of Christ or of redemption, we can call in its totality, a mystery of saving worship; a mystery of praise (the upward movement) and of salvation (the downward movement).[80]

At the same time Schillebeeckx registered awareness of a tendency among theologians, presumably himself included, to focus on the divine in Jesus and to pass cursorily over the human life of Christ.[81]

In the 1960s and early 1970s, Schillebeeckx changed his theological methods and so he no longer thought and wrote in his earlier idiom of metaphysical categories of classical Christology, in other words a Christological method that started 'from above'. In a change of method from a primary focus on *sacra doctrina* to a search of the New Testament texts with the tools of historical criticism and hermeneutics, he made an exhaustive Christological study and came face to face, as it were, with Jesus in his earthly human ministry. His later Christological method, therefore, was one which started 'from below', but method, as was pointed out above, is distinct from substance. In *Jesus* Schillebeeckx's purpose was 'to follow the way of Jesus from Nazareth, along with his disciples as it were, right up to his death and in that way ... to share the birth of the faith-inspired interpretation of Jesus the Christ'.[82] Schillebeeckx states how the first Christians understood 'Jesus ... to be the very essence of final salvation'.[83] In the second book, *Christ*, he is directly concerned with two aims, the first is 'the question how *New Testament Christianity* experienced and analysed salvation in and through Jesus'[84] and the second is to probe 'the extent to which the New Testament witnesses provide a normative orientation for contemporary Christians in their own interpretations of Jesus' salvific relevance'.[85] In the third book of the trilogy, Schillebeeckx explains that Jesus is God himself bringing his salvation to human beings in his praxis of the reign of God. The praxis of the reign of God shows what God is and does: compassionate in healing and liberating those who are suffering, giving unimagined new leases and levels of life, and challenging people who exploit, oppress and exclude others. God the Creator and Jesus are one in saving action. Christians know Jesus and increasingly get to know God when they, in turn,

---

80. Ibid., 13 [20].
81. Ibid., 30 [50].
82. Schillebeeckx, *Jesus*, 229 [258].
83. Ibid., 33 [50].
84. Schillebeeckx, *Christ*, 8 [24].
85. Kennedy, *Schillebeeckx*, 109.

engage in the praxis of the kingdom of God. Despite Schillebeeckx's change in method, the substance of his Christology does not change: Jesus is salvation from God and God is the saving God in Jesus. Schillebeeckx never separates Jesus from God in his Christology.

In sharp contrast to Schillebeeckx, Jürgen Moltmann interprets the Trinitarian context for the theology of the crucifixion and death of Jesus as an event within the Trinity in which the Son is abandoned by the Father. Helen F. Bergin quotes Moltmann's grim statement, '"To say that Jesus was forsaken by the Father on the cross means that the Father cast him off and cursed him".'[86] Bergin's explanation of this statement by Moltmann is that it is meant to disturb 'in order that the horror of Jesus' death may be realised and that Jesus' God may be seen as directly involved', an argument which doubles the horror and implies that Jesus is not fully divine in the manner of God the Father. Schillebeeckx, consistently with his belief in the absolute presence of God, writes that the psalm, the first line of which Jesus prayed on the cross, according to the gospel accounts in Mark and Matthew, 'My God my God, why have you forsaken me?', 'ends in a prayer of thanksgiving for God's abiding, albeit silent, saving presence'.[87] God's silence is not absence or withdrawal. Bergin writes that Schillebeeckx's position is that any abandonment experienced by Jesus is 'not the effect of God's abandoning action, but the result of Jesus' utter assimilation and identification with forsaken human persons. … It is from the experience of complete identification with sinful humanity that Jesus seems abandoned by God.'[88] For Schillebeeckx 'Jesus' whole life is the actual interpretation [or hermeneusis] of his death.'[89] Jesus' caring and loving service of others, and the magnetic truth of his preaching in which he challenged hypocrisy and master/servant relations, provoked the anger, jealousy and fear of those in the religious and political establishments. They wanted to do away with him and so the manner of Jesus' death was the culmination of a life given to and for others. The crucifixion as crucifixion in itself is not salvific, as it were in isolation from Jesus' life, but with Schillebeeckx 'we can justifiably conclude that Jesus felt his death to relate (in some way) to salvation offered by God, a historical consequence of his caring and loving service to and solidarity with people'.[90]

---

86. Helen F. Bergin, 'The Death of Jesus and Its Impact on God – Jürgen Moltmann and Edward Schillebeeckx', *Irish Theological Quarterly*, 52 (1986): 193–211 (196).

87. Schillebeeckx, *Church*, 126 [128].

88. Bergin, 'The Death of Jesus and Its Impact on God – Jürgen Moltmann and Edward Schillebeeckx', 196.

89. Schillebeeckx, *Jesus*, 278 [311].

90. Ibid., 277 [310].

Chapter 6

CONTINUITY AND CHANGE IN SCHILLEBEECKX'S LATER CHRISTOLOGY: THE PRAXIS OF THE KINGDOM OF GOD AND THE HUMANITY OF JESUS CHRIST

The Praxis of the Kingdom of God

It is startling that Schillebeeckx's 'new' way of talking about God's salvation in Jesus is by using an ancient biblical expression and uncovering its riches. His understanding of the salvation that is found in Jesus does not consist of a theory of atonement whereby God's salvific action is enacted by Jesus in a propitiatory offering on the cross, a theory that could be said to separate Son from Father.[1] He agrees with 'the findings of recent biblical scholarship that the centre of Jesus' life and preaching was a message concerning the kingdom of God'.[2] What Jesus means by it is that God as sovereign Creator or 'king' 'is purveyor of salvation to that which he endowed with life'.[3] But God works through us and he 'looks to us humans to implement his "rule" in our world'.[4] In all Jesus' words and actions God's kingdom is brought about and God's saving nature is revealed. God's lordship, as Jesus understood and lived it, 'expresses the relationship between God and man, in the sense that "we are each other's happiness"'.[5] Schillebeeckx describes the Son of God in his humanity as living out God's resistance to sin and the suffering it causes. He avers that Jesus on earth was 'God's "no" to the history of human suffering'.[6] He

---

1. Schillebeeckx writes that we are tied to the reality which is Christ and not to articulations of that reality. Cf. p. 7: believing Christians seek 'to test Christian *conceptions* of the saving significance of Jesus' death in order to see if a Christian soteriology ties us to concepts like "ransom", "propitiation", "satisfaction" et cetera'. Schillebeeckx, *Jesus*, 285 [318]. From his own exegetical study of the New Testament Schillebeeckx avers that 'the soteriological interpretation of Jesus' death appears to have only a slender basis in the oldest strata of the tradition prior to the gospels'. Schillebeeckx, *Jesus*, 271 [303].

2. Kennedy, *Schillebeeckx*, 113.
3. Schillebeeckx, *Jesus*, 121 [142].
4. Ibid., 121–2 [142].
5. Ibid., 122 [142].
6. Ibid., 154 [178].

shows that 'God's essential being is anti-evil [actions], willing good'[7] or, expressed slightly differently, 'that God promotes good and opposes evil [actions], injustice and suffering'.[8] Jesus spoke and acted to unmask sin which excluded and burdened people, and he restored people to health and wholeness. Schillebeeckx 'explores God's own response to sin and suffering in and through the life-story of Jesus'.[9] In saving people from suffering and bringing them to wholeness, Jesus' words and deeds were perfectly in tune with one another and were the praxis of the reign of God in his particular historical context.

The kingdom of God

The kingdom of God is a multivocal expression and, in having various meanings about God the Creator (e.g. the saving presence of God and the revelation of God's 'no' to sin and suffering through the life story of Jesus) it also has profound and vital meaning for human beings. The kingdom of God is not something unilateral, a one-way action of God on recipients, but involves a dialectic between God and humanity. A one-way action of God on recipients would leave humanity passive, and Schillebeeckx's understanding of humanity being called and drawn into the experience of an active relationship with God in grace is precisely a structural aspect of his thinking as shown earlier. He writes of the dialectic between God and humanity,

> The kingdom of God is the saving presence of God, active and encouraging, as it is affirmed or welcomed among men and women. It is a saving presence offered by God and freely accepted by men and women which takes concrete form above all in justice and peaceful relationships among individuals and peoples, in the disappearance of sickness, injustice and oppression, in the restoration to life of all that was dead and dying.[10]

Schillebeeckx says, 'The Kingdom of God is a changed new relationship (*metanoia*) of men and women to God, the tangible and visible side of which is a new type of liberating relationship among men and women within a reconciling society in a peaceful natural environment.'[11] To enter into, and to work for, God's kingdom, in faith, entails a radical self-criticism, which implies *metanoia* which is 'repentance and … a right about-turn'.[12] Any boundary between humanity and God is always humanity's: 'The boundary between us and God is our boundary, not God's.'[13] Despite human beings' failures in the use of their freedom, Schillebeeckx writes,

---

7. Ibid.
8. Schillebeeckx, *GAU*, 99.
9. Mary Catherine Hilkert, '"Grace-Optimism": The Spirituality at the Heart of Schillebeeckx's Theology', *Spirituality Today*, 43, 3 (1991), 220–39 (227).
10. Schillebeeckx, *Church*, 110 [111–12].
11. Ibid., 110–11 [112].
12. Schillebeeckx, *Jesus*, 646 [747].
13. Schillebeeckx, *GAU*, 94.

'Despite everything, compassion is the deepest purpose that God seeks to fulfil in history. He wills men to live, wills their salvation, not their misery and death.'[14] Schillebeeckx explains, 'Our assignment and our burden within all finitude is to overcome suffering and evil everywhere we encounter it,' and, with regard to naturally caused suffering, 'with all possible means of science and technology.'[15] About suffering, which is caused by immoral decisions with regard to the use of natural resources that result in human and environmental disaster, he writes,

> Major world problems with deeply human connotations come to the attention of all of us, a development also encouraged by the obvious attention paid to them by the media: nuclear energy, nuclear armament, the pollution of the environment, the exhaustion of our natural resources, the oil crisis and the shifting of East-West conflict to the North-South conflict.[16]

To be a follower of Jesus, therefore, means to oppose the consequences of evil oppression (i.e. suffering) *sequela Jesu*. Schillebeeckx describes the Christian way *sequela Jesu* by using the image of a compass with the words, 'following Jesus [is] taking our bearings from him' but it is much more than that because it is

> allowing ourselves to be inspired by him, by sharing in his Abba experience and his selfless support for 'the least of my brethren' (Matt. 25:40), and thus entrusting our own destiny to God, we allow the history of Jesus, the living one, to continue in history as a piece of living Christology, the work of the Spirit among us, the Spirit of God and the Spirit of Christ.[17]

To live in discipleship *sequela Jesu* is to join him in the praxis of the kingdom of God.

Praxis

So, what exactly is praxis? Why did Schillebeeckx choose the word? The notion of praxis is crucial in Schillebeeckx's later Christology but the term is a philosophical-political one with a long history, starting with Aristotle, and found ubiquitously in Marxist, Western Marxist and Critical Theorist writings.[18] To most people it is a jargon word yet Schillebeeckx was writing for everyone. What is contained

---

14. Schillebeeckx, *Jesus*, 154 [177]. In the earlier translation, 'compassion' is given as 'mercy'.
15. Schillebeeckx, *IR*, 103 [118].
16. Schillebeeckx, *Church*, 223 [235].
17. Schillebeeckx, *Christ*, 630-1 [641].
18. Kennedy, *Schillebeeckx* (Aristotle) 33; 'Lukács held that Marx's most valuable discovery was that history is a mediating dialectic capable of conjugating human understanding and the concrete world of praxis.' Richard Kearney, *Modern Movements in European*

in the notion of praxis that causes Schillebeeckx to judge it to be the best way to express the dynamic of bringing about God's kingdom which, in scriptural terms, is loving God and loving one's neighbour as oneself? As a term used in his writings it is elusive, because he nowhere gives a comprehensive definition of the meaning he attaches to it. At the end of the *Jesus* book, in the list of some technical and unfamiliar terms for which he gives explanations, orthopraxis is given but praxis is not. Is praxis, correctly practised, orthopraxis?[19] As has already been seen, Schillebeeckx is not always scrupulous in his differentiation between words which denote overlapping concepts or where one word might denote a depth dimension of the concept of another word (e.g. contingency and finitude, and sin, evil and suffering).

There is some controversy over the exact meaning of the word praxis, and how it relates to theory, as Schillebeeckx uses it. Poulsom observes that praxis 'is often treated as interchangeable with practice in Schillebeeckx's writings' and he gives examples from Donald J. Goergen. He writes that Goergen 'speaks of the "preoccupation with orthopraxis" in his later works, which "raises the question of how to bridge the gulf between theory and practice" '.[20] He also notes Goergen's remark that 'The earthly Jesus reacted to the prevailing attitude of his day, "in which theory and practice had drifted apart", by refusing to sanction an orthodoxy separated from an orthopraxis.'[21] William L. Portier, however, emphasizes that Schillebeeckx used praxis precisely to differentiate it from practice. He writes,

> The unfamiliar term praxis is used deliberately, to avoid the connotations of practice. The latter implies a prior pure theory that we then apply practically; praxis, by contrast, is understood as co-constituent of theory likewise conceived. The ethical moment is, therefore, inseparable from theory or reflection. This is a contemporary rendering or recovery of the biblical and patristic truism that Christian thinking arises from and must return to Christian living.[22]

Philosophy: Phenomenology, Critical Theory, Structuralism (Manchester: Manchester University Press, 1986), 139.

19. The definition of orthopraxis that Schillebeeckx gives in the technical information at the end of *Jesus* is: 'Literally "right action". In this book orthopraxis always means action or conduct consonant with the standard or "directives" of the kingdom of God (the criteria and directives of which are examined in this book.' *Jesus*, 646 [747].

20. Poulsom, *Dialectics*, 112, citing Donald J. Goergen, 'Spirituality', in *The Praxis of the Reign of God: An Introduction to the Theology of Edward Schillebeeckx*, ed. Mary Catherine Hilkert and Robert J. Schreiter (New York: Fordham University Press, 2002), 117–31 (122).

21. Ibid.

22. William L. Portier, 'Interpretation and Method', in *The Praxis of the Reign of God: An Introduction to the Theology of Edward Schillebeeckx*, 2nd edn, ed. Mary Catherine Hilkert and Robert J. Schreiter (New York: Fordham University Press, 2002), 19–36 (30).

The sources in which Schillebeeckx came across the term praxis are the writings of the Critical Theorists. Although Kennedy makes the point that Schillebeeckx's understanding of Critical Theory (and its use of the term praxis) is mainly derived from the earlier works of Habermas, two elements which Schillebeeckx draws on are illuminated by Antonio Gramsci and Georg Lukács.[23] George Hoare and Nathan Sperber draw attention to what they call *'the intimacy of theory and practice'* as Gramsci's essential postulate above all others: 'For Gramsci, theory is called on to provide a rational basis for practice, and practice is necessary to actualise theory.'[24] There is a reciprocal dynamic between practice and theory and each nourishes the other. Poulsom identifies this dynamic as 'the relational dialectic of the two'. He writes,

> Schillebeeckx opposes what might be called 'mere' orthopraxis …: simply appealing to practical conduct as being what Christianity is all about is as artificial as appealing to the unchanging essence of Christianity in doctrine. Both extremes miss the point that the praxis of the kingdom of God is distinct from both orthopraxis and orthodoxy. It is, in fact, found in the relational dialectic of the two; hence Christianity's message must be both realized (practically) and articulated (theoretically).[25]

Poulsom draws attention to Schillebeeckx's statement that 'It is in [praxis] that the idea develops that God reveals himself as the mystery and the very heart of humanity's striving for liberation, wholeness and soundness.'[26] Poulsom, therefore, interprets Schillebeeckx's notion of praxis as involving three terms: theory, practice and the dialectical interacting of the two.[27] The model of praxis in Critical Theory and Christianity might also be said to be a relational trialectic between three elements, the situation, theory and action. Like the conundrum of chicken and egg, it is debatable as to which comes first. In terms of Marxist philosophy, it could be argued that it is the situation of suffering and exploitation that comes first. For the Christian, also, it may be that the pain of suffering and exploitation (of self and/or others) also comes first, but it is reflected on, analysed and acted upon in the light of faith that the believer already enjoys. The suggestion is that the sequence in the process of Christian praxis is this: there is a statement of faith about God, according to which action is taken; in the relational dialectic between the original statement of faith and the resulting practice, the concept of God can be more clearly discerned and so

---

23. For Kennedy on Schillebeeckx and Habermas, see *Schillebeeckx*, 50.
24. George Hoare and Nathan Sperber, *An Introduction to Antonio Gramsci: His Life, Thought and Legacy* (London: Bloomsbury Academic, 2016), 81.
25. Poulsom, *Dialectics*, 117.
26. Ibid., 116.
27. Ibid., 114.

is fed back into the statement about God (the theory). So, a reflection in faith precedes practice which results in praxis which in turn becomes prior to the next stage of theological reflection on faith.

Two themes in Gramsci's 'practical-critical activity' or praxis which echo crucial elements of Schillebeeckx's creation faith

As Hoare and Sperber reflect on Gramsci's 'practical-critical activity' or praxis two themes emerge which strongly echo crucial elements in Schillebeeckx's creation faith which are carried over into his theology of the praxis of the reign of God. They write that when 'Gramsci attempts to think through what it means to put human "practical-critical" activity or *praxis*, at the heart of Marxist philosophy', a note in one of his prison notebooks titled 'What Is Man?'[28] may provide a possible answer. One theme is that a human being (who has an identity) is not a fixed thing. For Gramsci 'man is above all a *social and historical animal* whose reality is constituted by the relations that tie the individual to others'.[29] Although overlaps with Schillebeeckx's thinking only go so far and no further, they still go some distance before they stop short of understandings based on belief in God the Creator. For Schillebeeckx (in agreement with Irenaeus' thinking) human beings are in a state of becoming (*fiunt*) and in that sense are not fixed things; they are temporal and historical creatures. Praxis is a way of 'becoming' or, as Poulsom refers to it, a 'way of life – a form of life, perhaps'.[30] Critical Theory's refusal to identify freedom with any fixed system of thought and its insistence that thought must respond to the new problems and the new possibilities for liberation that arise from changing historical circumstances chimed with Schillebeeckx's developing sense of the historical nature of existence and the fact that cultural historical forms are the constitutive vehicles of both the message and praxis of the gospel. The liberation that Jesus brought to people when he walked on earth was emancipation from the consequences of sin and from suffering. This liberation led to a wholeness of life that is God's intention for creation, and which Christ continues to bring about through people, in the Church and the world. The second echo, this time of Schillebeeckx's theological anthropology, is that of Gramsci's relational ontology 'in which [human] being can only be understood by reference to a set of relations'.[31] In Schillebeeckx's Christian creation faith, human beings are understood by reference to their relation to God and their relationship with God, expressed through their relationships with each other.

---

28. Hoare and Sperber, *An Introduction to Antonio Gramsci*, 82.
29. Ibid.
30. Poulsom, *Dialectics*, 118.
31. Hoare and Sperber, *An Introduction to Antonio Gramsci*, 82.

Features common to Critical Theory and Schillebeeckx's account of Christianity

Critical Theory was an intellectual influence on Schillebeeckx's Christological response to the puzzle and challenge of suffering and sin. There are several features of Critical Theory that occupy common ground with Christianity. The first is attentiveness to the world and its suffering. Common to the members of the Frankfurt School and to Schillebeeckx was a keen awareness of people in wider society, beyond the members of the Frankfurt School and the confines of the Church, respectively. Crucially, all people, everywhere, experience suffering, albeit to varying degrees. The members of the Frankfurt School saw the disorders of society as 'exploitation, repression, and alienation embedded within Western Civilisation'.[32] Schillebeeckx describes the disorders of the world as 'oppression and repression [which] taunt and mortally wound, subjugate and torture human beings'.[33] Critical Theorists recognized that people are often not even 'aware of their unfreedom, brought about by the manipulation of individuals through modern mass media'.[34]

The second feature of the approach of Critical Theorists that chimes with Schillebeeckx's Christian approach is that their focus on the world was not simply disinterested theory. While traditional theory and philosophy is seen as disinterested, Critical Theory is determined by an interest in human emancipation and so it is committed to seeking radical social change. Famously, Karl Marx's Eleventh Thesis on Feuerbach summed up the idea of thinking about social problems within history rather than outside it as detached theory. He wrote, 'Philosophers have only interpreted the world in various ways; the point is to change it.'[35] The Critical Theorists' philosophy was one that turned outwards towards society and scrutinized aspects of the existing order so that they might take appropriate action to alleviate suffering. Richard Kearney tells how early political experiences convinced the Critical Theorist Georg Lukács of the inseparability of 'contemplation' and action: 'the concrete political experience of his early years ... impressed upon [Lukács] that "contemplation" and "speculation" were not in themselves enough: that spiritual liberation had to be accompanied

---

32. Stephen Eric Bronner, *Critical Theory: A Very Short Introduction* (Oxford: Oxford University Press, 2011), 1.

33. Schillebeeckx, *Essays*, 155.

34. 'Frankfurt School', in *Dictionary of Philosophy*, ed. Thomas Mautner (London: Penguin Reference, 2005), 233.

35. Seen in large gold lettering above the double staircase in the entrance hall of the main building of Humboldt University in Unter den Linden Straße, Berlin, October 1993: 'Die Philosophen haben die Welt nur verschieden interpretiert, es kommt aber darauf an, sie zu verändern.' The statement was fastened to the wall above the staircase in 1953. Karl Marx and Friedrich Engels, 'Theses on Feuerbach', in *The German Ideology* ed. C. J. Arthur, trans. Lawrence and Wishart (London: Electric Book Company, 1970), 170.

by a correlative material liberation from the constraints of social oppression.'³⁶ Schillebeeckx insists that 'God must always be thought of in such a way that he is never *just* thought of; speaking about God is subordinate to the primacy of praxis. It is subordinate to the question: "Where are we going?" '³⁷ He argues against a polarization either way: neither must God be thought of in such a way that he is only just thought of, nor must he be spoken of only in terms of social and political liberation. In Christian faith and theology there is not a dilemma which imposes a choice between, on the one hand, social-cum-political liberation and, on the other hand, mystical liberation. He writes, 'In fact, I deny the proposed dilemma: political liberation or mystical liberation. … the two cannot be contrasted with each other. Restructuring and inner conversion form a dialectical process.'³⁸

Thirdly, Critical Theorists were convinced that change is possible in society as a result of a commitment to seeking radical social change, in order to emancipate human beings from what oppresses them. A strong sense of 'making history' is common to Critical Theory and to the Christian understanding of the task God has assigned to humanity. Schillebeeckx writes,

> The transformation of the world, the designing of a better society for men to live in, and a new earth lie in the hands of man himself; … Based on a correct belief in creation, we cannot pass off our task in this world on to God.³⁹

Lukács considered that 'idealists and positivists alike fail to appreciate the dynamic transformative tendencies with which the factual world is charged'.⁴⁰ He argued against the so-called facts of the capitalist system 'being regarded fatalistically as *what is given*; and in this way reality [being] divested of its human potential for change'.⁴¹ From the suppositions of Christian creation faith (contingency, human autonomy) Schillebeeckx argues that creation faith is not an explanation of the 'facts' of aspects of the finitude of human life (such as disease) and, therefore, that there are no grounds for attributing them in a fatalistic way to God.⁴² Rather they are a reality with a potential for change in human hands. Lukács talked about 'a "potential" for human praxis and consciousness residing within the world as

---

36. Richard Kearney, *Modern Movements in European Philosophy: Phenomenology, Critical Theory, Structuralism* (Manchester: Manchester University Press, 1986), 137. Georg Lukács, a Hungarian Marxist philosopher, 1885–1971.
37. Schillebeeckx, *IR*, 105 [120].
38. Ibid., *IR*, 93 [105].
39. Ibid., 103.
40. Kearney, *Modern Movements in European Phil*, 140.
41. Ibid.
42. Cf. Schillebeeckx, *GAU*, 94, 'the Jewish-Christian creation faith does not give us any explanation of our world and our humanity' and 'creation faith sets us free for own task in the world'.

history'.[43] Central to Christianity is the belief that, on the one hand, change for the better in terms of personal *metanoia* and reform (commonly called redemption) and in building a better world is possible, but, on the other hand, that it is not the case that 'history *per se* mean[s] progress'.[44]

The difference between Critical Theorists and Christians in their attitudes to the achievability of change for the better lies in the Christian recognition and acknowledgement of sin and the need for a continuous reliance on the grace of God to bring about such change. Schillebeeckx's creation faith, and his whole theology, is determined by trust and confidence that God, in his absolute presence, is constantly offering human beings emancipation from sin and from the suffering it causes if they commit themselves to seeking radical salvation in Christ. Where Critical Theory has an optimism of reason, Christianity's optimism of reason is transcended in a pessimism that is transformed by God into an optimism of grace. Where grace is operative 'one of the fundamental signs of an authentic Christian community is its faithful activity on behalf of God's reign where justice, peace, and the integrity of creation can flourish'.[45]

A change at the conjunctural level: The Christian understanding of God's original justice as something to be fulfilled in the future which is rooted in the praxis of the kingdom of God now

A fourth feature of Critical Theory that shares common ground with Schillebeeckx's thinking about theology and the praxis of the kingdom of God is its orientation towards the future. He writes,

> So the interpretation of faith and theology cannot be reduced to a purely theoretical interpretation of the Christian past. There is a dialectical relationship between the present, the past and the future still to be made, a relationship between praxis and theory.[46]

This statement of Schillebeeckx's introduces another, temporal, layer of dialectical relationship in praxis. Writing in 1968, Schillebeeckx observed the rapid changes in the societies of North America and Europe and said that the prevalent culture was one which was no longer orientated towards the past but 'which [was] resolutely turned towards the future as something that it [meant] to make'.[47] The

---

43. Kearney, *Modern Movements in European Phil*, 139. Lukács argued that 'meaning is *neither* something simply created by the human subject over against the real objective world … *nor* something determined by anonymous laws of natural causality, but a "potential" for human praxis and conscious residing within this world as *history*'.

44. Schillebeeckx, *GAU*, 97.

45. Hilkert, *Grace Optimism*, 225.

46. Schillebeeckx, *Church*, 34 [34–5].

47. Schillebeeckx, *GFoM*, 109 [181].

constant developments in scientific technology raise human beings' expectations for material and social amelioration. Schillebeeckx writes, 'Whether we like it or not, the ever-increasing importance in modern life of the natural sciences, technology, and the behavioural sciences is thrusting man towards the future. ... Human society ... is clearly becoming orientated towards a new future.'[48] Rather than associating God's transcendence with a notion of unchanging eternity 'out there', followers of Jesus Christ, within this culture, turn to the transcendent God because they know that within divine transcendence is found the absolute saving presence of the Creator God, the Source of power and grace to build a better world: '[God] shows himself as the God who gives us in Jesus Christ the possibility of making the future – that is, of making everything new and transcending our sinful past and that of all men.'[49] As well as common ground, there is, however, a crucial difference between the atheist's or the agnostic's attitude to the future, in comparison with the Christian's. For the atheist, both the individual and the collective future stop at death, whereas the Christian believes that new and eternal life has already begun on earth and that it will be brought to fulfilment on the far side of death.[50] As Kennedy points out, to speak of God as the future of humanity is 'actually a rediscovery of an ancient biblical image: God is humanity's future, and its promise'.[51]

In McManus's terms, this future, glimpsed and kept alive in hope by negative contrast experiences on earth, could be said to be God's original justice. On no account, in Schillebeeckx's theology and Christology, is the post-death future of humanity, individually and collectively, understood as a desirable escape from the present constraints of finitude, in other words, as a spiritual escapism. Unlike a concept of original justice which looks backwards to an Eden of the past, as in a lapsarian understanding of the Incarnation, Schillebeeckx's forward-looking understanding of original justice (an expression he does not in fact use) in no way implies that God's creation is intrinsically flawed in the present. Implicit in Schillebeeckx's ideas about humanity's task of the transformation of the world by means of the praxis of the reign of God is a deeply biblical sense of the unbreakable connection of human time on earth with what happens beyond death. Schillebeeckx suggests an eschatology of interrelation, between the praxis of the reign of God in the present and the fulfilment of that reign in God's heavenly kingdom. In contrast, medieval doom paintings, still preserved in the upper part

---

48. Ibid., 104 [172-3].

49. Ibid.

50. It has been suggested that the burgeoning and dominance of eulogies at contemporary funerals in Britain (eulogies which have been categorized as the 'Curriculum Vitae', the hagiographical and the jocular 'best man's speech') are a means of cementing past memories which gain importance as agnosticism or absence of belief in life beyond death increases. For Christian belief that new and eternal life has already begun on earth see: Jn 3.36; 5.24; 6.47; 11.25-26.

51. Kennedy, *Schillebeeckx*, 45.

of chancel arches in some ancient churches, suggest an eschatology of rupture in which the present and the future are related but not interrelated. In St Peter's Church in Wenhaston, Suffolk, and St Thomas' Church in Salisbury, the conduct of human beings on earth certainly determines their individual fates after death, but there is no hint of a continuum between the establishment of God's kingdom on earth and its fulfilment in God's heaven.[52] Earth and heaven appear as two separate realms with a line of judgement dividing them. Schillebeeckx's emphasis on the arrival of the kingdom of God in Jesus, and its continuing establishment, however stumbling, by his followers, traces a continuum between this world and the next. It is noteworthy that in speaking of the continuity and interrelatedness of God's saving action in the praxis of his reign or kingdom, Schillebeeckx, in fact, makes a distinction between God's rule and his kingdom as two aspects of the same saving reality:

> God's lordship or rule and the kingdom of God … are two aspects of one and the same reality. His lordship refers to the dynamic, here-and-now character of his rule; the kingdom of God refers to the final state of bliss which forms the basis of his saving action. Thus present and future are essentially interrelated.[53]

The task of the praxis of the reign/kingdom of God is to work with God to implement the conditions for human flourishing to his greater glory, both here and after death.

Rodenborn's analysis is that in the 'future-oriented dynamic that came to the fore in modernity', Metz and Schillebeeckx 'turned to the category of eschatology', Schillebeeckx to a prophetic eschatology and Metz to an apocalyptic eschatology.[54] Despite the different trajectories of their work, he traces three common developments that emerged in their writings at the end of the 1960s. The first was a 'recognition that the central problem endangering the viability of Christian hope was not the crisis of faith that accompanied what they had described as the process of secularization but the unrelenting crisis of history's suffering people'.[55] A second shared concern in Metz's and Schillebeeckx's projects was what Rodenborn calls 'the turn to a practical eschatology'.[56] Schillebeeckx was concerned that Christian eschatological hope must 'find support in historical reality, in both the kingdom praxis of Jesus and the ongoing liberating praxis of his disciples'.[57] Rodenborn couches what he considers to be the third element in

---

52. St Peter's Church, Wenhaston, in Suffolk and St Thomas' Church in Salisbury have fine examples of doom paintings. The emphasis on judgement in eschatology is also vigorously depicted in the sculptures above the west door of Bourges Cathedral in France.
53. Schillebeeckx, *Jesus*, 121 [141].
54. Rodenborn, *Hope in Action*, 5.
55. Ibid., 310.
56. Ibid., 311.
57. Ibid., 180.

common between the two theologians in words that are, in fact, Metz's, namely, that 'a trace of something unreconciled hovers over Christianity', by which he means the 'still unreconciled character of the Christian hope'.[58] He then offers, as a corresponding quote, Schillebeeckx's words, 'expectation of the future is only a name for *hoping*' and juxtaposes the following words of his own (Rodenborn's) in parenthesis, 'similarly pointing to the individual's experience of ever-pending death'. This last remark, however, is misleading because it bears no relation to anything said in the context from which Schillebeeckx's words above are taken. It is worth quoting some of the paragraphs to which the words, in fact, belong because the general tenor of what Schillebeeckx says is infused with an unmistakable grace-optimism:

> In conclusion I should like to say a word about the atmosphere of our expectation of the future. Our responsibility for the future is no more than a transposition to the human register of what is heard in the register of the vox coelestis – grace. We do not simply possess the future. Expectation of the future is only a human name for hoping, man's religious attitude to life.[59]

Schillebeeckx then goes on to describe in a way that is extraordinarily confident in its reliance on God, the dialectic between religious confidence in the future and the praxis of the kingdom of God:

> The more clearly our free commitment here and now to the future expresses a religious confidence, the more effectively will we, by our human activity, fashion the definitive future. Our courageous, free and competent movement towards the future is basically a question of being borne by God towards a kingdom of peace, love and joy. We work together with God at the future.[60]

It is important to add that Schillebeeckx considers the

> most striking and characteristic of Jesus' orientation to the future as 'God's potentiality', hence crucial to his understanding of God's lordship, is his utter indifference to a person's sinful past. When the point is raised (as in the case of the adulterous woman) Jesus displays extreme reserve. He condemns no-one; his concern is with the potential for the future in the 'now' of the metanoia.[61]

---

58. Ibid., 312.
59. Schillebeeckx, *W & C*, 216 [281].
60. Ibid. Poulsom considers that part of what Schillebeeckx is doing when he alludes to a dialectic between a present commitment to shaping the future and a religious confidence in being borne by God is countering the claim of humanism that faith in God holds back humanity such that humanity, in order to fashion a truly human future, must free itself from God (comment: 12 July 2017).
61. Schillebeeckx, *Jesus*, 125 [145–6].

A final element in Critical Theory that coincides, to some degree, with Schillebeeckx's thinking about the kingdom of God is the concern with domination. Theodor Adorno and Max Horkheimer, leading lights of the Frankfurt School, co-authored *Dialectic of Enlightenment*, in which their concern was the fact of domination in advanced state capitalism which they identified with both fascist and Soviet totalitarianism.[62] Schillebeeckx's response to human domination, not as a sociologist or cultural historian but as a theologian, was to advocate the revolution of the gospel, namely the abolition of master–servant relationships. He writes, 'According to the New Testament there must be a fundamental solidarity and equality among Christians, without master-servant relationships, though this does not in any way exclude authority and leadership in the community.'[63] He talks about Jesus' announcement of the bankruptcy of the Jewish religious rulers of his time 'who are set on gathering together a pure community of God through separation and selection and leaving the mass of people to their fate.'[64] The same can be said of people in positions of religious and secular power in subsequent history who, in their domination, have excluded and oppressed people. In human and therefore spiritual terms they are bankrupt. Jesus himself does not exclude but brings his message to all without exception. It is 'a message and a praxis that proclaim God's universal love, God's true lordship with no "remnants"'.[65] Schillebeeckx writes that 'Equally, Jesus repudiates the apocalyptic reversal of power structures, in other words the poor becoming the boss and those who are now rich becoming the oppressed.' The kingdom of God is 'the abrogation of all abusive power structures'.[66]

Schillebeeckx says that 'the concrete content of the kingdom of God transcends our human power of imagination'.[67] We get a 'vague' idea of it from a combination of experiences of goodness and justice, of meaning and love, and 'reflected in our opposition to situations in which we feel the human in us, personal and social, to be threatened, enslaved and dishonoured'.[68] The vision of what the kingdom of God can be for men and women only takes shape 'against the horizon illuminated by Jesus' life: his message, conveyed above all in parables of the kingdom of God, his personal pioneering praxis of the kingdom of God which he maintained to the death'.[69] Schillebeeckx describes Jesus as 'God's exegete' who interpreted God using words, 'theoretically' so to speak, and who was also the 'practitioner' who

---

62. Kearney, *Modern Movements in European Phil*, 220.

63. Schillebeeckx, *The Church with a Human Face*, trans. John Bowden, extensively edited and corrected by Ted Schoof, The Collected Works of Edward Schillebeeckx 9 (London: Bloomsbury, 2014), 38 [41].

64. Schillebeeckx, *Jesus*, 124–5 [145].

65. Ibid., 125 [145].

66. Ibid.

67. Schillebeeckx, *Church*, 111 [112].

68. Ibid.

69. Ibid.

lived a way of life in accordance with God's kingdom.[70] He did not work from a blueprint or a well-defined concept of eschatological and definitive salvation.[71] Instead, 'in and through his own historical and thus situationally limited praxis of "going about doing good" [Jesus] ... threw light on a distant vision of definitive, perfect and universal salvation'.[72]

The humanity of Jesus Christ

The humanity of Jesus is part of the unity of divine-in-human of Jesus which is as much a structural element of Schillebeeckx's Christology as it is of the dogmatic tradition of the Church. In *CSEG* Schillebeeckx differentiates between what can be called God's strategy in creation and his tactic. God's strategy, his 'ultimate purpose was [and is] to call a faithful people into life'.[73] Implicit in this statement is the twofold action of God: his creative action which holds people in existence and his salvific action which enables a fullness of life over and above biological existence and the life-draining and distorting tendency to sin. The two are inseparable because not only does God want the creation that he freely holds in existence but he loves it. His deepest desire is that human beings should flourish to his greater glory. God's tactic is the humanity of Jesus, that is, God's own humanity in Jesus:

> The humanity of Jesus is concretely intended by God as the fulfilment of his salvation; it is a messianic reality. This messianic and redemptive purpose of the Incarnation implies that the encounter between Jesus and his contemporaries was always on his part an offering of grace in a human form. For the love [issuing from] the man Jesus is the human incarnation of the redeeming love of God: an advent of God's love in visible form.[74]

In this passage and context Schillebeeckx explains that the humanity of Jesus is the means by which God's redeeming grace is brought to human beings. He does not treat salvation in Jesus as focused and channelled through the passion and crucifixion of the God-man, in a lapsarian way. Instead all of Jesus' human actions 'possess ... of their nature a divine and saving power'.[75] Schillebeeckx never lets go of the divinity in the humanity of Jesus and writes,

> Precisely because these human deeds of Jesus are divine deeds, personal acts of the Son of God, divine acts in visible human form, they possess of their nature a

---

70. Schillebeeckx, *IR*, 108 [124].
71. Ibid.
72. Ibid.
73. Schillebeeckx, *CSEG*, 9 [12].
74. Ibid., 10 [14].
75. Ibid.

divine saving power, and consequently they bring salvation; they are 'the cause of grace'.[76]

All the actions, words and deeds, of the man Jesus, are saving and 'this truth is realized in a most particular way in the great mysteries of his life: his passion, death, resurrection and exaltation to the side of the Father'.[77] Schillebeeckx attributes this way of understanding to Aquinas.[78] He views the sacraments through the lens of his Christology. Jesus himself, in his humanity 'as the personal visible realization of the divine grace of redemption, is the ... primordial sacrament'.[79] In conclusion, although Schillebeeckx talks here in 'an amalgam of Aquinas' insights, historical *ressourcement*, and De Petters' phenomenology' the humanity of Jesus is already treated as of equal and essential importance to the divinity of Jesus in his Christology.[80]

A change at the conjunctural level: The meaning of Jesus' humanity for us

Kennedy points out that, for Schillebeeckx, there is no condescension in God's contact with human beings. Writing about Schillebeeckx's understanding of the knowability of God, he avers,

> The linchpin of Schillebeeckx's treatment of cognitional approaches to God is the view that in order for God to be knowable, God's reality itself must include a human element [referred to above as God's 'tactic']; and in order for human knowledge to make cognitional contact with the reality of God it must involve an indescribable but vaguely visualised divinizing element. Within such a scheme humanity is declared to be the nature of God. Otherwise expressed, Schillebeeckx's theology specifies humanity as the fundamental symbol of God (imago Dei).[81]

In *CSEG* Schillebeeckx uses a Thomist paradigm to talk about Jesus and already brings Jesus' humanity to the fore as an intrinsic part of, and on an equal footing with, his divinity: God's divinity is expressed in his humanity. God expresses his love for humanity in his own humanity in Jesus. With the changes to his theological methods of the 1960s, Schillebeeckx closely scrutinizes the biblical portrayal of Jesus and the conclusion he reaches is something of a reversal of the perhaps more common approach to assessing the humanity of Jesus. He writes that Jesus 'might

---

76. Ibid.
77. Ibid.
78. Ibid., note 11 for references to the *Summa Theologiae*, III, q. 48, a. 6; q. 8, a. 1, ad 1; q. 78, a. 4. And the remark, 'Here St. Thomas is relying above all on Greek patrology.'
79. Schillebeeckx, *CSEG*, 11.
80. Kennedy, *Schillebeeckx*, 44.
81. Kennedy, *Deus Humanissimus*, 23–4.

well teach us what it really means to be human, in other words, that the measure for assessing Jesus is not our idea of humanity but that *his* humanity is the measure by which we ought to judge ourselves'.[82] Schillebeeckx sees the unity of the divine-in-human in Jesus as requiring us 'to be open to Jesus' own interpretative experience [on the one hand] of the reality of God which he manifests in his humanity'[83] and, on the other hand, 'to [be open to] the true nature of man [as lived by Jesus], in such a way that the former is achieved via the latter'.[84] Schillebeeckx, open in his faith to meeting the historical person of Jesus through a hermeneutical study of the New Testament, starts with Jesus and through him interprets what it is to be human. In other words, he presents a Christological anthropology which '"proclaims Jesus Christ as the origin and end of true humanity", as the one mystery who unlocks the mystery of human life'.[85] Jesus' humanity is God's salvation, or making whole of human beings, which, in turn, enables them to become fully human.

Kennedy unfolds Schillebeeckx's argument that

> if humanity is the fundamental symbol of God' then God may be 'contacted' in an activity that strives to bring about a more human situation in the midst of an inhuman predicament; and, for Schillebeeckx, within such a striving, the hidden God, the Deus absconditus, becomes known as a Deus humanissimus, as the One who is more human than any human being.[86]

The activity that 'strives to bring about a more human situation in the midst of an inhuman predicament' is precisely the praxis of the kingdom of God.[87] This last remark demonstrates the inseparable interconnectedness between the themes of suffering, the praxis of the kingdom of God and humanity in Schillebeeckx's later Christology. As Poulsom writes, Schillebeeckx's account of what is genuinely human changes in a conjunctural shift. In his earlier Christology he 'posit[s] a theological definition of man to complement and complete secular ones'[88] (such as the definition he gives in *Dialogue with God and Christian Secularity* [1958][89]).

---

82. Schillebeeckx, *Jesus*, 564 [601].
83. Ibid., 567 [604].
84. Ibid., 566 [603].
85. Mary Catherine Hilkert, 'The Mystery of Being Human', in *The Theology of Cardinal Walter Kasper*, ed. Kristin M. Colberg and Robert A. Krieg (Collegeville, MN: Liturgical Press, 2014), 59–78, 62, quoting Kasper in the 'Theological Anthropology of *Gaudium et Spes*', *Communio* 23 (Spring 1996): 129–40, 137.
86. Kennedy, *Deus Humanissimus*, 24.
87. Ibid.
88. Poulsom, *Dialectics*, 132.
89. *Dialogue with God and Secularity* was first published under the title 'God and Man', in *Verslagboek van de Theologische week over de mens*, Nijmegen, 1958, 3–21. This was later published in the English translation by Edward Fitzgerald and Peter Tomlinson as Chapter 5 in *God and Man* (London: Sheed and Ward, 1969), 210–33.

A theological definition, by reason of being a definition, suggests an exact description of the unchanging nature of something. Schillebeeckx, increasingly aware of the historical nature of human existence, influenced by existentialism and the ideas of Critical Theory, combined with an understanding of the contingency of God-given freedom, became more conscious of 'man's being [as] a being of possibility', in Irenaean terms, a work of clay in progress in the hands of God.[90] Schillebeeckx writes, 'being man is a *becoming* man … a task and not a reality which is already given and finished, as it were, behind our body, even before we make our appearance actively in the world'.[91] Poulsom writes,

> The conjunctural shift to a more critical stance is recognizable in Schillebeeckx's acknowledgement that the 'Christian has as little positive idea [of what is truly worthy of man] as the non-Christian'. It finds definitive expression, nonetheless, in his insistence that there is no 'pre-existing definition of humanity – indeed for Christians it is not only a future, but an eschatological reality'.[92]

In saying this, Schillebeeckx is referring to norms and ethical imperatives of humanity that change on the conjunctural, or even ephemeral, plane. Given that each human being finds him/herself in the flux and ambiguity of history, in a complex entanglement of phenomena, and that 'the critical force of human reason is dependent on the historical circumstances of human reason', it is both impossible and illogical to try to nail down one positive definition of what constitutes full humanity.

Schillebeeckx, however, borrowed the term *humanum*, which had been coined in the Frankfurt School of Philosophy, to indicate in general terms what it means to be human. Kevin Considine describes it as 'a term that points to the fullness of humanity, its wholeness, healing, and reconciliation, that is present in fragments and is always endangered'.[93] Schillebeeckx, therefore, advocates a set of *anthropological constants* which could be said to be the structural elements (in the *Annales* sense) of what constitutes humanity (although he does not explicitly refer to the threefold *Annales* model in his discussion of structural elements of what constitutes human nature). The anthropological constants are wholly rooted in the creation. Salvation applies to our human bodiliness and through our bodiliness, it must inform humanity's relationship to nature and the ecological environment.[94] Salvation is the life blood of relationships to other, fellow human beings. Schillebeeckx describes a

90. Schillebeeckx, *W&C*, 185 [241].
91. Ibid.
92. Poulsom, *Dialectics*, 132. Poulsom is citing Schillebeeckx, *Christ*, 725 [731].
93. Kevin P. Considine, *Salvation for the Sinned-Against: Han and Schillebeeckx in Intercultural Dialogue* (Eugene, OR: Pickwick, 2015), 51.
94. Although some individuals have accused Schillebeeckx of following a theological fashion by writing about humanity's partnership with nature and the environment only in his later theology, he refutes the charge saying, 'I was already writing substantially the same

dialectic between the development of individual personhood through encounter in intersubjectivity with fellow human beings. He observes of the human face, 'The human face in particular – a man never sees his *own* face – already indicates that man is *directed towards* others, is *destined for* others and not for himself. The face is an image of ourselves *for others.*'[95] Salvation embraces human beings' connection with social and institutional structures; it infuses conditioning by time and place and is achieved through the mutual relationship of theory and practice. The sixth anthropological constant is the religious and parareligious consciousness of human beings. The seventh and final anthropological constant is the synthesis of the six, a synthesis which heals human beings and brings them salvation.[96] Schillebeeckx writes about the anthropological constants,

> In very general terms these anthropological constants point to permanent human impulses and orientations, values and spheres of value, but at the same time do not provide us with directly specific norms or ethical imperatives in accordance with which true and liveable humanity would have to be called into existence here and now.[97]

He seems clearly to be alluding to structural and conjunctural aspects when he writes,

> Taking into account the particular socio-historical forms of a particular society, and in the light of these spheres of values recognized as constant (in our time-conditioned awareness of the problem), it is in fact possible to establish specific norms for human action over a middle or longer term.[98]

Establishing 'specific norms for human action' is intended to make for the *humanum*.

The more Schillebeeckx explicates the meaning of the *humanum*, the more he talks about God and Jesus. He links Jesus Christ, both in his work on earth and in his resurrection, to 'God's business', that is, creation. God's business is the *humanum*, the well-being and happiness of human beings in a world that is flourishing. Jesus is intent on it. It is to seek God for his own sake and, above all, about delighting in God himself. For Jesus, as for humanity, the *humanum* is to understand the lordship of God in a way that expresses the relationship between God and human beings so that 'we are each other's happiness'.[99] Humanity's recognition of God's

---

thing [about humanity and the environment] in 1974 and even in 1960'. *Church*, 237 [240], note 4.

95. Schillebeeckx, *Christ*, 731 [737].
96. Ibid., 728 [734]–737 [743] on anthropological constants.
97. Schillebeeckx, *Christ*, 727 [733].
98. Ibid., 727–8 [733].
99. Schillebeeckx, *Jesus*, 122 [142].

creative lordship 'engenders the truly human condition, the salvation [flourishing and happiness] of humankind'.[100] McManus describes the *humanum* as 'that full human flourishing that fulfils the divine will at the heart of creation'[101] and which Irenaeus avers is to the glory of God.[102]

Christology is concentrated creation

Towards the end of his book *Christ*, Schillebeeckx concludes that four fundamental elements, constituent of a Christological soteriology, can be derived from a study of the New Testament 'relationship between God's universal will for salvation and the human experience of the ultimate meaning of life'[103] found in Jesus Christ. The four elements are both rooted in the apostolic tradition and are relevant to the present historical situation.

The first of these elements is God and his history with human beings. This is both a theological and an anthropological element. Jesus and his first followers were Jewish and inherited their Jewish faith from within the history of God's revelation to and relationship with his people. They had a rocklike faith in God that, whatever the sufferings and disasters of human life, God is working for the salvation of his people in history. In this faith, God is a God of humanity.[104] That God's self-revelation to humanity is to be found in history and not somewhere beyond is a theme central to Schillebeeckx's theology and is also one which Irenaeus expresses forcefully when he writes that 'it is the greatest possible slight to God to disparage the historical self-revelation of his immeasurable love and to look behind it for a non-existent access to the unknown God'.[105] In terms of Christian anthropology, human beings are the creatures who by their very relation to the Creator are made precisely for relationship with God. God 'wants to be the deepest meaning, the salvation and happiness of human life'.[106]

The second fundamental element of a Christological soteriology is that the nucleus of God's history with humanity can be found in the person and life of Jesus of Nazareth. To call Jesus the nucleus of God's history is a dense and powerful metaphor. Just as the nucleus is the information centre of the cell, Jesus is, as it were, the information centre of God's creation and of God's history with humanity. God's bodily entry into the world in the person of Jesus of Nazareth, his culminating self-revelation and self-gift in love in the person

---

100. McManus, *Unbroken Communion*, 7, note 5.
101. Ibid., 8.
102. Irenaeus, *Adversus Haereses*, IV.xxxiv.7 (Harvey's edition, 219).
103. Schillebeeckx, *Christ*, 627 [638].
104. Old and New Testaments are agreed: 'Yahweh is a God of man.' Ibid., 628 [639].
105. Balthasar, *The Glory of the Lord*, 61.
106. Schillebeeckx, *GAU*, 104.

of Jesus, is the pivot from which God's 'nature' and purposes in creation are revealed in a concentrated way. Looking back in time, the history of God's people, God's covenant with the people of Israel, was the preparation for the coming of the longed-for Messiah, Jesus Christ. The pivotal point was Christ's life on earth. On earth Jesus in person was God's salvation. In their encounters with Jesus, people experienced release from their suffering and alienation, to find themselves transformed with new life, salvation directly from God himself. This experience of God's salvation, which is concerned with the wholeness and happiness of humanity and which opposes suffering and injustice, is God's aim in creation. Through the person, career and destiny of Jesus, 'the meaning and destiny of human beings, prepared for and intended from of old by God, has been disclosed'.[107]

The third fundamental element of a soteriology that is constituent of Christology is 'our history, following Jesus'.[108] Looking forward from the pivotal point that is Jesus' life, the resurrection of Jesus was the start of the story of the followers of Jesus Christ making history with God. They were and are called, in the power of the Spirit of God and the same Spirit of Christ, to enact God's healing and life-giving deeds and words *sequela Jesu*, in their own historical contexts. In Jesus is a concentration of what God longs for in his creation, namely, that 'taking our bearings from [Jesus], and allow[ing] ourselves to be inspired by him, by sharing in his *Abba* experience and his selfless support for "the least of my brethren" '.[109] In this way not only do we 'entrust[ing] our own destiny to God, we allow the history of Jesus, the living one, to continue in history as a piece of living Christology'.[110] This is a living out of the Eucharistic doxology, 'Through him and with him and in him, in the unity of the Holy Spirit, all glory and honour is yours, almighty Father, for ever and ever.' Through relationship with God in prayer and contemplation, Christians are propelled into engagement with the world. Jesus showed that the setting and material for humanity's task of receiving God's salvation and, at the same time, of being his agents to bring salvation to each other is the world itself. In direct proportion to Jesus' and his followers' involvement and participation in the depths and heights of human life in the material world, in accordance with his Father's will, God the Creator is glorified.

The fourth and final element of God's saving history with humanity in Jesus is that it is a history without historical end.[111] Christians believe in life everlasting. Human death does not cause God's creative activity of holding his creatures in existence to cease. Rather, God destines his human beings to be happy with him

---

107. Schillebeeckx, *Christ*, 628 [639].
108. Ibid., 630 [641].
109. Ibid.
110. Ibid., 630.
111. Ibid., 631 [642].

forever in the life that is to come beyond death. This aspect of God's creative plan has been powerfully demonstrated in the raising of Jesus from the dead. God's plan to raise all humanity is concentrated in Christ who, as 'the first fruits of those who have died',[112] sends his Holy Spirit to his followers as they work with God bringing in his kingdom on earth.

---

112. 1 Cor. 15.20.

Part III

SCHILLEBEECKX'S IDEAS AND METHODS IN
DIALOGUE WITH NEW CONTEXTS

Chapter 7

SCHILLEBEECKX'S IDEAS AND METHODS IN DIALOGUE WITH NEW CONTEXTS: THE FEMINICIDE IN CIUDAD JUÁREZ

In this and the following chapter examples of the work of two theologians are taken, Nancy Pineda-Madrid and Lieven Boeve, and are examined and analysed in terms of how their work continues and develops some of the key ideas and methods of Schillebeeckx. In this chapter Nancy Pineda-Madrid's account of salvation in the midst of the suffering in Ciudad Juárez is examined and in Chapter 8 a study is made of Lieven Boeve's proposal of the Catholic Dialogue School.

Suffering and salvation in Ciudad Juárez

The whole of Schillebeeckx's theology is rooted in his creation faith. He believes that God's constant creative action is at the same time an assurance of God's continuous, saving presence with his creation. This belief is a structural element of his theology which endured over his entire career. At the same time, Schillebeeckx's theological evolution translated a classical tradition of talking in conceptual terms about God and salvation in Christ into a concrete language of Christian praxis in the world opposed to suffering, *sequela Jesu*. To talk theologically of salvation in terms of opposing suffering in the world is to transform soteriology from being a church-centred focus on personal salvation to becoming a world-centred, societal theology. Schillebeeckx chose to focus in a major way on suffering because to suffer is a universal and ubiquitous experience, albeit in varying degrees and in various ways. On the one hand, suffering provides common ground from which to engage in dialogue with those who might not share traditional concepts and assumptions of Christian faith. On the other hand, for those with Christian faith, to engage with suffering in praxis is to throw open the doors of the Church and to meet Christ in the suffering people of the world and to bring his healing in solidarity: *nulla salus extra mundum*.

Kathleen McManus shows the wide embrace of 'suffering' when she explains the scope of the term in the introduction to her study of the place and meaning of suffering in Schillebeeckx's theology. Among other examples of suffering that she touches upon, she names 'one person's excruciating battle with a terminal illness, and another's agonizing loss of a loved one to sickness and death' and the suffering that may afflict whole peoples as a result of the unfathomable horrors of war, genocide, abuse of human rights and unresolved centuries-old hatred between nations.[1] To judge by the 'slaughter bench' of history (to use Hegel's expression),[2] human suffering on this earth is not going to disappear. The relevance of a focus on suffering in theology is set to last.

In the 1980s the first cases of feminicide were reported in Mexico. Nancy Pineda-Madrid defines *feminicide* as 'a term widely used by feminist social scientists, to refer to the killing of girls and women by men in an exceptionally brutal manner, on a massive scale, and with impunity for the perpetrators'.[3] From the mid-1990s international media began to report hundreds of such killings and in 2009 a second wave of killings started. The feminicide in Ciudad Juárez is an egregious case of suffering with elements common to other contexts in the world. In the last decades of the twentieth century and into the twenty-first century the borderlands of Ciudad Juárez became a place of rapid industrialization. Poverty compelled families to move from rural areas to Juárez in search of work in the industrialized zone along the border with the United States. *Maquiladoras* (assembly plants or factories) sprang up in Mexico, run by foreign, mainly US, companies which export the products to those companies' countries of origin. The managers of the *maquiladoras* were keen to employ young women for their labour force because they had 'fresh energy for work, had a great deal of manual dexterity, did not question authority, and did not complain about sudden changes in their work shift or about demanding work quotas'.[4] In the 1990s it became clear that, within the high murder rates of both men and women in the borderlands of Ciudad Juárez, there was a pattern to the frequent sexual assaults, torture and killings of young women who had no part whatsoever in any form of criminal activity. Owing to the corruption of police and civil authorities, these crimes were committed with impunity. Pineda-Madrid studies the beginnings of salvation for the women of Ciudad Juárez in the midst of their suffering.

Naming suffering and naming sin

Pineda-Madrid, in confronting the particular suffering in Juárez caused by the brutal, sexualized murders of young women, and the mutilation of their bodies, raises the question for theology as to whether we can hope for salvation from suffering caused by such cruel and heinous sin. To use the metaphor of the coin, when humanly caused suffering is one side of the coin, the other side is sin. An account of the suffering of the girls and women and their families reveals a

---

1. McManus, *Unbroken Communion*, 2.
2. Georg Wilhelm Friedrich Hegel, *The Philosophy of History*, trans. J. Sibree (New York: Dover Publications, 1956), 21.
3. Nancy Pineda-Madrid, *Suffering and Salvation in Ciudad Juárez* (Minneapolis, MN: Fortress Press, 2011), 1–2.
4. Ibid., 36.

complex of interwoven layers not only of sinful atrocities committed by individuals and gangs but also of interlocking webs of corruption among civil authorities which prevent the perpetrators being called to justice. Schillebeeckx's emphasis in understanding sin as being not only a matter of individual wrongdoing but also, often at the same time, as being a societal collusion or tacit acquiescence in wrongdoing is of capital relevance. About systemic sin he writes that healthy and life-affirming communications and relationships between people at a societal level are disrupted or prevented by 'sexism, racism, and fascism, antisemitism, hostility to and attacks on immigrant workers, and the Western cultural and religious sense of superiority'.[5] Pineda-Madrid names the breakdown of society caused by such catastrophic disruption, in this case the feminicide, as sociocide, and develops the idea that community must be a condition of the possibility of our knowing salvation or the 'healthy and life-affirming communications and relationships' that Schillebeeckx refers to when she writes,

> When we are faced with the breakdown and collapse of our social bonds, with the destruction of our sense of interrelatedness with other human beings and with the whole of creation, then we see ever more sharply how community must be a condition of the possibility of our knowing salvation.[6]

It is pertinent to examine the causes of the feminicide, described by Pineda-Madrid, because they demonstrate the interplay between individual actions, and political systems and economic structures which cause suffering. Schillebeeckx's focus on suffering means he never loses sight of the heavy reality of sin and Pineda-Madrid's analysis highlights the depths and extent of individuals' complicity in webs of action and inaction that are instrumental in inflicting dire suffering on others.

The context

The geographical position of Ciudad Juárez is central to understanding how suffering in the city has been caused for economic and political reasons. Juárez is divided from El Paso in Texas by the stream of the Rio Bravo/Rio Grande. In 1965 Mexico announced the Border Industrialization Program as a result of which numerous enterprises were established, most of them subsidiaries of US firms.[7] Decades before the passage of the North American Free Trade Agreement (NAFTA) in 1993, Mexico experimented with political projects that would suspend national sovereignty in the border space in favour of attracting foreign

---

5. Schillebeeckx, *Church*, 130 [132].
6. Pineda-Madrid, *Suffering and Salvation in Ciudad Juárez*, 61.
7. Anna-Stina Ericson, 'An Analysis of Mexico's Border Industrialization Program', *Monthly Labor Review*, 93:5 (May 1970): 33–40 (33).

exchange. The militarization of the borderland by the US government, coupled with the porous border as a result of NAFTA, 'has generated a new wave of criminal organisations who use the desert for clandestine commercial activity that traffics in human beings, [activities] dubbed "illegal" by the United States'. Alicia Schmidt Camacho claims that such borderlands or denationalized spaces, rife with criminality, are conducive to producing 'a climate where sociality is defined less by national belonging than by the atomizing force of collective fear' and writes that 'we need to situate the feminicide in the context of the borderlands, not merely in Ciudad Juárez or Mexico'.[8]

In the case of Juárez, although the economic dimension to the suffering is indisputable, Pineda-Madrid observes that the economic interests involved 'constitute[s] one of the most fiercely debated perceptual terrains'.[9] Rosa-Linda Fregoso recounts, how, after the passage of NAFTA in 1993,

> During the 1990s, Ciudad Juárez [became] the largest export-processing zone on the border, host to roughly 350 manufacturing plants owned primarily by U.S. transnational corporations. These plants employed roughly 180,000 workers who were paid around $23 per week in take-home pay, a little less than $4 per day, or fifty cents per hour. ... Antiglobalization perspectives provide valuable insight into how Juárez figures as the 'local' embodiment of the [nature] of global-neoliberalism (market-based development) under the co-ordination and direction of the Group of Eight (G8), the IMF (International Monetary Fund), and the WTO (World Trade Organization), and the World Bank; of the concentration of economic power in transnational corporations; of the internationalization of social divisions; and of the subordination of national economies to global forces. Without doubt, global and transnational dynamics implode into the geography of Ciudad Juárez.[10]

While Fregoso writes that it is true that global and transnational dynamics imploded into the geography of Ciudad Juárez, she reports that it is, in fact, the case that 'only a small number of the victims ... worked in Juárez's *maquiladoras*'.[11]

---

8. Alicia Schmidt Camacho, 'Ciudadana X: Gender Violence and the Denationalization of Women's Rights in Ciudad Juárez, Mexico', *New Centennial Review*, 5 (2005): 255–92.

9. Pineda-Madrid, *Suffering and Salvation in Ciudad Juárez*, 29.

10. Rosa Linda Fregoso, *Mexicana Encounters: The Making of Social Identities on the Borderlands* (Berkeley: University of California Press, 2003), 7. In a report, 'Disappearing Daughters', in *The Seattle Times* it was stated that 'By the time NAFTA was implemented in 1994, formally incentivizing trade between the U.S. and Mexico, the structures that targeted women for violence were already well-established.' 'Disappearing Daughters', *The Seattle Times*, a project combining visual journalism with visual poetry to highlight the strength of the women of Juárez, by Corinne Chin and Erika Schultz, International Women's Day, 8 March 2020.

11. Fregoso, 'Toward a Planetry Civil Society', 40–2.

The problem with erroneously connecting all victims of the feminicide to the *maquiladora* industry is that they may be viewed 'as passive victims, poor, brown, women unfortunately caught up on the wrong side of inevitable, capitalist "change and progress"'.[12] The double danger here is that the individual women become objectified as statistics within a view of history against which Schillebeeckx argued forcefully, namely, an 'unChristian ... belief in progress'. He writes that some 'cherish an optimistic view of "change". ... They think that the social, economic, political and other cultural features of our history at a particular period disappear, in a process of ups and downs, because life and history *per se* mean progress.'[13] 'Thinking that there is an evolutionary course of history is to misunderstand the contingent nature of economic and historical forms.'[14]

Criminal trafficking in Juárez is both of people and of drugs. In the late 1980s the city became the centre of major and rival drug cartels, the largest being the Sinaloa Cartel which 'became the biggest supplier of illegal drugs to the U.S. during [Joaquin] Guzmán's long reign as leader',[15] trafficking cocaine, heroin and marijuana to feed a US market. The rivalry between drug cartels is violent and, at its peak, the cause of several homicides a week. An execrable aspect of the murder of women and girls was that killing them and mutilating their dead bodies was a 'sport', 'a competition', 'or ... a way for drug cartels to mark their territory or to "celebrate" successful drug runs across the border'.[16] Politically, the drug cartel activity aggravated the already existing, deeply rooted corruption of the police and officials at every level of government and within the judiciary which, in turn, made the violence, lawlessness and impunity for wrongdoers normative. One drug gang counted municipal and state police among its members.[17]

The church as a social institution has not been without its share of criticism in the context of Ciudad Juárez. Julia Monárrez Fragoso argues that 'as late as 2003 churches in Juárez – Catholic and Protestant (mainline and evangelical) – had not publicly taken a position in support of the murdered girls and women'.[18] For years the church authorities scandalously remained silent concerning the feminicide and even deployed the same shameful tactic used by the police in blaming the victims for provoking their killers' sexual aggression by their 'immodesty'. Catholic Church

---

12. Pineda-Madrid, *Suffering and Salvation in Ciudad-Juárez*, 30.

13. Schillebeeckx, *GAU*, 97.

14. Ibid.

15. BBC news website report, 'Mexico Cartels: Which Are the Biggest and Most Powerful?', 24 October 2019. Joaquin 'El Chapo' Guzman, the founder and leader of the Sinaloa cartel, was found guilty of trafficking tonnes of cocaine, heroin and marijuana and engaging in multiple murder conspiracies in February 2019, and sentenced to life in prison in July 2019, following a trial in the United States.

16. Pineda-Madrid, *Suffering and Salvation in Ciudad Juárez*, 15–16. This information was given by perpetrators under interrogation.

17. Ibid., 33.

18. Ibid., 35.

officials also criticized the mothers who protested their daughters' murders, alleging that these mothers created divisions in society by means of their criticism of civil authorities. When, however, a Mexican cardinal was assassinated in 1993, the same Catholic authorities expressed their outrage against civil authorities.[19] Subsequently in 2009, the Bishops' Conference in Mexico issued a major pastoral exhortation and the Chihuahuan bishops issued their own statement imploring people to turn to God and work towards an end to the violence.[20] Where the institutional church was slow to come to the aid of the victims and their families, individual Catholics had been working for years taking independent initiatives in support of those afflicted by the breakdown of society in the borderlands of Ciudad Juárez. Outstanding among them were the Carmelite priest Peter Hinde and the Mercy Sister Betty Campbell, who lived and worked in solidarity with the poor at Casa Tabor.[21] This contrast between individual and institutional responses to the suffering in Ciudad Juárez only serves to emphasize how individuals within the composite structure of an institution can be lulled into a complicit inertia or denial with regard to the suffering of others. In a plea for humanity in the church, Schillebeeckx writes,

> Humanity's cause is God's cause and God's cause is humanity's cause. As an institution, the church is the servant of the true salvation, the true happiness of men and women. Moreover, the church as an institution can be measured by the liberating power of the gospel. It can also be criticized. According to the New Testament there must be a fundamental solidarity and equality among Christians, without master-servant relationships, though this does not in any way exclude authority and leadership in the community.[22]

As already mentioned, it is precisely because suffering is a universal experience that Schillebeeckx chose it as a way of talking about God because God as revealed in his humanity in Jesus is, above all, opposed to suffering. Expressed positively, God in his humanity shows himself as the giver of fullness of life. Elements of Schillebeeckx's theology are central to debate about the infliction of any kind of suffering. The elements are closely linked. On the one hand, it is the inescapable fact of the reality of sin in the world. It is human beings' propensity to sin, a propensity which is like a 'malignant cancerous tumour that is constantly spreading',[23] as

---

19. Graciela Atencio, 'El Feminicidio es el Exterminio de la Mujer en la Patriarcado: Monárrez Fragoso', *La Jornado*, 1 September 2003. http://www.jornada.unam.mx/2003/09/01articulos/61_juarez_monarrez.htm. Cardinal Juan Jésus Posadas Ocampo was assassinated in May 1993 in what is thought to have been a case of mistaken identity. *New York Times*, 25 May 1993.

20. Pineda-Madrid, *Suffering and Salvation in Ciudad Juárez*, 35.

21. *The Catholic Universe*, 17 November 2020.

22. Schillebeeckx, *Church*, 38 [41].

23. Schillebeeckx, *W&C*, 9 [12].

Schillebeeckx expresses it, known as original sin, and which, when yielded to, results in personal acts of sin. On the other hand, there is the contingency of human free will.[24] Sin and free will are linked because there can be no harmful or sinful action without human agency and human agency is contingent: human beings can act against suffering and resist sin, or they can inflict suffering by their actions or by default. These facts (the propensity to sin and to yield to that propensity) tie in with Pineda-Madrid's identification in the Mexico of Ciudad Juárez of a 'hegemonic imaginary worldview' which allows an appropriation of suffering within society with the result that the suffering of those who suffer is ignored and is accepted as inevitable.

Imaginal social existence

In an attempt to crack the puzzle of why a society can acquiesce in the enduring and abhorrent suffering of its victims, Pineda-Madrid uses a social-suffering hermeneutic and alights upon what can be seen as a development of Schillebeeckx's understanding of the insidiousness and collectivity of original sin. She starts by drawing on Charles Taylor's idea of 'the ubiquitous character' of our 'imaginal social existence' and 'the ways ordinary people imagine their social space in precognitive and prethematic fashion', in other words, 'our shared operative sense of how things in society do proceed'.[25] In noting the important differences between social imaginary and social theory, Charles Taylor writes, 'the social imaginary is that common understanding that makes possible common practices and a widely shared sense of legitimacy'.[26] He warns that 'the social imaginary can be full of self-serving fiction and suppression, but it is also an essential constituent of the real. It cannot be reduced to an insubstantial dream.'[27] There is a 'dissonance between the social, moral society we imagine ourselves to be and the social world we have de facto created'.[28] When the 'social world we have de facto created' is a world where terror, torture and suffering are inflicted with impunity as at Ciudad Juárez, a central theological theme of Schillebeeckx confronts us. Such a world of suffering ('world' in both the micro and the macro senses) is the absolute opposite of what God wants. In the Old Testament scriptures God is shown to be a God who, in an unbreakable covenant of love, protects and defends his people and wills for them to enjoy all the blessings of peace. Supremely in his humanity in the person of

24. See Chapter 1.
25. Pineda-Madrid, *Suffering and Salvation in Ciudad Juárez*, 41. In addition to Charles Taylor, Pineda-Madrid also takes Octavio Paz and Emilie Townes to develop the exploration of Taylor's concept of 'false consciousness'.
26. Charles Taylor, *Modern Social Imaginaries* (Durham, NC: Duke University Press, 2004), 23.
27. Ibid., 183.
28. Pineda-Madrid, *Suffering and Salvation in Ciudad Juárez*, 43.

Jesus, God shows that he lifts people out of any situation that causes them to lead a deadened life, whether it be from afflictions of physical or mental health; the loss, through death, of a child; social ostracism; or oppression by a social institution (the religious hierarchy of his day).

Pineda-Madrid acknowledges the value of Taylor's construct to help us 'to recognize the significance of people imagining their social existence and the precognitive dynamic of social imaginaries'[29] but she goes further. She makes an analysis of what constitutes the false consciousness and distortion of the social imaginary in Latin America. She finds that Octavio Paz, whom she describes as 'the ever-controversial Nobel Prize Laureate', 'foregrounds gender constructions, particularly in relation to violence and suffering'.[30] Controversial and limited though his reading of the Mexican social imaginary may be, it nonetheless 'offers a glimpse of a tenacious, hegemonic worldview that keeps the notion of Latina suffering deeply rooted'.[31] Schillebeeckx's insistence that God is absolutely opposed to suffering requires development: situations of suffering, not only in Ciudad Juárez but everywhere, must be laid bare not only by the concrete facts of exploitation and cruelty but also by identifying the less tangible aspects of any false consciousness of peoples' social imaginaries. The approach of the Christian social ethicist Emilie Townes, which draws on Michel Foucault's understanding of the imagination and Antonio Gramsci's use of hegemony, shows how the hegemonic imagination generates 'caricatures and stereotypes'. Townes argues that what she describes as 'structural evil', in other words structural sin, is embedded not only in rational mechanisms but is also 'maintained by more heuristic forces that emerge from the imagination as emotion, intuition and yearning'.[32] Stereotypes of any sort including those of Latina femaleness, Pineda-Madrid avers, operate as these heuristic forces.[33]

Schillebeeckx talks of God in terms of a praxis of the reign of God. Jesus' followers are called to do the same as he did and, in doing so will, like Christ, build God's kingdom. The praxis of God's reign, like the social imaginary, is no insubstantial dream. Rather, it calls on us in Christ to imagine 'something new, constructive, opening new possibilities'[34] by breaking down stereotypes, changing habitual ways of thinking and putting on the mind of Christ. There is limitless scope for theological exploration and application of this element of Schillebeeckx's theology, current and still to be undertaken, in how human beings learn to confront the fact of suffering in their societies, unearthing the complex layers of

---

29. Ibid.
30. Ibid.
31. Ibid., 44.
32. Emilie M. Townes, *Womanist Ethics and the Cultural Production of Evil* (New York: Palgrave Macmillan, 2006), 18.
33. Pineda-Madrid, *Suffering and Salvation in Ciudad Juárez*, 45.
34. Taylor, *Modern Social Imaginaries*, 183.

self-interest, individual and societal, that cause untold suffering while despoiling the earth on which we all depend.

Once caricatures and stereotypes are generated, they can become cultural representations that are woven into narrative accounts that serve the interests of the most powerful while the poor are written off.[35] In this way, structures that give rise to social suffering can lead to those who hold the power within a society telling history in a way that refuses to recognize atrocities for what they are and even in a way that justifies them. Such ill use of hegemonic power is a manifestation of a pervasive cause of suffering to others, or (in theological language) a manifestation of original and personal sin. In an extension of Schillebeeckx's morbid simile when he likens original sin to a cancer, it is not misplaced to transpose his simile into sociocultural terms by describing one of the manifestations of original sin as a false or warped social imaginary. Without explicitly using the theological language of sin, Pineda-Madrid has developed an understanding of original sin precisely by highlighting in sociocultural terms the unconscious interplay between individual, subjective wrongdoing and societal, institutional, collective wrongdoing through the work of Taylor, La Paz and Townes. As argued in Chapter 5, however, there is no such thing as an entity 'Evil'. Schillebeeckx's keen sense of contingency, the critical power of the contingency of each human individual's free will, and his acute sense that ultimately it is each human being that has to accept responsibility for the way he or she has acted and acts need to be brought to the foreground.

Salvation as liberation from suffering into fullness of life is a leitmotif of Schillebeeckx's later work. The contemporary followers of Jesus Christ, who had, in Jesus, experienced the salvation that comes directly from God, in turn proclaimed and practised a love that liberated sufferers and set them free into fullness of life in the power of the Holy Spirit. Militating against this kind of solidarity of empowerment in the Holy Spirit in order to overcome and banish suffering is a strand in Christian spirituality that exalts the individual endurance of suffering. The agony and helplessness of Christ, depicted nailed and unable to move on the cross, has been and is a focus of intense devotion. Images of the crucified Christ have often become not just a symbol or 'book' from which to read the lengths to which God in his love for humanity was prepared to go. On the one hand, for those followers of Jesus who are enduring extremes of suffering, and who are physically as constrained and tortured as Jesus was on the cross, spiritual strength may well be derived from calling to him as their crucified Saviour. On the other hand, there are those who may be suffering abhorrent treatment, yet for whom there might be the possibility of movement out of their suffering, yet who are nevertheless told by those who wish to preserve the status quo that they are powerless to change their situation and they the victims are encouraged to cultivate endurance by meditating on the crucified Christ.

In the Mexican context, there are two master narratives that condense models of womanhood and which reinforce a fatalistic attitude to suffering: the Virgin of

---

35. Ibid., 45–6.

Guadalupe and La Malinche. In this binary La Malinche is said to be the indigenous Aztec woman who was Hernan Cortés's translator and mistress, who helped him in his conquest of Tenochtítlan. She is, therefore, the traitor who betrays her people, and leads them to destruction while her sexuality is tainted by immorality. La Guadalupe, on the other hand, is a title given to Mary, Mother of Jesus, after apparitions of her are said to have been seen by Juan Diego in 1531. Devotional focus on the Virgin of Guadalupe, in combination with Church teachings about the virtue of self-denial and service of others, has led to an attitude of acceptance of suffering. The veneration of the Virgin of Guadalupe has encouraged women to follow the 'example set by Mary' who stood silently, in tormented sorrow at the foot of the cross.[36] She had been helpless to change the course of events that led to her Son's crucifixion. *Marianismo*, the so-called veneration of the Virgin Mary, has been operative in encouraging women to model themselves on Mary in her suffering at the crucifixion: to be silent, passive and enduring in their own suffering. Women, in their turn, should model 'self-sacrifice, self-effacement, and self-subordination' and by so doing become 'spiritually superior'.[37] The point that emerges here is that a Mexican woman has often been, and may still be, categorized as either a 'Guadalupe' or a 'Malinche'. Anna Nieto-Gómez gives forceful expression to the effects of '*marianismo*'. She writes that a woman would ideally come to understand herself

> as a virgin, as a saintly mother, as a wife-sex object, as a martyr ... Church teachings have directed women to identify with the emotional suffering of the pure, passive bystander: the Virgin Mary. ... In order to be a slave or a servant, a woman cannot be assertive, independent, and self-defining. She is told to act fatalistically ... She is led to believe it natural to be dependent psychologically and economically, and she is not to do for herself but to yield to the needs of others – the patron, the family, her father, her boyfriend, her husband, her God. [... *Marianismo* portrays] the woman as semi-divine, morally superior, and spiritually stronger than her master because of her ability to endure pain and sorrow.[38]

The recontextualization of salvation

Schillebeeckx's understanding of salvation is that God's creative action and his saving action are two inseparable aspects of one dynamic: 'From the beginning

---

36. Pineda-Madrid, *Suffering and Salvation in Ciudad Juárez*, 49.

37. Betta Esperana Hernandez-Truyol, 'Culture and Economic Violence', in *The Latino Condition: A Critical Reader*, ed. Richard Delgado and Jean Stefancic (New York: New York University Press, 1998), 536–8.

38. Anna Nieto-Gómez, 'La Chicana – Legacy of Suffering and Self-Denial', in *Chicana Feminist Thought: The Basic Historical Writings*, ed. Alma M. García (New York: Routledge, 1977), 48–9.

of creation God also began on the realization of salvation – including religious salvation – for human beings in our history.'[39] He warns that salvation is not coterminous with what religions and churches may define nor that it is merely 'inward':

> It was the exclusivist coupling of salvation with religion and the church instead of the recognition of a deeper basis of the beginning of salvation from God in the world – the association of human salvation with the human world – that often resulted in an intellectualistic, idealistic, sacramentalistic and Neoplatonic-hierarchical view of God's system of salvation; at the same time there was also a one-sided concentration of salvation on inwardness.[40]

An example of one-sided concentration of salvation on inwardness is the intense individual devotion focused on the crucified Christ as a source of 'comfort' by those who are subjugated and suffering.

So much for what salvation is not. Schillebeeckx avers that the origin and source, the *Ursprung* of salvation, lies in the God-given human 'No!' to pain. Physically pain is necessary for the defence and protection of the body, for the survival of the human being, for life itself. A normally healthy newborn baby does not suffer any physical pain until pangs of hunger or wind make themselves felt. The baby will instinctively and noisily react to discomfort when it experiences thirst or the terror of sensing that it is not being held securely. The same response is true of emotional and psychological pain. As the baby grows to child and young person, emotional and psychological pain will manifest itself in symptoms and behaviour which ideally will be resolved with the help of parents, and those around the child. Whenever something is wrong, a physical injury or a psychological hurt, a sense of pain alerts the human being. When afflicted and affected by the chaos and injustice of the world, the adult human being has the same reaction, 'namely, that of a "no" to the world as it is'.[41] Schillebeeckx regards this reaction of 'no' to negative experiences, that is, experiences of disorder, injustice and suffering in the world, 'as being a pre-religious experience … accessible to all human beings'.[42] The inbuilt reverse of the 'No!' to experiences of suffering is 'Yes!' to the contrasting situations where pain is removed and there is no suffering. Schillebeeckx calls this 'Yes!' a consensus with 'the unknown', 'a better other world, which in fact does not yet exist anywhere' and he expresses it in another way by saying that this 'yes' is the 'assumption of the possibility of improving our world'; it is 'openness to the unknown and the better'.[43] This double-edged experience he calls a negative experience of contrast and says that the 'yes' is inherently stronger than

---

39. Schillebeeckx, *JWC*, 7.
40. Ibid., 9.
41. Schillebeeckx, *Church*, 5 [5].
42. Ibid.
43. Ibid., 6.

the 'no': 'The fundamental human "no" to evil [deeds and situations] therefore discloses an unfulfilled and thus "open yes" which is as intractable as the human "no", indeed even stronger, because the "open yes" is the basis of that opposition which makes it [the "no"] possible.'[44]

Believers, agnostics and all humanity share together in the pre-religious experience of salvation of saying 'no' to suffering, a 'no' which God has implanted in human beings. Schillebeeckx says that this 'is a rational basis for solidarity between all people and for common commitment to a better world with a human face'.[45] For those who believe in God,

> the 'open yes' then takes on a more precise direction. Its origin is not so much, or at least not directly, the transcendence of the divine (which is inexpressible and anonymous and cannot be put into words) as (at least for Christians) the recognizable human face of this transcendence which has appeared among us in the man Jesus, confessed as Christ and Son of God.[46]

Schillebeeckx's idea of negative experiences of contrast is a concise foundational idea and it is born of his Christian creation faith based on the belief that God the Creator has made human beings to want to flourish and God invites them into fuller life and freedom in relationship with Godself. The awareness of hope in the midst of suffering, whether an inchoate or a formulated hope, exists as the first step towards a worthy, human situation. It is the first firm step towards a recontextualization of salvation. In resistance to suffering the awareness of hope and its realization can be compared to the initial sketches for a painting. The fundamental idea is clear but to accomplish it requires perseverance in working out the composition and perspective in order that a bare canvas be transformed into an oil painting. The journey from the 'No-to-suffering' to the 'Yes-to-a-better-situation' is completed, in terms of the simile, by choosing and painstakingly mixing colours to bring about the desired perspective and composition of the picture. In the real terms of Ciudad Juárez, Pineda-Madrid makes a theological analysis of suffering and shows how the women of Ciudad Juárez resist their suffering step by arduous step to reach a safer place.

In the task of saying 'No!' to suffering, to alleviating, abolishing and preventing it, Pineda-Madrid avers that 'how we regard suffering matters theologically'.[47] What are we to make of it? How are we to understand it? It is inadequate to see it merely as an aberration and to see healing from it as something needed by those directly affected by it. Likewise suffering in general cannot simplistically be reduced to the effect of the sufferers' own personal sin (in Juárez, religious and civil

---

44. Ibid.
45. Ibid.
46. Schillebeeckx, *Church*, 6.
47. Pineda-Madrid, *Suffering and Salvation in Ciudad Juárez*, 4.

authorities made just such an argument). A third way to regard suffering is to see it as the by-product of social structures – economic, political, religious, cultural. Paul Farmer says of structural violence, 'The term is apt because such suffering is "structured" by historically given (and often economically driven) processes and forces that conspire – whether through routine, ritual, or, as is more commonly the case, the hard surfaces of life – to constrain agency.'[48] Suffering as the result of social structures is no more inevitable than individual sin. Identifying suffering as the result of structural violence or sin is sharpened by using the relational dialectic that is the habitual characteristic of Schillebeeckx's thought: structural violence or sin comes about through an interplay between, on the one hand, individual sin or wrongdoing and, on the other hand, systemic or institutional collusion or alliance in sin, and the two coalesce together and feed off each other. Chiming with Schillebeeckx's strong idea of the power of God-given subjective choice Farmer writes,

> The afflictions [of AIDS and political violence in Haiti] are not the result of accident or *force majeure*; they are the consequence, direct or indirect, of human agency. When the Artibonite Valley was flooded, depriving families … of their land, a human decision was behind it; when the Haitian army was endowed with money and unfettered power, human decisions were behind that, too.[49]

If followers of Jesus are to bring his healing to those who suffer, they must attempt to understand the mechanisms that produce the suffering. Schillebeeckx writes,

> It is striking that in a process in which people experience both suffering and hope the distinctive ideas a people have about 'salvation' are attempts to probe and interpret, not only the depth and unbounded extent of hardship, suffering, evil and death, endured and enduring, but also their causes, origin and effects. Where salvation is hoped for, it is in the express form of this expectation that evil and suffering are unmasked.[50]

Those who do not hunger or thirst, who lead comfortable, secure lives, need not only to write cheques or to make electronic donations but to unmask the far-reaching and interlocking chains of harmful, that is, sinful, decisions by politicians and executives in industry and financial institutions.

Relevant to understanding the sometimes-complex causes of systemic sin and the widespread human suffering of the world in postmodern times is how we perceive the media and the commercial, political and technical interests behind it. The media in itself is neutral: it is potentially either a power for good or a power

---

48. Paul Farmer, *Pathologies of Power: Health, Human Rights, and the New War on the Poor* (Berkeley: University of California Press, 2005), 40.
49. Farmer, *Pathologies of Power*, 40.
50. Schillebeeckx, *Jesus*, 3–4 [20].

for ill. Modern technology allows news of people's suffering to be flashed around the world either as it happens or minutes later. Such speedy communication is beneficial when it prompts offers of international help in the wake of a natural disaster or when mobile telephone video of the killing of protesters is shown to the world and shames the dictator into holding fire. On the other hand, the dangers are several: we the 'consumers' may 'become desensitized to and overwhelmed by serious suffering yet grateful that it is not readily visible in our own neighbourhoods';[51] the stream of images of suffering can 'produce moral fatigue, exhaustion of empathy, and political despair'.[52] We may be 'left feeling that there is far too much suffering; it is too complex to be readily understood and too complicated to alleviate'.[53] As Pineda-Madrid forcefully concludes, 'This undermines any attempt at creating more just structures. We can find ourselves unable to respond.... It is as if we are in a catatonic state.'[54] Here the Schillebeeckian insights into the power of our freedom and Christian hope are vital. Before even tackling the causes of suffering, a first step is to avoid either being overwhelmed by news reports of suffering, or, as a news junkie, to avoid becoming desensitized to reports of suffering; instead, it is necessary to develop 'media intelligence', the ability to understand the vested interests behind the various media outlets. Hand in hand with being media savvy is hope.

A social-suffering hermeneutic

Interpreting suffering by 'linking personal accounts of extreme suffering *to* the social matrix that precipitates them, has been termed by some theorists [and theologians] "social suffering"'.[55] How does the feminicide, and any suffering, when viewed through the lens of a social-suffering hermeneutic, recontextualize salvation? Two elements of a social-suffering hermeneutic, already touched upon, develop Schillebeeckx's ideas: contingency and systemic and collusive sin. Contingency is core to Schillebeeckx's understanding of creation: the contingency of God's free creative action in holding the universe in existence and the contingency of human autonomy, even within the limits of finitude, mean that there is no predetermination to the way that the human world is as it is. A core feature of a social-suffering hermeneutic is the praxiological nature of the experience of suffering.[56] Pineda-Madrid refers to 'the integral relation that exists

---

51. Pineda-Madrid, *Suffering and Salvation in Ciudad Juárez*, 20.
52. Arthur Kleinman and Joan Kleinman, 'The Appeal to Experience: The Dismay of Images: Cultural Appropriations of Suffering in Our Times', in *Social Suffering*, ed. Arthur Kleinman, Veena Das and Margaret Lock (Berkeley: University of California Press, 1997), 2.
53. Pineda-Madrid, *Suffering and Salvation in Ciudad Juárez*, 20.
54. Ibid.
55. Ibid., 21.
56. Ibid.

between human thought and action (or practice)' and then goes on to explain that to say 'suffering is necessarily and unavoidably praxiological means that we do not unreflectively assume that the experience of suffering is merely a given. ... With interpretation comes some active purpose or interest.'[57] Suffering is to do with realities and the theories or interpretations as they relate to those realities. To ignore the praxiological nature of suffering would be in effect a denial of suffering or a kind of neutrality that in practice equates with an unthinking acceptance of the suffering. Either of these responses is to be complicit in the suffering. Suffering must first of all be named and then interpreted. What are the facts and patterns of the horrendous rape and murder and the mutilations of the murdered bodies of the women of Juárez? Uncovering the facts is the necessary start, but more is needed because the experience of suffering, as Paul Farmer notes, 'is not effectively conveyed by statistics or graphs' unless the ' "texture" of dire affliction is better felt in the gritty details of biography'.[58] In the interpretation of suffering and the sin that causes it, both statistics and individual stories are needed.

The causes of the suffering must be laid bare. A social-suffering hermeneutic recognizes the presence of interests in our naming of suffering. Those interests may be economic, political, social or ecclesiastical and whichever they may be, they influence how we understand and respond to suffering. For example, those with the responsibility for building a dam which displaces whole villages of people and floods the fertile land on which they grew their food, may nevertheless present the suffering imposed as necessary for the greater prosperity of the country as a whole. In Ciudad Juárez, a narrative of those in power attempted to 'explain away' the horror that befell the women with lies about the roles of the women or denials of the facts. How suffering is represented '[prefigures] what we will, or will not do, to intervene'.[59] The motives and interests behind differing and opposing interpretations need to be understood and the truth sought. In opposing suffering, an analysis of the motives and interests behind different interpretations provides signposts to point the way, step by arduous step, to its abolition. Grappling in this concrete way with the facts of the suffering – naming it, understanding the differing interpretations offered for it and following signs of hope in order to abolish it – is an enactment of what Schillebeeckx calls a negative contrast experience. That the world is filled with suffering caused by human beings' treatment of each other is not inevitable. Human beings have caused that suffering by the way they use their freedom. Drawing on Aquinas' doctrine of double agency Schillebeeckx stresses that human actions are genuinely causes despite the restraints of human finitude. Human beings are genuinely free and they could prevent suffering and many, in fact, can, and do, work to prevent, alleviate and eliminate it.

57. Ibid., 22.
58. Farmer, *Pathologies of Power*, 31.
59. Arthur Kleiman and Joan Kleinman, 'The Appeal to Experience; The Dismay of Images: Cultural Appropriations of Suffering in Our Times', xii-xiii.

Another distinguishing feature of a social-suffering hermeneutic that is particularly relevant to the development of Schillebeeckx's thinking is that it 'attends to the interplay between societal problems and personal suffering'.[60] Attention has been drawn to Schillebeeckx's emphasis on understanding sin as being not only a matter of individual wrongdoing but also, often, at the same time, as being collective and systemic.[61] In order to recontextualize salvation the thread of people's decision-making within institutions (financial, political, civic) needs to be understood. Every decision made along the line is a moral act. Unless it is not worth making because it changes nothing, a decision will either improve life for people or cause suffering. The causes of public suffering on a large scale such as genocide and cultural decimation, and widespread poverty and ill health, are traceable, to a series of decisions by individuals, who form networks of systemic collusion over time, and the individuals in those networks are, each one, the actual cause of suffering.[62]

Salvation as societal

Just as Schillebeeckx analyses sin to be both individual and also systemic, so too with salvation. Describing salvation, and its opposite, namely, disaster, as societal he writes,

> Where good is promoted and evil is fought against for the healing of humanity, this historical praxis in fact confirms the nature of God – God as salvation for men and women, the basis of universal hope – and people moreover receive God's salvation: in and through a love which is put into practice. The history of human beings, the social life of human beings is the place where the cause of salvation or disaster is decided.[63]

---

60. Pineda-Madrid, *Suffering and Salvation in Ciudad Juárez*, 21.
61. 'Schillebeeckx's understanding of sin and its consequences in causing suffering, widened from something which appeared confined to an individual to something that is often, at the same time, endemic in society and its institutional systems.' This is a quote from before note 59 Ch. 5 p. 3.
62. Pineda-Madrid writes that

> we may identify four distinguishing factors in a social-suffering hermeneutic: (1) it foregrounds the praxiological nature of the experience of suffering; (2) it recognizes the presence of our interests in the naming of suffering; (3) it attends to the interplay between societal problems and personal suffering; and (4) it discerns the ways in which 'core symbol systems and cultural discourses' are used to mediate suffering as a social experience.

63. Schillebeeckx, *JWC*, 9–10. Italics added.

One element of salvation is to break out of the isolation of bearing suffering alone and in that way to find the freedom to act in solidarity with others, 'in the social life of human beings'.[64] Far too often, 'and to great destructive effect, suffering has been viewed as "one's cross" ' and therefore to be endured on one's own, even abandoned, as Jesus was when he endured his suffering on the cross.[65] In writing about one of the tasks of theology, namely, 'to safeguard belief in and ... hope for a liberating saving power which loves men and women and which will overcome [suffering]' Schillebeeckx writes that the 'liberating God is concerned for humankind and its humanity in a social and historical context'.[66]

In her study of salvation from the horror of the social and historical context of the feminicide, Pineda-Madrid calls attention to 'the primacy of a social dimension in our understanding of salvation'[67] and indicates the form of the social dimension in her analysis. The parents and families of the murdered women of Ciudad Juárez provide a courageous and inspiring model of solidarity, an interactive unity of feeling and action, in their acute suffering. Theirs was and is a solidarity which not only means that they can reach out to each other in the agony of their grief, but it also enables them to oppose the actions of the people who continue with impunity to cause suffering. In accordance with Paul Farmer's point that 'the "texture" of dire affliction is [more keenly] felt in the gritty details of biography',[68] Pineda-Madrid tells the harrowing story of the seventeen-year-old María Sagrario González Flores who was killed on her way home from the *maquiladora* plant on 16 April 1998. Sagrario's story not only tells of the horror of what she suffered but indicates the cumulative societal solidarity in the wake of her murder in stark contrast to the systemic sin of the cruel inaction of police and officials. When Sagrario did not return home, her frantic father, Jesús González, first searched for her with his eldest daughter, Guillermina. When they could not find her, they went to the local police in central Juárez, to ask them to help and start a search for Sagrario. The police made it clear, in a patronizing way, that 'they would do nothing in the effort to find Sagrario, even though over the previous five years Juárez had a rapidly growing list of missing young women who turned up tortured, raped and dead'.[69] Jesús González next went to the offices of the district attorney and the state police, 'offices ... charged with handling the investigations of the string of murdered women' but was rebuffed again and told 'that he had to wait twenty-four hours before he could file a missing person's report. He argued

---

64. Ibid.
65. Pineda-Madrid, *Suffering and Salvation in Ciudad Juárez*, 64.
66. Schillebeeckx, *Church*, 4 [4].
67. Pineda-Madrid, *Suffering and Salvation in Ciudad Juárez*, 98.
68. Farmer, *Pathologies of Power*, 31.
69. Details taken from Diana Washington Valdez, *The Killing Fields: Harvest of Women: The Truth about Mexico's Bloody Border Legacy* (Burbank: Peace at the Border, 2006), 35–42; Rodríguez, Montané, and Pulitzer, *Daughters of Juárez*, 75–90, recounted by Pineda-Madrid, *Suffering and Salvation in Ciudad Juárez*, 13–15.

that he was looking for his daughter alive, not dead, but to no avail.'[70] After they had checked the local area hospitals, Jesús and his son, Juan, began their own search along the path that Sagrario normally took. 'Fairly quickly the family sought the help of neighbours, who organized themselves and began a search in the desert where other victims had been found.'[71] The family and neighbours had been searching for two weeks when word came that a body had been found in the desert area called Loma Blanca. Sagrario's mother, Paula, and her brother, Juan, went to the police station on May 1 to identify the body. The 'young woman's body was clothed [in] a company smock with the name Sagrario embroidered on it' and despite the level of decomposition it was ascertained that she had been stabbed five times and strangled. The police thought that Sagrario had probably been raped 'but her body was too decomposed for them to make a definitive judgement'.[72]

Apart from rare, isolated exceptions, there was no attempt by 'officials', that is individual people, at every possible level of government to bring the murderers of the girls and young women to justice. 'Officialdom', free human beings holding public office with the responsibility to protect the population, acted as one colluding collective. This colluding collective is a prime example of horrendous systemic sin. An example of an exception to this closing of ranks in collusion was Oscar Maynez Grijalva, the forensics chief and criminologist, who 'began investigating the crimes in 1994 only to have his reports consistently ignored by his superiors in the Chihuahua state attorney general's office'.[73] When he refused to obey his superiors' instruction 'to plant evidence to incriminate innocent men he began receiving death threats and was eventually forced to resign'.[74] The families of the victims of the feminicide met with a blank wall of inaction and incompetence from people at every possible level of government. Far from fighting to alleviate their suffering and bringing the perpetrators to justice, officials were the cause of the suffering of the people whom they were charged to protect.

Resistance to suffering

The beginnings of salvation in such a seeming dead-end of suffering came in resistance to that suffering, not by the people notionally charged to protect them but by the sufferers themselves and their supporters. Groups and networks formed.

70. Ibid.
71. Ibid.
72. Ibid.
73. Pineda-Madrid, *Suffering and Salvation in Ciudad Juárez*, 13.
74. Ibid., drawing on Teresa Rodríguez, Diana Montané and Lisa Pulitzer, *The Daughters of Juárez: A True Story of Serial Murder South of the Border* (New York: Atria, 2007), 39–41, 199–203, 211.

A feminist group, the *Ocho de Marzo* (8th March), was the 'first group "actively to document and denounce the violence against women in Ciudad Juárez"' when a pattern began to emerge.[75] Once the pattern in the growing number of murders of girls and young women was identified in the mid-1990s, mothers, fathers, families, friends and others who became aware of the feminicide set up networks of protesters to resist the violence and demand public accountability. In 2001 the circle of resistance widened with the increasing involvement of society, and the protesters turned to 'performance activism' which took the form of rituals and dramas scheduled on seasonal days such as *Dia de los Muertos* (1 November), International Women's Day (8 March), International Day for the Elimination of Violence against Women (25 November) and Valentine's Day (14 February). By these means the parents, and their supporters (women and men), in solidarity, enacted resistance to suffering in public space, in the streets of Ciudad Juárez. Salvation was to be found by action in solidarity with fellow sufferers and empathizers, not simply in church but in the world itself: *salus in mundo*. The active resistance to the suffering gives powerful and full witness to God's opposition to suffering, the opposition that Schillebeeckx so strongly affirms: 'The Jewish-Christian tradition defines God as pure positivity; in other words, it rejects all names and images of God which injure and enslave human beings instead of liberating them.'[76] God the Creator's love is for the whole of his creation and all its people. He wills salvation, full life and flourishing, for everyone in the world. However, the absolute saving presence of God confessed by believers 'is itself as such simply an offer and a gift; by virtue of that it is not yet his presence, endorsed, received and welcomed'.[77] Schillebeeckx writes that salvation is not something that happens to a person as a passive recipient but that it is appropriated as an experienced reality. The women who protest against the feminicide are, in their united resistance, appropriating God's offer of salvation. They become channels of God's salvation, both receiving and imparting it. They started their public resistance to suffering by breaking the reign of terror that the murderers and their accomplices held over them. To do that required courage and they gave courage to one another. Schillebeeckx wrote about God's gift of courage in a Eucharistic prayer which he composed, and how it enables people to give themselves to each other: 'We remember that wherever your Jesus came, [people] rediscovered their humanity, and so were filled with new riches, so that they, given new courage in their lives, could give themselves to one another.'

The women's processions and performances in protest against the violence of the feminicide were public acts, outside the confines of home and church. As one mother of a missing daughter said,

---

75. Pineda-Madrid, *Suffering and Salvation in Ciudad Juárez*, 99, drawing on Mark Ensalaco, 'Murder in Ciudad Juárez: A Parable of Women's Struggle for Human Rights', *Violence against Women*, 12:5 (May 2006): 428.

76. Schillebeeckx, *Church*, 73 [75].

77. Schillebeeckx, *JWC*, 8.

When we go out on the streets, we spread our testimony to stop young girls from dying, right? We have to make young girls aware of this to prevent it. Going out on the streets, screaming out their names … we feel like we are actually doing something to find them, that we are fighting [against the evil suffering of feminicide], and that we won't stop until we find them.[78]

They were and are implementing and appropriating the first stages of God's salvation in the world itself, in this case, in the streets of Ciudad Juárez. Their screams of protest, their fight against the suffering of feminicide and their determination not to give up embody God's attitude to suffering. Jesus did not specifically and formally address structures but 'the closest [he] comes to [doing so] are his diatribes against Pharisees and lawyers who have gone too far in yoking simple people with burdens of religious legality without ever acting to ease their lot'.[79] God is a God of pure positivity and in human flesh Jesus acted and protested so firmly against the oppression they caused that the Pharisees and chief priests did away with him.[80] Likewise for the women of Juárez, in the liberation of protesting publicly against their suffering came risk and danger. The women faced retaliation: 'While the identity of the perpetrators is not entirely clear, many of those who stood up to them have been threatened and, in several cases, killed.'[81] When, in 2002, the marchers reached the city limits of Ciudad Juárez towards the end of their major 230 mile march from Chihuahua city to the Paso del Norte International Bridge in Ciudad Juárez, a walk which symbolized the Israelites' walk from the slavery of Egypt to freedom, 'they were met by a group of "political thugs" who attempted to intimidate the women by pushing some of them to the ground and denying them the right to march into the city of Juárez'.[82] According to Diana Washington Valdez, 'Several men who accompanied the women intervened. They created a physical wedge between the two groups, and that permitted the marchers to continue into Juárez without further problems.'[83]

The message of the processions and performances of the women of Juárez is clear: It is 'Not one more!' to the killing of their daughters; it is a 'No!' to the intolerable impunity of the perpetrators and a 'No!' to the corruption of the police and the civic authorities. It is also a 'Yes!' to accountability of the police and civic authorities, a 'Yes!' to bringing the perpetrators to justice and a 'Yes!' to making Ciudad Juárez a safe place. From the start of their processions and performances

---

78. Perla Janina Reyes Loya, whose daughter Jocelyn Calderón Reyes, thirteen, disappeared on 30 December 2012. She is still missing.

79. McManus, *Unbroken Communion*, 132.

80. Schillebeeckx, '[Jesus'] suffering and death were consequences of the conflict aroused during his life' and, quoting Mk 11.18, 'It is not the Pharisees and Herodians but in particular "the high priests and scribes" who contemplate destroying Jesus.' *Jesus*, 263–4 [295].

81. Pineda-Madrid, *Suffering and Salvation in Ciudad Juárez*, 105.

82. Ibid., 102.

83. Valdez, *Killing Fields*, 74–5.

of protest against their suffering, the women have expressed the negativity of their suffering and the contrast to that negativity visually. They have taken the central symbol of Christianity, the cross, and used two colours, black and pink. The crosses they have carried, painted and planted on the sites of the murders of their daughters have been either pure black or pure pink. They are profoundly religious symbols used in a way that strikingly develops and reflects both Schillebeeckx's method and his ideas of the cross and theology of salvation. Schillebeeckx writes, 'religious belief seeks to rescue us from this fatal experience' of human beings' 'theoretical and practical failure in the face of evil and suffering', by

> giving our action new meaning by breaking its impotence in the light of a new possibility from God: thanks to the proclamatory reminiscence of Jesus as the story of a crucified man who is now alive, through whom a future is given to those who have come to grief in history.[84]

The 'proclamatory reminiscence of Jesus as the story of a crucified man who is now alive, through whom a future is given to those who have come to grief' is powerful. The black and pink crosses of the women of Ciudad Juárez do not have the figure of the crucified Christ on them. They are blank, although the pink ones often have the name of a murdered victim painted on the crossbar. Despite the militarized use of the cross by Constantine and the Crusaders, the Christian connotation of a cross is Jesus Christ's suffering. In Roman times crucifixion was considered so cruel and degrading that Roman citizens were exempt from it. It was reserved for slaves, who in Roman law were defined as property not persons, for criminals and for those of the lowest social status. Martin Hengel argues that this form of torture and execution was used primarily as a deterrent. The cross is a powerful metaphor for the suffering of the girls and women of Ciudad Juárez. Like Jesus, the women who have been murdered are without the protection of citizenship and, like slaves, they have been treated as disposable as though they are no more than things. They have been crucified. One mother 'described her experience of being involved in the mothers' movement as a "calvary"'.[85] The perpetrators use their killings to generate fear as a deterrent so that the families of the murdered women will not dare to challenge them or their accomplices among the police and officials in civic government. The stark black crosses of the women of Ciudad Juárez are charged with meaning: they speak of the horror of the sin and cruelty of Jesus' crucifixion and, at the same time, of the women's demand for reform in the wake of the sin and depravity of the killing of their daughters. The mothers' implicit reinterpretation is that Jesus' crucifixion was not a sacrifice of atonement but the consequence of a brutal political system and the murderous intent of malignant enemies. They know

---

84. Schillebeeckx, *Christ*, 720-1 [727-8].
85. Pineda-Madrid, *Suffering and Salvation in Ciudad Juárez*, 104, quoting Camacho, 'Ciudadana X', 33-4.

only too well that the tortured deaths of their own daughters are the consequence of brutal political systems and the actions of violent murderers.

While one woman explained 'that black stood for death', the colour of the pink crosses stands 'for the promise of life and youth'.[86] The pink in juxtaposition with the black is a visual representation of Schillebeeckx's idea of negative experiences of contrast. Nothing can undo the fact of a person's murder. The untold suffering of the young women who met death by torture and murder can never be undone. On the other hand, the vocal or stifled cries of the women and girls who were killed, who screamed out against the evil actions of the killers, have been taken up by their mothers and communities in active resistance against their suffering, sometimes in actual screams naming their daughters in the streets of Ciudad Juárez as described by Perla Janina Reyes Loya.[87] When a cross is black it speaks of the bleakness and unfathomable cruelty of the killing of a girl or a young woman and the corresponding grief of their mothers and families. When a cross is pink it sharpens the horror that a young woman, a beloved daughter, has been brutally cut down in her youth and speaks of the life that should have been. The shade of pink of the crosses 'is commonly associated with female humanity, youth and vitality, the season of spring, and the hope of a bright future'.[88] At the same time, a pink cross speaks of the fragmentary glimpses of how life might become better in contrast to what has happened. It speaks of the importance of keeping that young woman's memory alive and fresh in order that the community, in solidarity, may prevent another murder happening. For those with faith in the resurrection it points to the risen life of their daughters beyond death. In other practices of resistance, activists painted utility poles pink and tied black ribbons around them, and they painted black crosses against a large pink background on telegraph poles. When the protesters of the 230-mile-long pilgrimage-march, from Chihuahua city to the Paso del Norte International Bridge in Ciudad Juárez, arrived at the bridge, they erected a twelve-foot black cross at the start of the bridge, set against a larger pink board behind it.[89] Across the middle of the cross is a pink notice on which is written 'Ni Una [Muerte] Mas' (Not One More Death) and hammered into the pink board are large black nails each representing the death of a woman by feminicide.

86. Valdez, *Killing Fields*, 38.
87. Page 22, note 74. See note 77.
88. Pineda-Madrid, *Suffering and Salvation in Ciudad Juárez*, 114.
89. Ibid., 102, quoting Valdez, *The Killing Fields*, 75. Pilgrimages are, most commonly, although not always, journeys made by pilgrims to sacred and holy places. The pilgrimage-march from Chihuahua City to the Paso del Norte was to bring the horrors of the feminicide to the attention of a wider, international public. At the same time, the pilgrim-marchers hoped their walk would lead to freedom from slavery to the fear of feminicide, just as the ancient Israelites' walk out of Egypt led from slavery to freedom. A reversal of pilgrimage to holy places is made by Raymond Pelly in *Pilgrim to Unholy Places: Christians and Jews Re-visit the Holocaust* (Bern: Peter Lang AG, 2017) Pelly tells how he made a number of pilgrimages (1995–2008) to the extermination (and other camp) sites of the Third Reich,

Suffering and salvation in Ciudad Juárez, Pineda-Madrid and Schillebeeckx

Working inductively

Pineda-Madrid's theological study of suffering and salvation in Ciudad Juárez starts in response to a specific situation of suffering, the harrowing and unchecked violence of feminicide. The feminicide has caused and continues to cause untold suffering to the victims and their families. As a theologian Pineda-Madrid does not start her study with theodicy or a metaphysical doctrine of suffering. Rather her point of departure is inductive. She starts from the actual, concrete situation of suffering. Robert J. Schreiter points out that working inductively is Schillebeeckx's method:

> [Schillebeeckx's] method represents an inductive, rather than deductive point of departure. 'It began with an experience' is a phrase that echoes throughout his Christological writings. Even his eclectic use of different methodologies in his theology reflects the need to meet the situation on its own terms, rather than force the data into a predetermined form.[90]

He suggests that Schillebeeckx doubts that 'a great dogmatic system is possible any more. This sentiment does not grow out of … the impossibility of a plausible metaphysics ever undergirding a theological system.'[91] Rather,

> it would seem that [such doubts] represent an intuition into the basic pluralism that marked twentieth-century life and experience. For the gospel message to be heard in such a context of pluralism, it has to be able to touch the immediate and the concrete. It cannot be presumed that there is a common frame of reference.[92]

In this analysis it is not being suggested that Pineda-Madrid is consciously modelling her theology on Schillebeeckx's inductive method or, for that matter, that she is deliberately choosing to develop his theological ideas and themes. Rather, a study of her method and ideas in dialogue with the context of Ciudad Juárez discovers that both Schillebeeckx's method and ideas are apt tools with which to engage with the contemporary theological issues that the suffering in Ciudad Juárez raises. In using these ideas and method, Pineda-Madrid is developing and enriching them.

1933–45. These find expression in diary entries that describe the sites as they now are and scope the problems they raise for both Jews and Christians. The book thus places the Holocaust at the centre of Jewish–Christian dialogue.

90. Robert J. Schreiter, 'Edward Schillebeeckx: His Continuing Significance', in *The Praxis of the Reign of God: An Introduction to the Theology of* Edward *Schillebeeckx*, 2nd edn, ed. Mary Catherine Hilkert and Robert J. Schreiter (New York: Fordham University Press, 2002), 185–94 (187).

91. Ibid., 186.

92. Ibid.

Theological attitudes to suffering

Two earlier sections have touched on the theme of Schillebeeckx's choice of suffering as a common human experience from which to talk about God and his idea of negative experiences of contrast.[93] As Schillebeeckx observes, the very reason that he chose suffering as a major focus in his later theology is that it is an experience common to all humanity. Every human being experiences a natural aversion to suffering and, unless morally warped, is repelled by the suffering of others. The more grotesque the suffering inflicted on fellow human beings, the stronger the desire by others to eliminate the causes of that suffering. This is true at an anthropological level but what do Pineda-Madrid and Schillebeeckx say theologically about suffering?

Schillebeeckx takes a Christological route to suffering. He avers that God reveals himself most palpably in his humanity in Jesus and, it is in God's self-revelation in Jesus that God is seen, above all, to be opposed to suffering. As Kathleen McManus writes, 'The Jesus of the Gospels does not speculate about the origins of suffering and evil in sin but concerns himself with the concrete suffering in front of him.'[94] In his life in Jesus, God shows his nearness to be saving ('where Jesus appears, salvation begins to live'[95]) and also [his saving action] was for everyone 'made present through [Jesus'] historical life of care for his fellow men and women, without exception'.[96] He goes on to say that Jesus was little interested 'whether [a person's] suffering was the consequence of sin or was innocent suffering. He identified himself with the sufferer – *sāddīq* or not: neither piety nor lack of piety set any limits to his approach.'[97] Essential to Schillebeeckx's creation faith is belief in God the Creator who is, all the time and in every place, involved in the good and against suffering and injustice. The followers of Jesus are called to know God as a God not of the dead but of the living (Mt. 22.32), to recognize God as a God 'only of pure positivity', that is,

> By nature God promotes good and opposes evil, injustice and suffering. ... Seen in this light, for the person who believes in God the inspiration and orientation for all actions lie in a call to promote all goodness and righteousness and to oppose evil, injustice and suffering in all its forms.[98]

Pineda-Madrid as theologian plunges *in medias res*, into a critical situation of suffering in Ciudad Juárez that is part of a chain of related events. Just as Jesus concerns himself with the suffering in front of him, so Pineda-Madrid concerns herself with the suffering of the women and families caught up in the

---

93. Pages 143 and 38–9.
94. McManus, *Unbroken Communion*, 75.
95. Schillebeeckx, *Christ*, 791 [795].
96. Ibid.
97. Ibid.
98. Schillebeeckx, *GAU*, 99.

feminicide that confronts her. As a theologian her purpose, through analysis and interpretation, is to recontextualize salvation in the complexities of the context of Ciudad Juárez.

Human beings cannot be passive in the work of salvation

God's saving action or salvation is not showered upon an oblivious and passive humanity. To be sure, once they are born human beings automatically enjoy the gift of God-given biological life, but that life has to be nurtured and protected by the action of human beings in order to sustain life with the provision of food, water, clothing and (in colder climates) warmth; medicine and social structures are also necessary to protect people from disease and human violence. Activities and structures vital for the nurture and protection of human life are to be found and engaged in within any human society. But God wants to give more than physical existence to human creatures; he wants human beings to get to know him and love him. As Dorothy Jacko writes, 'Where the secular perspective sees finitude alone, faith in creation perceives finitude's ultimate source and ground, the Living God.'[99] Although the concept is somewhat elusive in Schillebeeckx, this is where what he refers to as the *surplus* becomes relevant: 'This faith perception shows that there is in creation a "surplus", something more than isolated finitude.'[100] The Jews of the Torah were open to and actively responded to God's revelation of himself. They entered into a dialectical, covenantal relationship with Yahweh. God's revelation culminated in the person of Jesus Christ, in whom his followers experienced salvation and a fullness and richness of life that comes straight from God. Jesus' followers, then and now, commit themselves, in free and conscious dependence on God, to confronting sin and suffering and to working to overcome it. As Pineda-Madrid observes, salvation, being saved from sin and suffering, begins with human beings' 'awareness of our abiding need for God'[101] and is realized in the efforts of people to alleviate, overcome and eliminate suffering. Salvation will not be achieved if people do nothing in the face of suffering. If in a situation of dire suffering men and women first have a glimmer of hope that there can be a better, contrasting situation, and they set out to realize it, they are actively appropriating salvation. By resisting the suffering that confronts them they are the human mediators of God's saving action. Schillebeeckx writes, 'The world of creation, our history within nature as an environment, is the sphere of God's saving action in and through human mediation.'[102]

---

99. Dorothy Jacko, *Salvation in the Context of Contemporary Secularized Historical Consciousness: The Later Theology of Edward Schillebeeckx*, A thesis submitted in partial fulfilment of the requirements for the degree of Doctor of Theology (Regis College, Toronto School of Theology, Toronto, Ontario, Canada, 1987), 103.
   100. Ibid., 103–4.
   101. Pineda-Madrid, *Suffering and Salvation in Ciudad Juárez*, 69.
   102. Schillebeeckx, *Church*, 12.

Pineda-Madrid's searching account and analysis of the bereaved mothers' and families' actions in Ciudad Juárez tells the story of a people determinedly 'endorsing and appropriating salvation'. If they had not risen in protest, both literally and metaphorically, the scale of the feminicide would have been altogether unchecked. As it is, in the slow and painfully achieved steps that Pineda-Madrid chronicles, the mothers, fathers, families and friends of the victims have become mediators of God's salvation through their actions. They are active in the work of salvation.

Continuity and change in understanding salvation

Central to Schillebeeckx's theology is the question of the expression and formulation of truths about reality: about God the Creator and human beings, about sin and suffering, about Jesus and the hope for and experience of salvation. In an analysis of his Christology, using the French historical–critical *Annales* model of change, it is found that change at one level may be compatible with continuity. Indeed, change may be necessary in order to give faithful expression to an unchanging reality. The theology of creation is the bedrock of Schillebeeckx's entire theology: God is Creator and Jesus Christ is the 'condensation of creation'. Central to his Christology is that those who followed and met Jesus while he was on earth experienced salvation from God in him, and subsequent generations of his followers likewise experience God's salvation in the living Christ. Drawing on his exhaustive, hermeneutical study of Jesus, Schillebeeckx emphasizes that the salvation that Jesus Christ imparts is rooted in the concrete situations of everyday life. It is not a private or merely individual affair but is concerned with relations within the community and society and only in that sense has a political dimension. This understanding of salvation diverges radically from Anselm's contribution to the doctrine of salvation, namely, his argument in *Cur Deus Homo*. Even if Schillebeeckx has a fundamental disagreement with a theological position, he tends not to take up a polar opposite position. Instead, he delves into and develops the grounds for a different perspective. In the case of atonement theory, here and there, appositely included in his writings, a trenchant, impersonal criticism of the inadequacy of atonement theory is to be found. Although the spur to this study was the need to look for a wider, and different, understanding of salvation from that provided by atonement theory, its focus has rather been to trace the evolution of Schillebeeckx's soteriological Christology.

When Pineda-Madrid is confronted by the suffering of the feminicide, she uses a social-suffering hermeneutic to try to understand what Christian salvation can mean and she scrutinizes 'the ability of Anselm's interpretation to respond to the concerns of our own time'.[103] She finds and argues that in the light of her study of the Juárez feminicide 'the paradigmatic, enduring and overriding Anselmian construal of salvation becomes far more problematic and, accordingly, less defensible'.[104] She

---

103. Pineda-Madrid, *Suffering and Salvation in Ciudad Juárez*, 70.
104. Ibid.

proceeds to make a thorough, hermeneutical appraisal of Anselm's atonement theory.[105] In her appraisal, which is both sensitive and nuanced, she reaches the conclusion that there is a need to rethink salvation.[106] In her examination of the 'relative adequacy of Anselm's *Cur Deus Homo* and the gaps generated in its wake'[107] with regard to the Ciudad Juárez feminicide, Pineda-Madrid stresses and develops Schillebeeckx's idea that the saving work of Jesus needs to be understood through a historical and faith hermeneutic of Jesus' life and the death he suffered by crucifixion, as recounted in the gospels. The significance of Jesus cannot be reduced to his death. Because *Cur Deus Homo* is ahistorical and based on an abstract theory 'the historical dimensions of Jesus' life, namely his efforts to bring about and exemplify the reign of God throughout his ministry, remain at best secondary'.[108] Bereft of Jesus' teaching, healing and challenges to oppressors, the ahistorical view of salvation through Jesus' death provides no guidance to the prophetic tension that the followers of Jesus are called to engage in from within contexts of suffering. As Pineda-Madrid remarks, 'For those who reap the benefit of the world as it is, this view of salvation [atonement theory] has marked appeal. For those on the underside of history, like the women in Juárez, it does not.'[109] Her reconstrual of salvation is a development of Schillebeeckx's soteriological Christology in which salvation is realized in a relational dialectic of prayer and social commitment, the praxis of the reign of God.

The theology of suffering and salvation in Ciudad Juárez

The situation of the feminicide in Ciudad Juárez is the *locus theologicus* in which the actions of the mothers of murdered daughters, and their families, who resist the suffering provide a pre-eminent source for the development of theological discourse on suffering and salvation. In Juárez the parents and families are both the victims of an agonizing bereavement caused by the heinous crimes committed against their daughters and sisters, and they are also the people who rise in resistance against the structural sin and corruption that lie at the root of those crimes. As victims, who was there to comfort them? Their lot was like that of Mary, mother of Jesus, who stood powerlessly, which is not to say with resignation or acceptance, at the foot of her Son's cross while he died from crucifixion. The gospels record St John as standing with Mary in her suffering. Who stood and stand with the bereaved mothers? What constitutes salvation for the bereaved parents and families of Ciudad Juárez? God's salvation is found to be mediated through each other and their neighbours and the wider community. God's positive

---

105. See *Suffering and Salvation in Ciudad Juárez*, Chapter 3, 'Anselm and Salvation', 69–95.
106. Ibid.
107. Pineda-Madrid, *Suffering and Salvation in Ciudad Juárez*, 86.
108. Ibid., 91.
109. Ibid., 92.

hope for something better is nurtured in the community. The societal dimension of salvation is experienced. The suffering of the feminicide is no longer a matter for an individual mother or family, but it is pain borne in solidarity by everyone in the community and beyond by, for example, journalists, theologians and aid workers. The pain, at both an individual and a societal level, is made public, its causes dissected in all their ramifications and voicing the pain leads to opposition to the suffering and the hope for a better situation.

The fearlessness of the bereaved women and families, who resist the perpetrators and the colluders in the feminicide, is a clear reflection of the fearless challenges of Jesus to the scribes and Pharisees who lorded over people by legalistic and life-denying insistence on keeping to the regulations. The women are bringing in God's kingdom *sequela Jesu*. They are exercising prophecy in calling out the abhorrent deeds of those who cause the suffering of the feminicide. They are subverting a status quo in which governments, drug dealers, police, lawyers and civil servants have exercised a reign of terror with impunity either by acting or failing to act (a few people in these latter professions have been brave and honourable exceptions). Just as Jesus sought the liberation from oppression that God wants for all human beings, so the women of Ciudad Juárez seek God's liberation from the paralysing fear of murder that takes hold in a feminicide. Just as Jesus left no theological writings, these women do not write theology, rather they do it. In her probing and compassionate theological analysis Pineda-Madrid shows how these women raise prophetic voices, subvert the status quo and embody the hope of realizing God's kingdom, *sequela Jesu*, all themes central to Schillebeeckx's Christology.

Chapter 8

SCHILLEBEECKX'S IDEAS AND METHODS IN DIALOGUE WITH NEW CONTEXTS: THE CATHOLIC DIALOGUE SCHOOL IN FLANDERS

In this chapter a study is made of the project of the Catholic Dialogue School as described by Lieven Boeve. It is examined from three perspectives: first, cultural context as constituent of theology; secondly, recontextualization and tradition; and, thirdly, the dialogical and relational dialectic in the Catholic Dialogue School.

What is theology?

Posing this question at the start of the final chapter rather than in the first chapter may seem perverse. The reason, however, is to recapitulate what Schillebeeckx understood the activity of theology to be, and to compare his understanding with that of Lieven Boeve. From there an analysis is made of the rich development of Schillebeeckx's ideas and methods in Boeve's project of the Catholic Dialogue School.

For Schillebeeckx faith is the sine qua non of theology. It is an 'inner demand of theology'.[1] He says that theology begins with reflection and that the reflection which is inherent in the life of faith can take two forms. The first is 'the spontaneous, undeliberate reflection on faith which all Christians pursue' and the second is when that spontaneous reflection is extended to a 'deliberate, methodical, and systematic reflection, [which] is precisely theology'.[2] William L. Portier writes that Schillebeeckx 'rarely addresses the methodological question that so exercises contemporary theology' and considers that this may be 'perhaps because of his long tenure in the state-supported Catholic faculty of theology at Nijmegen [1957–1982], [where] he has not had to face the question of theology's legitimacy in the academy'.[3] Portier goes on to say that Schillebeeckx 'is therefore quite

---

1. Schillebeeckx, *R&T*, 71. Cf. page 90.
2. Ibid., 73.
3. William L. Portier, 'Interpretation and Method', in *The Praxis of the Reign of God: An Introduction to the theology of Edward Schillebeeckx*, 2nd edn, ed. Mary Catherine Hilkert and Robert Schreiter (New York: Fordham University Press, 2002), 22.

comfortable describing himself in traditional terms, as a believer who reflects. His methodological interludes often contain variations on the Anselmian *fides quaerens intellectum* ("faith seeking understanding"). He feels no need to offer a reasoned defence of faith's constitutive role in theology.[4] That said, however, in his later writings Schillebeeckx became increasingly aware of the historical nature of human existence and was responsive to what he perceived as a crisis of faith among people who lived in societies being changed by forceful currents of secularization and pluralization such as in the United States.[5] In the long run Schillebeeckx is not concerned 'to unravel philosophical[-theological] enigmas once and for all. His impelling ambition is at once more modest and pastoral. His works are driven by a concern to help people who find Christian faith either incredible, meaningless or destructive.'[6] He says that in 'the critical and constructive aspects of my theological thought, I have sought to bear testimony to others about the hope and joy within me', a theological task in which he was 'a truly happy man'.[7] It was St Peter's exhortation, 'Always be prepared to make a defence to anyone who calls you to account for the hope that is in you' (Pet. 3.15b), that sustained him throughout his life as a theologian.

As for Schillebeeckx, so for Boeve, faith is the raison d'être of theology. In his essay *Christian Faith in a Postmodern Context*, he writes,

> Theology is the result of what Anselm of Canterbury described as fides quaerens intellectum: 'faith seeking understanding' or better still, 'the one who participates in reality as a believer wants to make his or her faith a source of insight in order to arrive at a Christian understanding of reality'.[8]

Closely echoing Schillebeeckx's description of the theologian's task, he writes, 'In a systematic and plausible manner, the theologian endeavours to put the life of faith into words and to express his or her participation as a Christian believer in reality.'[9]

A key difference with regard to the theology of Schillebeeckx and of Boeve, however, is the context in which the theology of each is embedded. Schillebeeckx was born in 1914 in Belgium where, until more or less the middle of the twentieth century, there was a culture and society with a 'nearly total Catholic horizon of meaning'.[10] Boeve, on the other hand, was born in Belgium in the 1960s, precisely

---

4. Ibid., 23.
5. Kennedy, *Schillebeeckx*, 43.
6. Ibid., 34.
7. Schillebeeckx, *HT*, 81.
8. Lieven Boeve, *Interrupting Tradition: An Essay on Christian Faith in a Postmodern Context*, trans. Brian Doyle, Louvain Theological and Pastoral Monographs 30 (Louvain: Peeters Press, 2003), 24–5 (henceforth *Interrupting Tradition*).
9. Ibid., 25.
10. Lieven Boeve, *Theology at the Crossroads of University, Church and Society: Dialogue, Difference and Catholic Identity* (London: T&T Clark, 2016, paperback edn, 2018), 34 (henceforth *Crossroads*).

at a time when Schillebeeckx was punctuating his writings with three words with reference to the radical cultural changes occurring at that time in Europe and America: 'crisis, newness and change'.[11] By 2000 Boeve, in his post as professor of Systematic Theology at the Katholieke Universiteit Leuven, set up a research group *Theology in a Postmodern Context*. As Boeve explains, theology's plausibility and relevance are no longer commonly evident in the 'current (generally) post-Christian and post-secular society' and its place and role in the university and church are challenged.[12] Gone is the 'nearly total Catholic horizon of meaning'[13] of Schillebeeckx's earlier life.

In what follows a Schillebeeckian prism is used to test whether and how his approach and ideas are relevant and can be developed in a contemporary situation. In the first section, an examination is made of how Boeve understands context as constitutive of theology (contemporary context understood as history in the making), an idea that was a central element of Schillebeeckx's thinking. In the second section Boeve is found to give a fully developed, concrete example of theological recontextualization, a process which Schillebeeckx refers to as reactivation of tradition. The third section first shows that a central theme of Schillebeeckx's creation faith, namely that God's continuing revelation is a dialogue between Creator and creatures in every sociocultural and historical context, is the dialogical foundation of the Catholic Dialogue School. Secondly, it identifies how a particular pattern of thought and discourse, relational dialectic, which is the underlying pattern of Schillebeeckx's theological thought, is brought to the fore by Boeve in framing the method for dialogue in the project of the Catholic Dialogue School.

Cultural context as constitutive of theology

Like the voices of a two-part musical invention, theology and the contexts within which it develops interweave. The first voice sings the melody of theological thought with the accompanying context in counterpoint. Sometimes the voices switch, and the second voice, context, sounds strongly and requires a contrapuntal response from the theology.[14] Pivotal to both Schillebeeckx's and Boeve's theology is that they engage in dialogue with their respective contexts. The interplay between theology, indeed between all human knowledge, and historical context

---

11. Kennedy, *Schillebeeckx*, 34.
12. Boeve, *Crossroads*, 54.
13. Ibid., 34.
14. 'Bach ordinarily presents his material in invertible counterpoint, where either voice can sit above the other. The crucial factor of [the analogy] here is the mutually [engaging] nature of the dialogue where no one part (of the two) is occluded by the other, but also not uninflected.' Edward Higginbottom, Conductor, (email, 20 May 2021), commenting on the analogy.

was strikingly identified for Schillebeeckx by the Dominican, Marie-Dominique Chenu. It was through Chenu's lecture course on Thomas Aquinas' theology and the medieval historical context of the Middle Ages at the École des Hautes Études of the Sorbonne[15] (during Schillebeeckx's year at Le Saulchoir, near Paris, from 1945 to 1946) that he learnt to appreciate theological texts and problems from a historical perspective. Schillebeeckx avers that '[The human person] is a being caught up in history.'[16] Just as the *nature* of a person 'is itself a history, a historical event, and is not simply *given*',[17] so too the nature of communities, societies and peoples is that they are histories in the making and, with the passing of time, their histories are recorded. The idea that 'the *nature* of a person is itself history' derives ultimately from Christian creation faith. It points to the underlying awareness that Schillebeeckx has of God's creative purpose: God invites human beings, in the contingency of their free will and in the contingency of the creation, to enter into covenantal relationship with Godself, in order to work in the Spirit of Christ to build a world in which the values of God's kingdom are lived out. Human beings both shape and are shaped by their contexts in time and place. God's self-revelation is through the concrete events and experiences of history. A fundamental principle of Schillebeeckx was to take revelation seriously as a historical event: God made, and makes, Godself known through human beings and as a human being (the Incarnation). For Schillebeeckx 'the secular event becomes the material of "the word of God".'[18] In other words, God reveals Godself through the concrete circumstances of our daily life provided we humans are receptive and that we open ourselves to God's revelation. Unless history is integrated into the practice of theology, theology remains a meta-historical system rather than an incarnated faith.[19] Chenu set about 'introducing history into the [medieval and Thomistic] theological endeavour as a fully-fledged partner in terms of both content and methodology'.[20] For him 'the historical sciences and the historical-critical method are referred to … as the *ancillae* (handmaids) of theology'.[21]

Whereas the material of historical study relates to past time, a hermeneutical study may give history its relevance to the present. Crucial to analysis of history is an understanding of historical context. Through Chenu, Schillebeeckx placed theological reflection in its historical context.[22] An analysis of historical context

15. Kennedy, *Schillebeeckx*, 22.
16. Schillebeeckx, *Christ*, 726 [732].
17. Ibid.
18. Schillebeeckx, *Church*, 6 [7].
19. Jürgen Mettepenningen, *Nouvelle Théologie New Theology: Inheritor of Modernism, Precursor of Vatican II* (London: T&T Clark, 2010), 10.
20. Ibid., 49.
21. Ibid., 53.
22. Kennedy points out that while it was through Chenu that Schillebeeckx placed theological reflection in a historical context, it was through De Petter that Schillebeeckx placed theological reflection in a human-experiential context. *Schillebeeckx*, 22.

is necessary for an appreciation of the way theologians of earlier epochs articulate and rearticulate statements about reality in response to the intellectual and social changes of their contemporary cultural context. In the analysis in earlier chapters,[23] the threefold model of change of the *Annales* school of French historiography was used to demonstrate Schillebeeckx's insight into the fact that, over the centuries, it may be necessary to rearticulate statements of theological understanding, in order to ensure faithfulness to the truth of the unchanging realities that they attempt to describe. Borgman writes,

> In the portrait [of Thomas Aquinas] that Chenu painted of him with much accuracy, Thomas was described as a theologian who tried to express the faith for his own time on the basis of the contemporary situation. By doing this, according to Chenu he performed the task which as a theologian par excellence he had to do. In this sense, for him Thomas Aquinas was a model theologian precisely as a thinker bound to medieval conditions.[24]

Schillebeeckx was above all impressed by how Chenu, in his turn, 'supremely embodied the powerful, living and open confrontation between Christian faith and contemporary culture' and 'by the way in which from his view of theology Chenu engaged concretely with critical initiatives, movements and (church) groups'.[25] At this point it is worth questioning (and bearing in mind) the choice of the word 'confrontation' used here. 'Confrontation' normally has a suggestion of hostility in the meeting between two parties. Need confrontation necessarily be hostile? Or can it be creative, powerful and effectively challenging in *dialogue* with the social and political movements of the day?

Two striking examples of Schillebeeckx's engagement with the cultural context of the faith crisis of the 1960s in Europe and the United States are his response to the book *Honest to God* by John A. T. Robinson, the Anglican Bishop of Woolwich, and his response to the question 'Is Christ really God?' that was repeatedly addressed to him on his lecture tours in the United States in the late 1960s. Robinson's book was published in 1963 during a period of radical social and cultural change and rapid secularization. Schillebeeckx was struck by the outstanding success of the book[26] and considered that the reason for its success was because Robinson expressed 'explosively' 'what a great many people felt', namely, that Christian 'belief, particularly where intellectuals [were] concerned, cannot be maintained within the framework of the old vision and experience'.[27] In the book Robinson quotes liberally from 'Paul Tillich, Dietrich Bonhoeffer and Rudolf Bultmann to

---

23. Chapters 3 and 4.
24. Borgman, *Edward Schillebeeckx*, 104.
25. Ibid., 105.
26. A total of 250,000 copies were sold in five editions within the space of a month, with edition after edition in several languages to follow. Schillebeeckx, *G&M*, 85.
27. Schillebeeckx, *G&M*, 87.

argue that the imagery in which God was presented made God unreal to people of a secular, scientific world'.[28] Schillebeeckx wrote two articles, published in 1963, in which he made a serious examination of *Honest to God* and in which he attempted 'to give a personal view of the problem of "Christian secularity" within the life of grace'.[29] The purpose of mentioning Robinson's book and Schillebeeckx's articles in connection with it is not to examine Schillebeeckx's critique of *Honest to God* but to note his immediate engagement with the public debate it caused. He wrote,

> The present reaction to secularization (which has been facilitated by our own outmoded theology, and above all by our factual experience of Christianity) is salutary – on condition that we keep our ears attuned to the word of God and remain humble towards his revelation of truth as an existential and saving revelation.[30]

By the mid-1960s the sentiments expressed in Robinson's book were freely floating in the streams of secularization. Believers found their faith radically challenged and hence the question that people asked Schillebeeckx on his US lecture tours, 'Is Christ really God?'.[31] Schillebeeckx responded to his audiences' concerns about the challenges to Christian faith in the context of secularization and was repeatedly asked whether the lectures he was giving would be published so that they could be read at leisure.[32] The lectures of his tour from November to December 1967 have been published in *God the Future of Man* and all but one of the chapters deal with secularization from different points of view:

> The theme of … the lectures was to a great extent that of religion and secularization, viewed from various vantage points – secularization and speaking of God, secularization and the problem of the Church's liturgy, secularization and the Church's new understanding of herself arising from this (the Church as dialogue) and, finally, secularization and the future of mankind on earth seen in the light of the eschaton (the Church and social politics).[33]

By 1978 rather than referring to the contemporary context as 'secularized', Schillebeeckx was describing it as 'the ever changing contemporary situation' and 'a modern world in which religion is no longer the cement of society, and is therefore no longer reinforced by social and cultural life'.[34] Schillebeeckx says that

---

28. See http://trinitycollegechapel.com>memorials>brasses.

29. Edward Schillebeeckx, 'Evangelische zuiverheid en menselijke waarachtigheid', *Tijdschrift voor Theologie*, 3 (1963): 283–325, and 'Herinterpretatie van het geloof in het licht van de seculariteit'. *Tijdschrift voor Theologie*, 4 (1964): 109–50.

30. Schillebeeckx, *G&M*, 94.

31. Edward Schillebeeckx, 'Catholic Life in the United States', *Worship*, 42 (1968): 134–49.

32. Schillebeeckx, *GFoM*, xvii.

33. Ibid.

34. Schillebeeckx, *IR*, 4.

before delving into the question of 'speaking of and to God in a secularized society' a distinction between two levels of the whole process of secularization needs to be made.[35] On the one hand, it is necessary 'to consider the process of secularization as a socio-cultural and historical phenomenon, in which the world and human society are conceived within the rational sphere of understanding'.[36] On the other hand, he writes 'secularity is interpreted as atheism and is, furthermore, interpreted as such *because* many think that faith in God remains an obstacle to secularization in the socio-cultural and historical sense'.[37] (This latter interpretation of secularity, it will be seen below, is disproved in the findings of reports on *European Values Studies*.)

Boeve proactively engages with the changing cultural and sociopolitical contexts in Europe in the late twentieth and early twenty-first century and makes an in-depth theological analysis of the sociocultural context, an approach that could be said to be a development of Schillebeeckx's more reactive engagement with the context of his time. Boeve examines what is entailed in the process of secularization as a sociocultural and historical phenomenon and analyses its consequences for university, church and society. Theology's credibility and relevance, which formerly shared in what was the little questioned character of a Christian horizon of meaning, are tested under the pressures of secularization and pluralization. He concludes that 'because of the processes of secularization and pluralization, the situation of Christian faith, and thus also of the church, is thoroughly changed in Europe'.[38] Boeve draws on the Belgian results of four reports that span twenty-eight years (1981 to 2009) that were part of the *European Values Study* to analyse cultural change.[39] In the research findings that relate particularly to religious matters he finds that

> in a relatively short period of time, Belgium has secularized and evolved from a culture and society with a nearly total Catholic horizon of meaning to a situation where this horizon determines to a much lesser degree the identity construction of individuals and groups.[40]

Of key importance to note is the fact that in a culture that changes from being one where there has been a nearly totally shared horizon of Christian meaning, to a new situation of secularization and pluralization, identity construction becomes a task for individuals and groups. The title of the third report, *Verloren Zekerheid (Lost Certainty)*, based on research from 1999 and published in 2000, indicates that 'classic patterns of identity and values formation' no longer continued and

35. Schillebeeckx, *GFoM*, 41.
36. Ibid.
37. Ibid., 41–2.
38. Boeve, *Crossroads*, 3.
39. Ibid., 33–8.
40. Ibid., 34.

the result was that people were uncertain of how to define their identity in terms of values. Critically, in the emerging sociocultural context, 'forming one's own identity has become an assignment'.[41] The picture that emerges is not simple. For example, the *European Values Study* of 2009 shows that '*unchurched does not mean by definition unbelieving or non-religious*, and that a distinction cannot be made between first generation and further-generation-unchurched persons on this point'.[42] While 'one-fifth of the unchurched indicated they are religious ... one quarter described themselves as convinced atheists', and

> Religious unchurched people are sensitive to the spiritual (81 per cent), say they have contact with the divine apart from churches (70 per cent); experience moments of meditation or prayer (54 per cent); and they attach importance to religious services at birth (60 per cent), marriage (55 per cent) and death (69 per cent).[43]

Boeve also draws attention to a paradox. On the one hand there has been a conspicuous drop in trust of the church as an institution (according to numbers from a survey conducted before the outbreak of the paedophilia scandal in 2010)[44] while, on the other hand, education, including Catholic education, has repeatedly scored first among the institutions in terms of public confidence. In surveys conducted in 1990, 1999 and 2009, 'the percentage of the population [in Belgium] expressing confidence in education increased from 72 per cent to 85 per cent'.[45]

Schillebeeckx had described the experience of encountering the effects of secularization as difficult: 'I have been brought face to face with the unmistakable difficulties of contemporary Christians in a "secularized world"', in 1960s America and earlier, at a personal level, with those who were called 'death of God theologians'.[46] He wrote that 'theology cannot be simply a question of scholarship pursued within the walls of one's study, it can only be built up in dialogue with one's fellow [men and women], a dialogue which involves our whole lives, whether we shut ourselves off in anxiety or think together with others in hoping and seeking openness'.[47] Schillebeeckx wrote those words in the late 1960s and Boeve takes up the baton fifty years later. In the second decade of the third millennium he describes the contemporary European[48] culture in several ways: post-Christian, postmodern

---

41. Ibid.
42. Ibid., 39.
43. Ibid.
44. Boeve, *Crossroads*, 38.
45. Ibid., 8.
46. Schillebeeckx, *GFoM*, 101 [169].
47. Ibid., 102 [170].
48. There are obviously variations between European countries but the findings of the *European Values Study* with regard to Belgium are broadly true for other European countries. The situations in the Unites States and Canada are appreciably different from but have much in common with Europe.

and post-secular. These descriptors can be, and are, daunting to Christians, on two counts, first, because of the speed of the sociocultural processes of recent decades that have brought about and continue to bring about changes to the context and, secondly, because of the detraditionalization, individualization and pluralization that they entail. Boeve defines detraditionalization as 'the fact that traditions are no longer self-evident',[49] or, more fully, as 'the process by which traditions, religious as well as other traditions (gender, family, professional context), no longer naturally transfer from one generation to another – a process that presses ahead in our society independent of individual preferences and decisions'.[50] He defines individualization as the 'other side of detraditionalization … the structural given that identity is no longer assigned, but that it should be actively taken on in increasing measure'[51] or, more briefly, the fact 'that identity formation requires the individual's choice and continuing effort'.[52] He defines pluralization as 'that there are a number of traditions, religions and philosophies at one's disposal to give shape to one's identity'.[53] He goes on to say that in a plural society no single religious tradition or ideological position can automatically claim the observer's position:

> All positions are participants and, as such, relate to one another. Pluralization implies that each identity is structurally challenged to conceive of itself in relation to difference and otherness – especially to the effect the other truth claims have on its own claim.[54]

Boeve emphasizes the distinction between traditionalization, individualization and pluralization, which are 'the *sociocultural processes* that have *structurally* changed – and continue to change – our culture and society'[55] and the possible reactions to them which are expressed by the same words with the different suffix, '-ism'. These '-isms' are (neo)traditionalism, individualism and pluralism which each have negative connotations. 'Traditionalism' denotes a 'reaction against the rationalism and individualism encouraged by the Enlightenment. … The traditionalists maintained that a revelation was granted to humanity at its origins and then transmitted in an unbroken way through subsequent history.'[56] The First Vatican Council (1869–70) repudiated the traditionalists' claim that 'knowledge of God can only come through [disincarnated] revelation and our faithful assent to

---

49. Boeve, *Crossroads*, 8.
50. Ibid., 44.
51. Ibid.
52. Ibid., 8.
53. Boeve, *Crossroads*, 8.
54. Ibid., 44.
55. Ibid., 43.
56. Gerald O'Collins, S.J. and Edward G. Farrugia, S.J., *A Concise Dictionary of Theology* (London: HarperCollins, 1991), 247.

it'.[57] One response to secularization may be traditionalism or neo-traditionalism which is a disregard of God's continuing revelation of Godself through the changing contexts of human history. 'Individualism' commonly denotes 'self-centred feeling or conduct as a principle; [it is] a mode of life in which the individual pursues his [or her] own ends or follows out his [or her] own ideas'.[58] In other words it is egoism rather than independent critical thinking. Pluralism (as opposed to pluralization) is a philosophical term denoting a theory or system that recognizes more than one ultimate principle yet in everyday language means 'relativistic': that is, 'there are no absolute truths or values but they are all *determined* by particular periods, cultures, societies and people'.[59] From this comparison of the -ization and -ism forms of the words 'tradition', 'individual' and 'plural' it can be seen how there might be confusion between the two. The distinction between them is crucial.

Boeve as a theologian unflinchingly faces the contemporary context in Europe, analysing theology's changed place and status. He finds that there is a 'thorough ambiguity' in the 'strange combination of ideas' which characterize the post-Christian, post-secular religious situation in Belgium. He writes,

> On the one hand, in the public sphere, a kind of post-Christian default-position of quasi-neutrality – influenced by secularization – is promoted. On the other hand, in the framework of the so-called multicultural society, a kind of post-secular pluralism of philosophical and religious convictions is avowed.[60]

He observes that the ambiguity arises, for example, when adherents of religions or ideologies want their convictions to matter in the public forum or, conversely, when individuals' and communities' ideological concepts or behaviour appear to disturb the quasi-neutral default-position. As he goes on to say, 'This also becomes clear as defenders of the quasi-neutral position react with incomprehension and even outrage when the specific value-laden presuppositions of this default-position are questioned, and its often soft-secularist character is criticized. Neutral, is, after all, not really neutral.'[61]

The process of Christian theology being pushed to the margins of university, church and society as a result of the changes to the European sociocultural context in the last few decades had already started in Schillebeeckx's lifetime but has gathered pace. Boeve argues, however, that theology can be credible and relevant 'when it takes its place starting from the margin, at the crossroads of university, church and society'.[62] In making this argument, Boeve is reading the

---

57. Ibid.
58. *The Oxford English Dictionary*, ed. James A. H. Murray and others, 2nd edn. Prepared by J. A. Simpson and E. S. C. Weiner, 20 vols (Oxford: Clarendon Press, 2004), xviii.
59. O'Collins and Farrugia, *A Concise Dictionary of Theology*, 203.
60. Boeve, *Crossroads*, 4.
61. Ibid., 4.
62. Ibid., 1.

present situation as a religious situation. Just as one of the basic convictions of Schillebeeckx's creation faith was of the absolute and saving presence of God in the world, a presence to be made known in the followers of Jesus (theologians among them), wherever they may be and whatever their unfolding history might be, so Boeve sees precisely the difficult place in the margins to which theology has been pushed as the very position from which it 'can make a contextually relevant and theologically credible contribution ... at the crossroads of each of these domains'.[63] He stresses the interconnectedness of theology's roles in these three domains: if theology's role in one of the domains suffers, it will also suffer in the other two. The world is God's and wherever there are people, however challenging or threatening the circumstances may be, there is the opportunity for seeking and talking about God and making God's salvation in Jesus Christ known. Confronted with the fact of sociocultural change and recognizing that all theology is by necessity practised within a context, the next step is to work out how to respond to the ensuing pressures that challenge theology. Boeve names theology's task of reflecting on 'the internal intelligibility and external plausibility of the Christian faith' in relation to challenging contextual changes as *recontextualization*.[64] In the example of the rise of religious studies in the university, which is discussed below, it will be seen that recontextualization does not mean selling out to the culture, retreating from the world or overthrowing tradition.

Recontextualization and tradition

On the occasion of his retirement from his post as professor of Dogmatics and the History of Theology at Nijmegen, Schillebeeckx gave a lecture in which he spoke about the theological interpretation of faith or theological hermeneutics. He said that a hermeneutic or actualizing theology, if it wants to remain true to the gospel of Jesus, has to deal with at least three problem areas. The first such area is that Christian theology concerns what Schillebeeckx calls 'two poles': tradition and situation. He says, 'Because of this polarity between old and new, theology is essentially a *hermeneutic process* of actualising the religious substance of both the Torah and the Gospels as we know them.'[65] The second problem area concerns the nature of theology and the task of theologians and leads Schillebeeckx to observe that theologians are 'social actors' and a salient question is, 'What is the theologian's position in society, in the university, the churches or Christian grassroots communities in everyday life?'[66] He adds that if fundamental changes in the sociocultural pattern and thought categories make it difficult for Christians to deal with the concrete form of their faith, then 'a historical break with the cultural

---

63. Ibid., 10.
64. Ibid., 2.
65. Schillebeeckx, *Essays*, 52.
66. Ibid., 53.

forms of that religion could be the only possible way to maintain Christian continuity and identity, the sole adapted version of evangelically accurate, actualised theology of the Christian religious tradition'.[67] The third problem area that Schillebeeckx notes is that 'while *what* is actualised merits great emphasis in theology, it becomes a living revelation only in present-day religious interpretation and corresponding praxis. We cannot "passively" receive our faith from others.'[68]

To use the analogy of mathematics as pure and applied, Schillebeeckx does 'pure' theology when he talks of the 'two poles' of Christian tradition and current situation, whereas Boeve not only does the 'pure' theology but he also applies it to the Flemish-speaking part of Belgium, one of the specific sociocultural contexts of northern Europe, and develops it. Where Schillebeeckx asks the salient question, 'What is the theologian's position in society, in the university, the churches or Christian grassroots communities in everyday life?',[69] Boeve answers the question: theology is at the margin of university, church and society, and he proposes that 'rather than abandoning the crossroads [where university, church and society meet], it should learn to re-examine its place and contribution precisely *from the margin* in each of these domains'.[70] Schillebeeckx's third problem area of how to 'convert' theology into corresponding Christian praxis will be looked at in the section following this one.

Boeve writes that 'since its inception theology as a method develops through contextualization. Christian faith is always thoroughly embedded in a specific historical context. ... When the context changes, the contextually embedded form of Christian faith comes under pressure'.[71] Furthermore, Boeve writes,

> Recontextualization is a continuous, never-finished theological programme and necessitates a consciously undertaken dialogue with the contextual critical consciousness. This consciousness, in turn, is an expression of the reflexive potential present in the context, of its sensitivities, attitudes, thinking patterns and ambiguities.[72]

Each specific historical context in which there are Christians necessarily contributes to the manner in which the Christian faith is known and lived out. Christian faith is lived in a context and experienced in a context yet it is not reduced to its context. 'Recontextualization' is the theological process of relating theological truth to a changed context.

In the previous section, the cultural context was identified as constitutive of theology and examples were given of how Schillebeeckx engaged theologically

---

67. Ibid.
68. Ibid., 54.
69. Ibid., 53.
70. Boeve, *Crossroads*, 9.
71. Ibid.
72. Ibid.

with the cultural context by making a critique of a landmark book that signalled a turning point in the religious culture of Europe and North America (John Robinson's 'Honest to God') and by engaging with the anxieties of Christians in his audiences who were searching for a plausible interpretation of their faith in the divinity and humanity of Christ. The marginalization of theology in the university had already begun in 1968 when Schillebeeckx made clear the distinction between theology and the study of Christianity, writing, 'It is possible to study Christianity scientifically outside [the Christian] faith, and even to study its dogmatic content (as, for example, Buddhism is studied in comparative religion).' He goes on to say that in such a scientific study 'we shall be concerned with a purely "human" activity, and not with theology proper, which is concerned with pronouncements about the supernatural reality as this *is* in itself'.[73] Given the context and the metaphysics of Schillebeeckx's initial theological training, this remark is comprehensible. It needs, however, to be developed for the third millennium. Not only was faith the raison d'être of theology for Schillebeeckx but he also sets hermeneutics within faith. In response to the opposite view that 'the hermeneutical principle is not concerned with faith', he tells, in 1964, how

> several people have already maintained that a separate theology faculty is an absurdity and that theology should be a branch of the faculty of 'philosophy and literature' because, in its interpretation of faith, theology recognizes no other scientific law than that of the exegesis and the interpretation of texts in general (applied in this case to the Bible, confessional texts and so on).[74]

In the time between the 1960s and the early decades of the third millennium, theology has indeed either been squeezed out of the university or pushed to the margin of its own faculty by religious studies. Coupled with the processes of detraditionalization, individualization and pluralization the academy's scientific ideals of empirical rationality and 'the illusion of the presumption of objectivity and transparency' associated with it[75] are relegating theology to the sidelines. In such a climate theology is under increasing pressure to justify 'the legitimacy of its strictly theological finality'.[76] In other words, because the position of faith is often not understood or accepted as a legitimate one, those who are *fidentes quaerentes intellectum* (theologians) in the university are under pressure to justify the legitimacy of theology's purpose. That said, it is not just theology but many of the humanities that are being affected by detraditionalization and pluralization in postmodern culture. The legacy of the metanarrative that everything is knowable through science, or that science is the most likely means to solve our human problems, combined with materialistic ambitions or angst about job security,

---

73. Schillebeeckx, *R&T*, 74.
74. Schillebeeckx, *GFoM*, 10–11 [15].
75. Boeve, *Crossroads*, 59.
76. Ibid., 57.

prompts students to choose 'hard science' or vocational degrees that will serve as qualifications for jobs. Long past are medieval times when theology was revered as the highest level of academic learning, the *regina scientiarum*, queen of the sciences, the summit of human knowledge with philosophy as her *ancilla* (handmaiden).

Boeve observes that the most common strategy for dealing with challenges to the legitimacy of theology in a university is defensive retreat. In this case theology relinquishes any preferential relations that it may have enjoyed historically, and withdraws, even completely, into the university, thus separating itself from church and society, and either moulds itself alongside or into religious studies or is altogether replaced by religious studies. As he remarks, 'religious studies seems poised to inherit theology's status as an academic discipline'.[77] Where Schillebeeckx had identified voices raised against the continuing existence of theology faculties in the university, Boeve takes on the specific challenges of the survival and role of theology in the university within the new context of religious studies being established in what were previously theology faculties. He 'strive[s] for a contemporary theology that can claim at the same time both a theological validity and a contextual plausibility',[78] in other words, *recontextualization*. What Boeve calls *recontextualization*, Schillebeeckx refers to as the *reactivation of tradition*. A new context is a hermeneutical situation in which a theological process of reinterpretative understanding of Christian faith takes place, which both safeguards and interprets the tradition of faith within that context.

There are two stages to recontextualization which 'cannot be distinctly separated, but which stand in a dynamic relationship with each other'.[79] First, an authentic acquaintance with the contextual critical consciousness needs to be reached via a series of key questions such as, 'How does the context define itself? How does the Christian faith make itself part of this context? How do changes in the context place the Christian faith under pressure?' This line of questioning should lead to discovering what the contextual critical consciousness reveals about the context and the Christian faith in relation to it. Boeve points out the importance of distinguishing between secularization and post-secularization. Secularization is the process of detraditionalization and post-secular means that modernization of society has not led to the disappearance of religion but rather to a multiplicity of faiths, ideologies or positions of doubt or disbelief and that 'unchurched does not mean by definition unbelieving or non-religious'.[80] Secondly, and equally importantly, recontextualization means 'searching for a *contextually founded religious self-understanding*'.[81] From this process a theology can be forged, from its own resources (i.e. from its tradition by means of *ressourcement*) which at the same time addresses the challenges that the context makes to Christian faith.

77. Ibid., 58.
78. Ibid., 2.
79. Ibid.
80. Boeve, *Crossroads*, 39.
81. Ibid.

It is in this way that theology aims at a 'theologically legitimate and contextually plausible understanding of faith'.[82] Thus the contextual critical consciousness 'compels' theology to a contemporary theological critical consciousness which is an *aggiornamento*. This pattern of *ressourcement* and *aggiornamento* is evident in Schillebeeckx's theology and undergirds Boeve's concept and practice of recontextualization.

Boeve makes clear the distinction between theology and religious studies; he says of theology:

> Theologians engage in a reflection on – and from within – [faith that seeks understanding]: a reflection nourished by way of an existential praxis, rooted in a tradition, embedded in a community and performed in actual historical, cultural, socio-political contexts, on a scale that ranges from the particularly local to the global.[83]

In contrast, 'by religious studies is meant the scientific study of the phenomenon of religion in all its diversity. This study's operating procedure consists of applying proven philosophical and (sociological) scientific methods to the phenomenon of religion.'[84] This is not to say that theology is not recognized as a scientific discipline because its curriculum is still offered in many academic institutions. It holds its own because 'it can legitimize its activities, for example, when applying for research funding, by calling upon the scientific methodologies of other sciences (philology, history, philosophy, psychology, etc.) or by its relevance (ethics, the study of world religions)'.[85] How, then, does theology retain its identity of theological purpose plausibly in a context where it would be only too easy to find itself being sucked into religious studies? That identity of theological purpose and activity is 'Christian faith seeking understanding' in which theologians 'engage explicitly in the Christian tradition and attempt to contribute to that tradition through their own reflections'.[86]

Boeve contends that to think in terms of a presupposed continuity or discontinuity between theology and religious studies is counterproductive. On a presumption of either one of these two, 'the theological project ultimately perishes'.[87] On the lack of continuity he writes, 'Methodologically, theology crashes when exegesis of the Old and New Testaments becomes the study of Christianity's sources, when liturgical studies and sacramentology become "ritual studies" and when systematic theology becomes the philosophy of religion.'[88] In religious

---

82. Ibid.
83. Boeve, *Crossroads*, 137.
84. Ibid.
85. Ibid., 56–7.
86. Ibid., 57.
87. Ibid., 144.
88. Ibid., 141.

studies a theological question is 'hardly developed, or is immediately repudiated as (too) confessional or parochial'.[89] If religious studies is not a survival strategy for theology, neither is the retreat of theology into itself. If it turns inwards, it becomes isolated and 'pastoralized' (geared to the education of pastors). Either way recontextualization becomes impossible and theology is robbed of its 'necessarily interdisciplinary underpinning, its dynamic link to the (religious) sciences'.[90]

How, then, to recontextualize theology? First, by understanding the post-secular, pluralized context and its critical consciousness. Science and scientific rationality, with its models and theories, its legitimations of efficiency and performativity remain constitutive of the (university) context, where religious studies, with its scientific methods, is also set to stay. Christianity finds itself increasingly one faith among others owing to the movements of peoples. Secondly, recontextualization is not a process of attack from a land of 'counter-culture' but rather of Christianity recognizing its place 'in an internally pluralized field' from where it 'should [not only] determine its position, in relation to others' but also speak in the strength of its own identity.[91] Theology and religious studies can meet in mutual respect and dialogue, mutually 'interrupting' each other's self-understanding, to strengthen their own objectives. Religious studies already forms part of the contextual critical consciousness and does not happen in a value-free environment. Religious studies 'also expresses at every turn how a society thinks about religion and exercises an influence on those views (e.g. renewed attention to world religions)'.[92] It is precisely in meeting and engaging with religious studies that theology is compelled to voice its own, different identity and purpose in the new context. In dialogue with religious studies, theology can identify itself, precisely from its unique perspective of *fides quaerens intellectum*, as committed to the scientific search for truth and knowledge in the university. As Boeve writes, 'When theology is fully academic and thus meets university standards, it may get the chance to bring the university itself to self-critique, and help it to look beyond itself.' And this, he adds, 'is precisely when or perhaps because, it is situated in the margins'.[93] It can 'point the academy towards the limits of its methodologies and discourses, and warn against certain reductionisms'; it can 'foster a more critical-hermeneutical consciousness in the entire university by recalling and explaining that knowledge is always already situated and tied to interests', for example, by questioning the supposed neutrality of religious studies or the hard sciences; it can 'bring to expression, explicate and discuss the often hidden questions of meaning, ethics and anthropology' and take part in contemporary ethical and ideological discussions such as the question of 'assisted dying' or the wearing of religious symbols or clothing.[94] Theology's 'specific critical-productive

---

89. Ibid., 143.
90. Ibid.
91. Ibid., 145.
92. Ibid., 138.
93. Ibid., 61.
94. Ibid.

task is to examine the faith understanding of God's people in the world today and to work together so that today's church can also enter into a dialogue with the contemporary world'.[95] The theological question which must be clearly stated at the beginning of research (but which is lost in a takeover by religious studies) is: 'Where and how does God reveal Godself? How can we think of God's saving presence today? How can the tradition – as witness to God's active involvement with people and history – become a reading and living key for Christians today?'[96] Theology can have a critical prophetic and productive voice, to challenge not only assumptions, institutions and practices of Christianity and other religions but also of society as a whole, in order to enable individuals freely to participate in building a better world in which diversity and difference are not a threat to a person's own identity.

The Catholic Dialogue School: Its dialogical foundation and relational dialectic

Schillebeeckx and Boeve each independently considers that the basis and purpose of theology is condensed in the axiom of Anselm that theology is 'faith seeking understanding'. Each also holds that context is constitutive of theology, and that through the centuries Christians have lived lives true to the Christian tradition while reactivating or recontextualizing it. Thomas Aquinas is perhaps the outstanding example of a theologian who, in the thirteenth century, reactivated or recontextualized the tradition of the Church. In what follows it is argued, first, that the recontextualization proposed in the model of the Catholic Dialogue School has a theological foundation derived from one of the core elements of creation faith in that it is a development and practical application of the dialogue which lies at the heart of God the Creator's revelation of Godself to humanity. The same understanding of dialogue is also a core element of Schillebeeckx's creation faith. Secondly, and more specifically, the inter-human dialogue envisaged in the Catholic Dialogue School follows the same pattern of relational dialect that is fundamental to Schillebeeckx's thinking. In short, as God engages with his creatures in their sociocultural contexts, whatever they may be, so God's people are invited to respond to God in the dialogue of faith through the medium of the plural context of Catholic schools in contemporary Flanders; at the same time, relational dialectic enables participants to engage in dialogue with each other in a non-polar way so that in the ground covered about their differences they may (re)discover and strengthen their own identities.

The Catholic Dialogue School is a project initiated in the Flemish-speaking part of Belgium, the aim of which is to recontextualize the Catholic faith tradition and identity in Catholic schools. As recounted above, the pupils and staff in Catholic schools in Flanders (and the same is true for many other countries and regions in

---

95. Ibid., 7.
96. Ibid., 146.

Europe) are no longer all Catholics but are 'characterised by [the] religious and philosophical pluralisation, social secularisation, and individual disengagement with traditional communities of religious belonging and believing' of the contemporary context.[97] The architects of the model of the Catholic Dialogue School have confronted and analysed the fact that the contemporary sociocultural context is postmodern and post-secular and is therefore thoroughly pluralized. The question is, 'How can Catholic schools once again profile themselves as Catholic in a world which is post-Christian and post-secular?'[98]

Boeve sketches four models to analyse both the intended identity of Catholic schools (and other institutions) and the practices by which those institutions aim to achieve their desired identity. He notes that the actual identity which emerges may differ from the intended identity. The first model is one of *institutional secularization* in which schools claim either to be neutral or plural. In this case 'a fundamental equivalence of all philosophical and religious positions' is assumed and 'any and all expressions of preference' are eliminated, 'positing a formal equality of all substantial differences (i.e. relativism)'.[99] In institutional secularization Boeve asks whether 'true pluralist education is not aiming too high' because 'Flemish people today seem to be embedded in processes of obscured identity far more than of identity profiling and respect for religious plurality and otherness'.[100] He adds that 'the liberated religious space [of, for example, a secularised school] is all too easily seized in an insidious manner by a kind of libertarian ideology of individual freedom that discredits every other value commitment or source of meaning in advance'.[101] The second model is of *institutional reconfessionalization*. Didier Pollefeyt and Jan Bouwens write that 'actively to promote again the confessional Catholic identity [of an educational institute]', what Boeve calls 'institutional reconfessionalization' 'is an obvious reaction'[102] to a post-secular, pluralized context. One of the key elements of an active strategy of reconfessionalization,

---

97. Didier Pollefeyt and Michael Richards, 'Catholic Dialogue Schools: Enhancing Catholic School Identity in Contemporary Contexts of Religious Pluralisation and Social and Individual Secularisation', *Ephemerides Theologicae Lovanienses*, 96:1 (2020): 77–113 (77). Doi: 10.2143/ETL.96.1.3287376.

98. Lieven Boeve, 'Faith in Dialogue: The Christian Voice in the Catholic Dialogue School', *International Studies in Catholic Education*, 11:1 (2019): 37–49 (39) (henceforth *Faith in Dialogue*).

99. Didier Pollefeyt and Jan Bouwens, 'Dialogue as the Future. A Catholic Answer to the "Colourisation" of the Educational Landscape', English translation of *Dialoog als Toekomst. Een Katholiek Antwoord op de Verklaring van het Onderwijslandschap*, in *Dialogschool in Actie! Mag ik er Zijn Voor U?*, ed. P. Keersmaekers, M. van Kerckhoven and K. Vanspeybroeck (Antwerpen: Halewijn/VSKO/VVKHO, 2013), 49–60.

100. Boeve, *Crossroads*, 161.

101. Ibid.

102. Didier Pollyfeyt and Jan Bouwens, 'Framing the Identity of Catholic Schools: Empirical Methodology for Quantitative Research on the Catholic Identity of an Education

however, is that 'it is taken for granted that a substantial part of the school population is practising Catholic or should be, and the aim is faith formation for all students in a Catholic environment'.[103] Given the current sociocultural context in Flanders, there is little support for reconfessionalization.[104] The third model is of *Christian values education* which 'reformulates the Catholic educational project to a set of so-called Christian values, which (may) also appeal to non-Christians or no-longer Christians'.[105] The common basis that is interpreted as being Christian is pre-eminently taken to be ethics. At a cultural level ethics are recognized as valuable to non-Christians and theologically 'there can be no contradiction between what is "truly human" and what is "truly Christian"'.[106] However, whereas Christian-inspired ethics are based on a vision of what is entailed by the original creation (Gen. 1.26; 2.15)[107] and the refashioning of humanity in Christ (Rom. 6.4; 8.28-30),[108] the values of a Christian values education are 'seldom said to be founded from within a personally experienced relationship with God'[109] which is informed by Scripture, philosophical reason and the traditional experience and teaching of the church. Boeve avers that recent history has shown that the search for the greatest common denominator in Christian values education 'overaccentuates ethics and *de facto* detaches the proposed set of values in the school's project from an experienced Christian way of life that is ultimately founded in the communal relationship to the God of Jesus Christ'.[110] The specificity of Christian faith has been found to be the first victim in Christian values education.

Boeve proposes a fourth model for a Catholic school according to which the school both identifies itself as Catholic and is open to dialogue in a context which is post-Christian, post-secular and pluralized. Plurality is today's context in Flanders as it is in much of Europe and North America. The members of the Catholic Dialogue School share in and represent the characteristics of its

---

Institute', published online: 8 September 2010, 193–211 (henceforth *Identity of Catholic Schools*).

103. Ibid.

104. Boeve, *Crossroads*, 162.

105. Ibid.

106. Ibid., 164.

107. Gen. 1.26; 2.15: 'Then God said, "Let us make human beings in our image, after our likeness, to have dominion over the fish in the sea, the birds of the air, the cattle, all wild animals on land, and everything that creeps on the earth"' and 'The Lord God took the man and put him in the garden of Eden to till it and look after it.' To have dominion is to exercise lordship over, in this case, human beings in God's image are entrusted to reflect God's love for his creation in their care for it.

108. O'Collins and Farrugia, *A Concise Dictionary of Theology*, 149. Further New Testament references to the refashioning of humanity in Christ include 1 Cor. 15.49; 2 Cor. 5.17; Eph. 4.24; Col. 3.10.

109. Ibid., 163.

110. Ibid., 164.

thoroughly detraditionalized and pluralized context. The project of the Catholic Dialogue School involves a fundamental change in perspective from 'an analysis in terms of secularisation (that extends religious positions on a continuum between "practising Christian" and "convinced atheist")' to an analysis in terms of pluralization.[111] This change of perspective means that in their plurality the positions in the school are seen to relate to each other: 'On such a plural field each person is already a participant and in relation to other positions. Identity and difference go hand in hand.'[112] The religious and non-religious plurality is acknowledged and perceived as the new context in which to be Christian and to recontextualize or reactivate the Christian tradition. The plural situation, which plays havoc with the old, secure, shared horizon of Christian meaning, is precisely where God continues to reveal Godself, in Boeve's words, 'as a God of interrupting love, concerned with human beings, questioning their false certainties, and calling for compassion, justice and peace; interrupting closed stories, rescuing people from sin, and creating perspectives beyond human expectation'.[113]

The foundation of the Catholic Dialogue School is (unsurprisingly) dialogue, and, when looked at through a Schillebeeckian prism, it is dialogue in two dimensions. First it is based on the profoundly Christian concept of the dialogue that is the process which lies at the heart of God the Creator's revelation of Godself to humanity. Schillebeeckx emphasizes the distinction that Christian creation faith makes between Creator and creature and that it is a human being's 'creation [which] is the beginning of a dialogue between God and the human person'.[114] The relation of creature to Creator that God brings about by his creative action provides the framework for dialogical relationship between the two. For Schillebeeckx, the Creator, infinite in his transcendence, creates in order to invite men, women and children through the dialogue of revelation, into a deeper sharing of God's life. The plural composition of the Catholic Dialogue School is a new context in which God's invitation to the dialogue of revelation continues. Boeve writes, 'The concept of "dialogue" in the Catholic dialogue school is not neutral. It has been shaped by a deep Christian notion of a God revealing Godself to humanity, which is narratively anchored in the Jewish-Christian interpretation [of] history and community.'[115] Secondly, the method of the inter-person dialogue that the project of the Catholic Dialogue School promotes and implements is, in fact, a dialogue of relational dialectic. Schillebeeckx himself never used the nomenclature 'relational dialectic' but, Poulsom, in his study of Schillebeeckx's account of creation, coined the term to describe the dialectic which he identified as the pattern of Schillebeeckx's thinking and as operative in his theology.[116] He writes, 'in Schillebeeckx's relational

---

111. Boeve, *Faith in Dialogue*, 39.
112. Ibid., 40.
113. Ibid., 44–5.
114. Schillebeeckx, *W&C*, 187 [244].
115. Boeve, *Faith in Dialogue*, 45.
116. Poulsom, *Dialectics of Creation*, xi.

dialectic, the constituent elements are not considered as polar opposites but aspects, allowing them to be described as co-constitutive' and in such a dialectic, 'a dynamism is recognized between the aspects, a synergy in which neither can be reduced to the other without loss'.[117] Boeve writes of the inter-person dialogue in the Catholic Dialogue School,

> In as much as the dialogue with the other is constitutive for the construction of one's own identity, the presence of the (non)-religious other can contribute to this project of identity formation. People with different world views might challenge our views and urge us to account for them, both for ourselves as well as to others. We can learn a lot about who we are when confronted with who we are not.[118]

Dialogue conducted as relational dialectic avoids the logjam of polarized argument and instead benefits from the 'critical and productive (and therefore positive) force'[119] discovered in the ground between the participants' different positions. The presence of other religious and non-religious positions is the means by which, in dialogue, Catholic identity can be urged to account for itself.

While the concept of dialogue in the Catholic Dialogue School is charged with a specific understanding of what it is to be human and to live in relationship with God and each other, how in practice does the school retain its Christian identity in a plural context? Boeve writes that the project of the Catholic Dialogue School 'resolutely holds that the recognition of interreligious plurality and openness to other [non-]religious positions does not necessarily lead to a blurring of identity'.[120] He writes that the school is Catholic in a double way because the content of Christian faith (*fides quae*) is intrinsically interwoven with the attitude of faith (*fides qua*) (another example, incidentally, of a relational dialectic). The content of faith is not watered down to a general human longing for meaning and significance, common values or a sense that there is 'something more' to life: Christians believe that 'the "Something More" has revealed Itself as love in the concrete history of human beings'[121] and supremely by God's human enfleshment in Jesus of Nazareth. The Christian narrative tradition speaks about faith in terms of response to God in the dialogue that God initiates, of recognition of our absolute dependence on God freely to exercise our God-given autonomy; it speaks of faith in terms of repentance when we get things wrong and hurt or destroy one another,

---

117. Ibid., 97, where Poulsom quotes Rafael Esteban: 'Any member of a particular group should be able to say to the members of others: "Without you we are no longer ourselves."' Rafael Esteban, 'An Experience of Priesthood in Two Continents', *Way Supplement*, 83 (Summer 1995): 25-33 (especially 28-31).
118. Boeve, *Faith in Dialogue*, 40-1.
119. Ibid., 95.
120. Ibid., 43.
121. Ibid., 44.

and it speaks of a commitment of love to God and to each other so that our lives reflect the life of Jesus.

The institution of the Catholic Dialogue School has the responsibility institutionally to safeguard the dialogue in which Christians (re)discover and strengthen their own faith while enabling their partner-participants to do the same in their own identity formation. In this way the Catholic Dialogue School enables the Christian faith community to recontextualize the Christian tradition in the contemporary context. Christians and non-Christians each have their parts to play in supporting the project. With regard to the numbers of Catholic members, 'the Catholic Dialogue School hopes to be able to count on a sufficient number of people who can bring the Christian voice themselves, who can testify to it, however varied and divergent, fragile, incomplete and provisional this may be'.[122] Individuals' and the institution's ongoing Catholic formation and steadfast commitment are necessary for the Catholic Dialogue School's inspiration and effectiveness. Boeve points out that for Christians, who 'have learnt over the last decennia, out of respect for the other, to keep silent about their faith' or 'eschewed using a too obviously Christian language', to enter into dialogue with the other may be daunting and requires 'situating themselves and their faith within [the] broad Christian history of narrative and interpretation' and equipping themselves with language to testify authentically to their faith.[123] To be able to bear testimony to others about the hope and joy within them, with gentleness and reverence, as St Peter urges, and which was Schillebeeckx's lodestar, is the assignment and task of the Catholic Dialogue School and its members.

---

122. Ibid., 48.
123. Ibid., 46.

CONCLUSION

In John's gospel the story is told of how John the Baptist pointed out Jesus to two of his own disciples, Andrew and another, and that they heard the Baptist and followed Jesus. When Jesus turned round and noticed them following him, he asked them 'What are you looking for?'[1] A play on words has started. Jesus is not asking a banal question as though the two following him might have lost some trivial thing. Rather, the question 'touches on the basic need of [human beings] that causes [them] to turn to God'.[2] The answer of the disciples also includes a subtle play on a word, which in the common English translation is more or less lost: 'Rabbi, where are you staying?' The Greek word for 'staying', *meneis* (μενεις), has a strong pedigree. The same word is found in Homer to mean to 'stand fast' in battle, and in Plato to stick to one's opinion or conviction. John 'likes to use *menein* to express the permanency of relationship between Father and Son and between Son and Christian'.[3] This story leads straight to 'the divine will of God at the heart of creation'.[4] God is the source of human existence and God is the fulfilment of human existence through relationship with God-in-the-living-Christ.

God's divine will at the heart of creation is the core of Schillebeeckx's creation faith which undergirds his entire theology. In his development of corollaries of Aquinas' creation faith, Schillebeeckx examines in depth the implications of the contingency of creation, human free will and the making of history. Creation 'is not a chronological event, somewhere at the beginning, but a lasting dynamic event'.[5] He emphasizes that the creation in itself is not flawed and that human finitude is a fact of the gift of life. Any human sense of oppression at the restraints of finitude is at the same time balanced by the absolute presence of God in and with the finite [non-pantheistically] revealed through the medium of the creation. The relatedness of the human creature to the Creator is the prerequisite of God's

---

1. Jn 1.38.
2. Raymond E. Brown, *The Gospel According to John (I-XII): A New Translation with Introduction and Commentary*, The Anchor Bible 29 (New York: Doubleday, 1966), 78.
3. Ibid., 510.
4. McManus, *Unbroken Communion*, 8.
5. Schillebeeckx, *GAU*, 94.

invitation to enter into relationship with him. Drawing from a *ressourcement* of Irenaeus, Schillebeeckx avers that creation faith 'sets us free for own task in the world'.[6] Keeping the clay of our hearts moist and pliable in the two hands of God (the Son and the Spirit) we progress in sharing the life of God, and by enjoying and loving 'what is worldly in the world, what is human in [God's human creatures] is to enjoy and love what makes God God. God's glory lies in the happiness and well-being of [humanity] in the world'.[7]

God who 'loves us without limits or conditions'[8] came in human person so that 'everything that is good in creation is seen most clearly in the figure of Jesus'.[9] In his public life Jesus healed, forgave, liberated and brought in the outcast. In Jesus people experienced salvation from God. Jesus gave short shrift to man-made rules that oppressed the poor and powerless and he openly berated scribes and Pharisees. He challenged the authority of the religious hierarchy and subverted it; he also attracted a large following and, as a result, the chief priests and the scribes in anger and jealousy looked for a way to arrest Jesus by stealth and kill him.[10] In conjunction with the Roman governor they succeeded in bringing him to his death by crucifixion. His death was both contingent (a result of the way Jesus led his life for others and of the plotting of his enemies) and a sign of the lengths to which he was prepared to go for the love of human beings. God is constantly revealing Godself but in Jesus of Nazareth God gives humanity the clearest and most explicit revelation of himself. At the same time, in Jesus is seen the fullest and perfect human response to God, hence Schillebeeckx's interpretation of Jesus as 'concentrated or condensed creation'.[11] In Jesus, God is both hidden (*Deus absconditus*) and more human than any human being (*Deus Humanissimus*).[12] In the suffering, sin and confusion of human life on earth, God in Jesus is seen to resist suffering and to bring healing and fullness of life. God's purpose and longing in his creation is that human beings open themselves to God to reach the fullness of their humanity by bringing a fullness of life to each other as Jesus did.

In the latter half of his theological career, Schillebeeckx focused on suffering as an experience common to every human being, albeit in varying degrees, from which to talk about God. At first glance this choice of focus is ironical given that the 'problem of suffering', more often called 'the problem of evil', is considered by many to be a major impediment to finding faith in God. Schillebeeckx, however, chooses the common human reaction of abhorrence to suffering, together with its contrast experience of hope for relief from it, as a way of talking about God and Jesus. It is based on the belief that God the Creator is a God of positivity and wills

---

6. Ibid.
7. Ibid.
8. Schillebeeckx, *GAU*, 104.
9. Kennedy, *Schillebeeckx*, 94.
10. Mk 14.1.
11. Kennedy, *Schillebeeckx*, 94.
12. Kennedy, *Deus Humanissimus*, 24.

humanity to flourish, and invites humanity to work with God to build a world in which things are done in God's way, that is, 'to do justly, to love kindness and to walk humbly with your God'.[13] Jesus of Nazareth is the supreme example of following his Father's commission, in a life of prayer and actions. Christian prayer, meditation and contemplation arise from and return to living life in God's way, *sequela Jesu*. The to and fro between prayer and action (in a relational dialectic) in Christian life is what Schillebeeckx calls praxis, a rich development of the biblical notion of the love of God and love of neighbour. Love of God and love of neighbour must be co-constitutive of each other: God works through human beings who attune themselves to God's way, shown supremely in Jesus, in order to bring liberation to those who suffer.

A prime example of theological research into suffering and salvation in which ideas and methods of Schillebeeckx converge but are profoundly expanded is Pineda-Madrid's analysis of suffering and salvation in Ciudad Juárez. It is, first, a vivid exposition of crimes so vile and violent that it is tempting to describe them as 'unspeakable' and yet that is precisely what must not be done. The first step to salvation is to name the crimes of the feminicide. In solidarity with the victims it is the task of journalists, theologians and social scientists to bring to public attention and to analyse the causes of the feminicide. Just as Schillebeeckx never loses sight of the heavy reality of sin and suffering, Pineda-Madrid engages profoundly and unflinchingly with the crimes and suffering of the feminicide. What is remarkable in her account is that the surviving victims, the suffering and bereaved mothers, fathers and families themselves, rise up to resist their oppressors in public demonstrations again and again in order to put pressure on the corrupt police and civil authorities to stop them allowing the murderers to act with impunity. They are saying 'No!' to suffering caused by sin that is both individual and systemic, and 'Yes!' to better possibilities. They are working to eradicate the suffering of the feminicide, suffering which is the opposite of what God wants. In their concrete and courageous actions they employ two main religious symbols, the cross of Christ and, on their pilgrimage of protest from Chihuahua city to the Paso del Norte, the idea of exodus from a land of suffering and from enslavement to terror. The beginnings of salvation are found in joining together in solidarity and bringing God's healing to one another in community and as a society.

Boeve's project of the Catholic Dialogue School is an example of a theological project very different from Pineda-Madrid's but one which richly develops other ideas and methods of Schillebeeckx. To return to the account of Andrew and his companion following Jesus in John's gospel, the Jews of John the Baptist's time were born into believing communities although surrounded by the sea of Roman polytheism. That is not to say that Judaism itself was uniform because within the Judaism of the time different movements, sects and communities proliferated. Within the plurality of Judaism, it is significant that Andrew and his companion were first of all disciples of John the Baptist until he pointed out

13. Mic. 6.8.

Jesus as the Lamb of God. On their own initiative John's disciples then followed Jesus, because they trusted the Baptist's direction and, as disciples, learning on the way, they sensed something exceptional about Jesus, a magnetism to do with his relationship with God, and hence their question, 'Rabbi, where do you live/where are you staying/where are you rooted?' Their discipleship with Jesus was to be a process of dialogue, learning who Jesus is and how to live like him and, like Jesus, finding their rootedness in God. This is the model for the Catholics in the Catholic Dialogue School.

In the secularized and plural context of early-twenty-first-century northern Europe (specifically the Flemish-speaking part of Belgium) the Catholic Dialogue School envisages that those with Catholic faith be disciples, learning on the way, not through turning inwards but like Christ by openness to those around them, whatever their religious or ideological background may be, and engaging in dialogue with them, thus enriching and strengthening their own Catholic identity. The Catholic Dialogue School is based on the fundamental experience of faith which understands human life to be a God-given gift and responsibility. It trusts that 'the deepest mystery of life is love' and aims to practice love in every aspect of daily life at school,[14] preparing its pupils for life in a plural society. To quote from its mission statement: 'The school itself, in words and praxis, brings the Christian voice into [its] conversation in a contemporary and challenging way while additionally creating room for those who do not get a chance to enter the conversation.'[15] In its method and aims it seeks to find the language to point to the God of creation and in Christ to live out God's task of building a world in which everyone is able to search for the full meaning of being human and to flourish as God wills.

---

14. Boeve, *Faith in Dialogue*, 38.
15. Ibid., 38–9.

BIBLIOGRAPHY

Aquinas, Thomas, *Summa Theologicae (Summa Theologica)*. Prima Pars, Question 1, Article 7, Reply to Objection 1, New English Translation by Alfred J. Freddoso, Notre Dame, IN: University of Notre Dame. Accessed on 12 July 2011. https://www3.nd.edu/~afreddos/summa-translation/Part%201/st1-ques01.pdf.

Aquinas, Thomas, *Summa Theologicae: Volume 8 (1a. 44–49) Creation, Variety and Evil.* Question 45, Articles 1–5, 8, pp. 25–51, 59–63, edited by Thomas Gilbey O.P., Cambridge: Cambridge University Press, n.d., Imprimi potest, 1967.

Aquinas, Thomas, *Summa Theologiae. A Concise Translation*, edited by Timothy McDermott. Notre Dame, IN: Christian Classics, 1991.

Atencio, Graciela, 'El Feminicidio es el Exterminio de la Mujer en la Patriarcado: Monárrez Fragoso', *La Jornado*, 1 September 2003. http://www.jornada.unam.mx/2003/09/01/articulos/61_juarez_monarrez.htm.8 October 2021

Augustine, *Enchiridion, On Faith, Hope and Love IV: 13*, translated by Albert C. Outler. Dallas, TX: Southern Methodist University, 1955. www.tertullian.org/fathers'augustine_enchiridion_o2_trans.htm. 22 September 2016.

Aulén, Gustav, *Christus Victor: An Historical Study of the Three Main Types of the Idea of the Atonement.* London: SPCK, 1978.

Balthasar, Hans Urs von, *The Glory of the Lord: A Theological Aesthetics, Studies in Theological Style: Clerical Styles*, edited by John Riches, translated by Andrew Louth, Francis McDonagh and Brian McNeil. The Glory of the Lord: A Theological Aesthetics 2. Edinburgh: T&T Clark, 1995, pp. 31–94.

Barrett, C. K., *The Second Epistle to the Corinthians*. London: Adam and Charles Black, 1973.

Bartelmus, G. in G. Johannes Botterweck, Helmer Ringgren and Heinz-Josef Fabry (eds), *Theological Dictionary of Old Testament*, 10 vols. Grand Rapids, MI: Eerdmans, volume 15, translated by David E. Green and Douglas W. Stott, 2006, pp. 204–36.

Bauerschmidt, Frederick Christian, *Thomas Aquinas: Faith, Reason and Following Christ.* Oxford: Oxford University Press, 2013.

BBC news website report, 'Mexico Cartels: Which Are the Biggest and Most Powerful?', 24 October 2019. Accessed on 21 September 2021. https://www.bbc.co.uk>world-latin-america-40480405.

Behr, John, *Asceticism and Anthropology in Irenaeus and Clement*. Oxford: Oxford University Press, 2007.

Behr, John, *Irenaeus of Lyons: Identifying Christianity. Christian Theology in Context.* Oxford: Oxford University Press, 2013.

Bergin, Helen F., 'The Death of Jesus and Its Impact on God – Jürgen Moltmann and Edward Schillebeeckx', *Irish Theological Quarterly*, 52 (1986): 193–211.

Boeve, Lieven, 'Faith in Dialogue: The Christian Voice in the Catholic Dialogue School', *International Studies in Catholic Education*, 11:1 (2019): 37–49.

Boeve, Lieven, *Interrupting Tradition: An Essay on Christian Faith in a Postmodern Context*, translated by Brian Doyle. Louvain Theological and Pastoral Monographs 30. Louvain: Peeters Press, 2003.

Boeve, Lieven, *Theology at the Crossroads of University, Church and Society: Dialogue, Difference and Catholic Identity*. London: T&T Clark, 2016, paperback edn, 2018.

Boeve, Lieven, Frederick Depoortere and Stephan van Erp (eds), *Edward Schillebeeckx and Contemporary Theology 4*. London: T&T Clark, 2012.

Borgman, Erik, *Edward Schillebeeckx: A Theologian in His History. Volume I: A Catholic Theology of Culture (1914–1965)*, translated by John Bowden. London: Continuum, 2003.

Borgman, Erik, 'Still Revealing Himself: How Jesus' Resurrection Enables Us to Be Public Theologians', in *Grace, Governance and Globalization*, edited by Stephan van Erp, Martin G. Poulsom and Lieven Boeve. London: Bloomsbury T&T Clark, 2017, pp. 102–13.

Bowden, John, *Edward Schillebeeckx: Portrait of a Theologian*. London: SCM Press, 1983.

Bronner, Stephen Eric, *Critical Theory: A Very Short Introduction*. Oxford: Oxford University Press, 2011.

Brown, Raymond E., *The Gospel According to John I-XII: A New Translation with Introduction and Commentary*. The Anchor Bible 29. New York: Doubleday, 1966.

Burrell, David B., 'Act of Creation with Its Theological Consequences', in *Aquinas on Doctrine: A Critical Introduction*, edited by Thomas G. Weinandy, Daniel A. Keating and John P. Yocum. London: T&T Clark, 2004, pp. 27–44.

Camacho, Alicia Schmidt, 'Ciudadana X: Gender Violence and the Denationalization of Women's Rights in Ciudad Juárez, Mexico', *New Centennial Review*, 5 (2005): 255–92.

Canlis, Julie, 'Being Made Human: The Significance of Creation for Irenaeus' Doctrine of Participation', *Scottish Journal of Theology*, 58 (2005): 434–54.

Carroll, Denis, 'An Essay in the Theology of Creation', in *The Critical Spirit: Theology at the Crossroads of Faith and Culture*, edited by Andrew Pierce and Geraldine Smyth. Dublin: The Columba Press, 2003, pp. 15–26.

Carroll, Maureen Patricia, 'Framework for a Theology of Christian Conversion in the Jesus-Project of Edward Schillebeeckx' (unpublished doctoral dissertation, Catholic University of America, 1985). Abstract in *Dissertation Abstracts International*, 46 (1985): 1007-A, ProQuest Dissertations & Theses A&I http://0-search.proquest.com. Abstract, paragraph 2 of 4.

Chin, Corinne and Erika Schultz, 'Disappearing Daughters', a Project Combining Visual Journalism with Visual Poetry to Highlight the Strength of the Women of Ciudad Juárez, *The Seattle Times*. International Women's Day, 8 March 2020.

Considine, Kevin P., *Salvation for the Sinned-Against: Han and Schillebeeckx in Intercultural Dialogue*. Eugene, OR: Pickwick, 2015.

Cooper, Jennifer, *Humanity in the Mystery of God: The Theological Anthropology of Edward Schillebeeckx*. T&T Clark Studies in Systematic Theology. London: T&T Clark, 2009.

Creamer, Deborah, *Disability and Christian Theology*. New York: Oxford University Press, 2009.

Daley, Brian E., 'Balthasar's Reading of the Church Fathers', in *The Cambridge Companion to Hans Urs von Balthasar*, edited by Edward T. Oakes and David Moss. Cambridge: Cambridge University Press, 2004. pp. 187–206.

Daly, Gabriel, *Creation and Redemption*. Wilmington, DE: Michael Glazier, 1989.

Daly, Gabriel, 'What Is Original Sin?', *The Tablet* (8 February 1997): 170–1.

Davies, Brian, *The Thought of Thomas Aquinas*. Oxford: Clarendon Press, 2009.

Davies, Brian, and Brian Leftow, eds, *The Companion Guide to Anselm*. Cambridge: Cambridge University Press, 2004.

Deane-Drummond, Celia E., 'Hans Urs von Balthasar (1905-1988) - A Theo-Drama', in *Creation and Salvation, Volume 2: A Companion on Recent Theological Movements*, edited by Ernst M. Conradie (Zürich: Lit Verlag 2012) Studies in Religion and the Environment, Vol. 6, pp. 71-6.

Dillon, Kevin, 'The Spiritual Growth of People with Intellectual Disabilities: Jean Vanier and John of the Cross'. Unpublished doctoral dissertation, Heythrop College, University of London, 2016, emailed to Rhona Lewis, 13 June 2016, p. 63.

Egan, Philip, *Philosophy and Catholic Theology: A Primer*. Collegeville, MN: Liturgical Press, 2009.

Endean, Philip, 'Erik Borgman: *Edward Schillebeeckx: A Theologian in His History, Volume One: A Catholic Theology of Culture (1914-1965)*', review in *Times Literary Supplement* (23 July 2004): 26.

Ensalaco, Mark, 'Murder in Ciudad Juárez: A Parable of Women's Struggle for Human Rights', *Violence against Women*, 12:5 (May 2006): 417-40.

Ericson, Anna-Stina, 'An Analysis of Mexico's Border Industrialization Program', *Monthly Labor Review*, 93:5 (May 1970): 33-40.

Esteban, Rafael, 'An Experience of Priesthood in Two Continents', *Way Supplement*, 83 (Summer 1995): 25-33.

Farmer, Paul, *Pathologies of Power: Health, Human Rights, and the New War on the Poor*. Berkeley: University of California Press, 2005.

Fiorenza, Francis Schüssler, 'The New Theology and Transcendental Thomism', in *Modern Christian Thought: The Twentieth Century*, edited by James C. Livingston, Francis Schüssler Fiorenza with Sarah Coakley and James H. Evans, Jr. Minneapolis, MN: Fortress Press, 2006, pp. 197-232.

Fitzmyer, Joseph A., *First Corinthians: A New Translation with Introduction and Commentary*. Yale: Yale University Press, 2008.

Fitzmyer, Joseph A., *The Gospel According to Luke*, edited by Joseph A. Fitzmyer. The Anchor Bible 28A. Garden City, NY: Doubleday, 1985.

Fitzmyer, Joseph A., *Romans*. The Anchor Bible 33. Garden City, NY: Doubleday, 1993.

Ford, David F. (ed.) with Rachel Muers, *The Modern Theologians: An Introduction to Christian Theology since 1918*, 3rd edn. Oxford: Blackwell, 2006.

Fregoso, Rosa Linda, 'Toward a Planetary Civil Society', in *Mexicana Encounters: The Making of Social Identities on the Borderlands*. Berkeley: University of California Press, 2003, pp. 1-28 (7).

Furnish, Victor Paul, *II Corinthians*. The Anchor Bible 32A. Garden City, NY: Doubleday, 1984.

Gallagher, Michael Paul, *Faith Maps*. London: Darton, Longman and Todd, 2010.

Galvin, John P., 'The Story of Jesus as the Story of God', in *The Praxis of the Reign of God: An Introduction to the Theology of Edward Schillebeeckx*, edited by Mary Catherine Hilkert and Robert J. Schreiter. New York: Fordham University Press, 2002, pp. 79-95.

Galvin, John P., 'The Uniqueness of Jesus and his "Abba Experience" in the Theology of Edward Schillebeeckx', *Heythrop Journal*, 18 (1977): 309-14.

Gibellini, Rosino, 'Introduction: Honest to the World. The Frontier Theology of Edward Schillebeeckx', in *I Am a Happy Theologian: Conversations with Francesco Strazzari*, edited by Edward Schillebeeckx, translated by John Bowden. London: SCM Press, 1994, pp. ix-xiv.

Goergen, Donald J., 'Spirituality', in *The Praxis of the Reign of God: An Introduction to the Theology of Edward Schillebeeckx*, 2nd edn, edited by Mary Catherine Hilkert and Robert J. Schreiter. New York: Fordham University Press, 2002, pp. 117–31.

Grant, Robert M., *Irenaeus of Lyons*, London: Routledge, 1997.

Grenet, Paul, *Teilhard de Chardin: The Man and His Theories*, translated by R. A. Rudoff. London: Souvenir Press, 1965.

Hardy, Daniel W., 'Karl Barth', in *The Modern Theologians: An Introduction to Christian Theology since 1918*, edited by David F. Ford with Rachel Muers. Oxford: Blackwell, 2006, pp. 21–42.

Hauerwas, Stanley, 'Timeful Friends: Living with the Handicapped', in *Critical Reflections on Stanley Hauerwas' Theology of Disability: Disabling Society, Enabling Theology*, edited by John Swinton. New York: Routledge, 2004, pp. 11–25.

Hegel, Georg Wilhelm Friedrich, *The Philosophy of History*, translated by J. Sibree. New York: Dover Publications, 1956.

Hernandez-Truyol, Berta Esperanza, 'Culture and Economic Violence', in *The Latino Condition: A Critical Reader*, edited by Richard Delgado and Jean Stefancic. New York: New York University Press, 1998, pp. 536–8.

Hilkert, Mary Catherine, ' "Grace-Optimism": The Spirituality at the Heart of Schillebeeckx's Theology', *Spirituality Today*, 43:3 (1991): 220–39.

Hilkert, Mary Catherine, 'The Mystery of Being Human', in *The Theology of Cardinal Walter Kasper*, edited by Kristin M. Colberg and Robert A. Krieg. Collegeville, MN: Liturgical Press, 2014, pp. 59–78.

Hoare, George, and Nathan Sperber, *An Introduction to Antonio Gramsci: His Life, Thought and Legacy*. London: Bloomsbury Academic, 2016.

Irenaeus, *Against the Heresies, Book 1*, translated and annotated by Dominic J. Unger, with further revisions by John J. Dillon, Ancient Christian Writers 55. New York: Paulist Press, 1992.

Irenaeus, *Against the Heresies, Book 2*, translated and annotated by Dominic J. Unger, with further revisions by John J. Dillon, Ancient Christian Writers 65. New York: Newman Press, 2012.

Irenaeus, *Against the Heresies, Book 3*, translated and annotated by Dominic J. Unger, with an introduction and further revisions by Irenaeus M. C. Steenberg, Ancient Christian Writers 64. New York: Newman Press, 2012.

The Editions which Balthasar Uses: He cites from Books 1, 2, 4 and 5 from Harvey's edition, and Book 3 from Sagnard's edition, in both cases by page.

Irenaeus: Sancti Irenaei, Episcopi Lugdunensis, *Libros Quinque adversus Haereses* Tom. I, edited by W. Wigan Harvey STB. Cantabrigiae: Typis Academicis, 1857. (Books 1 and 2).

Irenaeus: Sancti Irenaei, Episcopi Lugdunensis, *Libros Quinque adversus Haereses* Tom. II, edited by W. Wigan Harvey STB. Cantabrigiae: Typis Academicis, 1857. (Books 3, 4 and 5). Balthasar cites Book 3 from the critical edition of Francois Sagnard.

Irénée de Lyon, *Contre Les Hérésies, livre III*, Sources Chrétiennes, Texte Latine, Fragments Grecs, Introduction, Traduction et Notes de F. Sagnard O.P. Paris: Editions du Cerf, 1952. English translation by John Keble used in this thesis for Books 4 and 5: *Five Books of S. Irenaeus Bishop of Lyons, Against Heresies*, translated by The Rev. John Keble M.A. with the fragments that remain of his other works. Oxford: James Parker, 377 Strand; London, 1872.

Irenaeus's Demonstration of the Apostolic Preaching: A Theological Commentary and Translation. Iain M. MacKenzie with the translation of the text by J. Armitage Robinson. Aldershot: Ashgate, 2002.

Jacko, Dorothy, *Salvation in the Context of Contemporary Secularized Historical Consciousness: The Later Theology of Edward Schillebeeckx*, A thesis submitted in partial fulfilment of the requirements for the degree of Doctor of Theology. Regis College, Toronto School of Theology, Toronto, Ontario, Canada, 1987.

Jossua, Jean-Pierre, 'Immutabilité, Progrès ou Structurations Multiples des Doctrines Chrétiennes'. *Revue des Sciences Philosophiques et Théologiques* 52:2 (1968): 173–200.

Kasper, Walter, *Jesus the Christ*. Anonymous translator who thanks E. Quinn, W. J. O'Hara, Francis McDonagh and Rosaleen Ockenden for their help in producing the English version in a prefatory note, new edn. London: T&T Clark International, A Continuum Imprint, 2011.

Kasper, Walter, 'Theological Anthropology of *Gaudium et Spes*', *Communio*, 23 (Spring 1996): 129–40.

Kearney, Richard, *Modern Movements in European Philosophy: Phenomenology, Critical Theory, Structuralism*. Manchester: Manchester University Press, 1986.

Kennedy, Philip, 'Continuity Underlying Discontinuity: Schillebeeckx's Philosophical Background', *New Blackfriars*, 70 (1989): 264–77.

Kennedy, Philip, *Deus Humanissimus: The Knowability of God in the Theology of Edward Schillebeeckx*. Fribourg: University Press Fribourg, 1993.

Kennedy, Philip, 'God and Creation', in *The Praxis of the Reign of God: An Introduction to the Theology of Edward Schillebeeckx*, 2nd edn, edited by Mary Catherine Hilkert and Robert J. Schreiter. New York: Fordham University Press, 2002, pp. 37–58.

Kennedy, Philip, 'Human Beings as the Story of God: Schillebeeckx's Third Christology', *New Blackfriars*, 71 (1990): 120–31.

Kennedy, Philip, *Schillebeeckx*. London: Chapman, 1993.

Kenny, Anthony, *Aquinas*. Oxford Paperbacks. Oxford: Oxford University Press, 1991.

Kerr, Fergus, *After Aquinas, Versions of Thomism*. Oxford: Blackwell, 2002.

Kerr, Fergus, *Theology after Wittgenstein*. Oxford: Blackwell, 1986.

Kerr, Fergus, *Thomas Aquinas: A Very Short Introduction*. Oxford: Oxford University Press, 2009.

Kerr, Fergus, *Twentieth Century Catholic Theologians: From Neoscholasticism to Nuptial Mysticism*. Oxford: Blackwell, 2007.

Kilby, Karen, *The SPCK Introduction to Karl Rahner*. London: SPCK, 2007.

Kleinman, Arthur, and Joan Kleinman, 'The Appeal to Experience; The Dismay of Images: Cultural Appropriations of Suffering in Our Times', *Daedalus*, 125 (1996): 1–23.

Kuhn, Thomas S., *The Structure of Scientific Revolutions*, 50th anniversary edn. Chicago: University of Chicago Press, 2012.

Küng, Hans, 'Introduction', in *Paradigm Change in Theology*, edited by Hans Küng and David Tracy, translated by Margaret Kohl. Edinburgh: T&T Clark, 1989, pp. xv–xvi.

Lash, Nicholas, *Change in Focus: A Study of Doctrinal Change and Continuity*. London: Sheed and Ward, 1973.

Lewis, Christopher, 'Secularisation: An Outmoded Concept?', in *A Religious Atheist? Critical Essays on the Work of Lloyd Geering*, edited by Raymond Pelly and Peter Stuart. Dunedin: Otago, 2006, p. 73.

Lewis, C. S., *Mere Christianity*. New York: HarperCollins, 2001.

Martin, David, 'Everything Old Is New Again', *The Tablet* (1 November 2014), 20.
Martyn, J. Louis, *Galatians*. The Anchor Bible 33 A. Garden City, NY: Doubleday, 1997.
Marx, Karl, 'Theses on Feuerbach (Original Version)', in *The German Ideology*. Amherst: Prometheus Books, 1998, pp. 569–71.
McCabe, Herbert, *God Matters (London, 1987) – God Still Matters*. London: Continuum, 2005.
McGinn, Bernard, *Thomas Aquinas's Summa Theologiae: A Biography*. Princeton, NJ: Princeton University Press, 2014.
McManus, Kathleen Anne, 'Suffering in the Theology of Edward Schillebeeckx', *Theological Studies*, 60 (1999): 476–91.
McManus, Kathleen Anne, *Unbroken Communion: The Place and Meaning of Suffering in the Theology of Edward Schillebeeckx*. Lanham, MD: Rowman and Littlefield, 2003.
Metterpenningen, Jürgen, *Nouvelle Théologie New Theology: Inheritor of Modernism, Precursor of Vatican II*. London: T&T Clark, 2010.
Minns, Denis, *Irenaeus*. London: Geoffrey Chapman, 1994.
Nieto-Gómez, Anna, 'La Chicana – Legacy of Suffering and Self-Denial', in *Chicana Feminist Thought: The Basic Historical Writings*, edited by Alma M. García. New York: Routledge, 1977, pp. 48–50.
O'Collins, Gerald, *Christology*, 2nd edn. Oxford: Oxford University Press, 2009.
O'Collins, Gerald, *Jesus Our Redeemer: A Christian Approach to Salvation*. Oxford: Oxford University Press, 2007.
O'Collins, Gerald, and Edward G. Farrugia, *A Concise Dictionary of Theology*. London: HarperCollins, 1991.
O'Malley, John W., *What Happened at Vatican II*. Cambridge, MA: Belknap Press of Harvard University Press, 2010.
O'Meara, Janet M., 'Salvation: Living Communion with God', in *The Praxis of the Reign of God: An Introduction to the Theology of Edward Schillebeeckx*, 2nd edn, edited by Mary Catherine Hilkert and Robert J. Schreiter. New York: Fordham University Press, 2002, pp. 97–116.
O'Reilly, Cajetan, 'Père Gardeil Appreciation'. www.dominicanajournal.org/wp.../dominicanav17n1peregardeilappreciation.pdf.
Osborn, Eric, 'Irenaeus of Lyons', in *The First Christian Theologians*, edited by G. R. Evans. Malden: Blackwell, 2004, pp. 121–31.
Osborn, Eric, *Irenaeus of Lyons*. Cambridge: Cambridge University Press, 2005, 121–31.
Oxford Dictionary of the Christian Church, edited by F. L. Cross and E. A. Livingstone. Oxford: Oxford University Press, 1997, p. 315.
The Oxford English Dictionary, edited by James A. H. Murray and others, 2nd edn. Prepared by J. A. Simpson and E. S. C. Weiner, 20 vols. Oxford: Clarendon Press, 2004, p. xviii.
Pasnau, Robert, *Thomas Aquinas on Human Nature*. Cambridge: Cambridge University Press, 2002.
Philosophy: Penguin Dictionary of Philosophy, edited by Thomas Mautner. London: Penguin Books, 2005.
Pieper, Josef, *Guide to Thomas Aquinas*, translated by Richard and Clara Winston, 3rd rev. edn. San Francisco, CA: Ignatius Press, 1991; originally published as *Introduction to Thomas Aquinas*, translated by Richard and Clara Winston. London: Faber and Faber, 1963; original German title: *Hinführung zu Thomas von Aquin*. Munich: Kösel-Verlag.
Pineda-Madrid, Nancy, *Suffering and Salvation in Ciudad Juárez*. Minneapolis, MN: Fortress Press, 2011.

Pollyfeyt, Didier, and Jan Bouwens, 'Dialogue as the Future. A Catholic Answer to the "Colourisation" of the Educational Landscape', English translation of *Dialoog als Toekomst. Een Katholiek Antwoord op de Verkleuring van het Onderwijslandschap*, in *Dialogschool in Actie! Mag ik er Zijn Voor U?*, Antwerpen, Halewijn / VSKO / VVKHO, 2013, pp. 49–60.

Pollefeyt, Didier, and Jan Bouwens, 'Framing the Identity of Catholic Schools: Empirical Methodology for Quantitative Research on the Catholic Identity of an Education Institute', published online: 8 September 2010, pp. 193–211. https://doi.org/10.1080/19422539.2010.504034.

Pollefeyt, Didier, and Michael Richards, 'Catholic Dialogue Schools: Enhancing Catholic School Identity in Contemporary Contexts of Religious Pluralisation and Social and Individual Secularisation', *Ephemerides Theologicae Lovanienses*, 96:1 (2020): 77–113 (77). Doi: 10.2143/ETL.96.1.3287376. https://www.semanticscholar.org/paper/Catholic-Dialogue-Schools%3A-Enhancing-Catholic-in-of-Pollefeyt-Richards/83cc16061bbb5ac3f38187e78e5bf9a4759d07ff.

Portier, William L., 'Interpretation and Method', in *The Praxis of the Reign of God: An Introduction to the Theology of Edward Schillebeeckx*, 2nd edn, edited by Mary Catherine Hilkert and Robert J. Schreiter. New York: Fordham University Press, 2002, pp. 19–36.

Potts, Lauren, 'Remembering the York Minster Fire 30 Years On', BBC News. York and North Yorkshire, 9 July 2014.

Poulsom, Martin G., *The Dialectics of Creation: Creation and the Creator in Edward Schillebeeckx and David Burrell*. London: Bloomsbury T&T Clark, 2014.

Poulsom, Martin G., 'New Resonances in Classic Motifs: Finding Schillebeeckx's Theology in Translation', Review of *The Collected Works of Edward Schillebeeckx*. 11 vols. London: Bloomsbury T&T Clark, 2014, in *Louvain Studies*, 38 (2014): 370–81.

Poulsom, Martin G., 'The Place of Praxis in the Theology of Edward Schillebeeckx', in *Keeping Faith in Practice: Aspects of Catholic Pastoral Theology*, edited by James Sweeney, Gemma Simmonds and David Lonsdale. London: SCM Press, 2010, pp. 131–42.

Rego, Aloysius, *Suffering and Salvation: The Salvific Meaning of Suffering in the Later Theology of Edward Schillebeeckx*. Louvain Theological and Pastoral Monographs, 33. Louvain: Peeters, 2006.

Richard, Lucien, *What Are They Saying about the Theology of Suffering?* New York: Paulist Press, 1992.

Richards, Michael Pollefeyt, Didier and Michael Richards, 'Catholic Dialogue Schools: Enhancing Catholic School Identity in Contemporary Contexts of Religious Pluralisation and Social and Individual Secularisation', *Ephemerides Theologicae Lovanienses*, 96:1 (2020): 77–113.

Rodenborn, Steven M., *Hope in Action: Subversive Eschatology in the Theology of Edward Schillebeeckx and Johann Baptist Metz*. Minneapolis, MN: Fortress Press, 2014.

Rodriguez, Teresa, and Diana Montané with Lisa Pulitzer, *A True Story of Serial Murder South of the Border*. New York: Atria Books, 2007.

Rowland, Tracey, 'Christ, Culture and the New Evangelization', in *The New Evangelization: Faith, People, Context and Practice*, edited by Paul Grogan and Kersteen Kim. London: Bloomsbury T&T Clark, 2015.

Ruether, Rosemary Radford, 'The God of Possibilities: Immanence and Transcendence Rethought', *Concilium*, 2000/4 (2000): 45–54.

Russell, Norman, *The Doctrine of Deification in the Greek Patristic Tradition*. Oxford: Oxford University Press, 2006.

Sartre, Jean-Paul, *L'être et le néant: Essai d'ontologie phénoménologique*. Gallimard: Collections Tel, 1943.

Schoof, Ted, and Jan van de Westlaken, *Bibliography 1936–1996 of Edward Schillebeeckx*. Baarn: Nelissen, 1996.

Schillebeeckx, Edward, 'Catholic Life in the United States', *Worship*, 42 (1968): 134–49.

Schillebeeckx, Edward, *Christ: The Christian Experience in the Modern World*, translated by John Bowden, checked by Ted Schoof, unidentified new section translated by Marcelle Manley, The Collected Works of Edward Schillebeeckx 7. London: Bloomsbury, 2014.

Schillebeeckx, Edward, *Christ the Sacrament of the Encounter with God*, translated by Paul Barrett and Lawrence Bright. The Collected Works of Edward Schillebeeckx 1. London: Bloomsbury, 2014.

Schillebeeckx, Edward, *The Church with a Human Face*, translated by John Bowden, extensively edited and corrected by Ted Schoof. The Collected Works of Edward Schillebeeckx 9. London: Bloomsbury, 2014.

Schillebeeckx, Edward, *Church: The Human Story of God*, translated by John Bowden, checked by Ted Schoof. The Collected Works of Edward Schillebeeckx 10. London: Bloomsbury, 2014.

Schillebeeckx, Edward, *Essays: Ongoing Theological Quests*, translated by Marcelle Manley, except ch. 2, translated by Edward Fitzgerald and Peter Tomlinson. The Collected Works of Edward Schillebeeckx 11. London: Bloomsbury, 2014.

Schillebeeckx, Edward, 'Evangelische zuiverheid en menselijke waarachtigheid', *Tijdschrift voor Theologie*, 3 (1963): 283–325, and 'Herinterpretatie van het geloof in het licht Van de seculariteit', *Tijdschrift voor Theologie*, 4 (1964): 109–50.

Schillebeeckx, Edward, *For the Sake of the Gospel*, translated by John Bowden. London: SCM Press, 1989.

Schillebeeckx, Edward, *God among Us: The Gospel Proclaimed*, translated by John Bowden. London: SCM Press, 1983.

Schillebeeckx, Edward, *God, the Future of Man*, translated by N. D. Smith. The Collected Works of Edward Schillebeeckx 3. London: Bloomsbury, 2014.

Schillebeeckx, Edward, *God and Man*, translated by Edward Fitzgerald and Peter Tomlinson. London: Sheed and Ward, 1969.

Schillebeeckx, Edward, *God Is New Each Moment*, in conversation with Huub Oosterhuis and Piet Hoogeveen, translated by David Smith. London: Continuum, 2004.

Schillebeeckx, Edward, *I Am a Happy Theologian: Conversations with Francesco Strazzari*, translated by John Bowden. London: SCM Press, 1994.

Schillebeeckx, Edward, *Interim Report on the Books* Jesus *and* Christ, translated by John Bowden, checked by Ted Schoof. The Collected Works of Edward Schillebeeckx 8. London: Bloomsbury, 2014.

Schillebeeckx, Edward, *Jesus: An Experiment in Christology*, co-translators Hubert Hoskins and Marcelle Manley, edited by Joanna Dunham. The Collected Works of Edward Schillebeeckx 6. London: Bloomsbury, 2014.

Schillebeeckx, Edward, *Jesus in Our Western Culture: Mysticism, Ethics and Politics*, translated by John Bowden. London: SCM Press, 1987.

Schillebeeckx, Edward, *Revelation and Theology*, translated by N. D. Smith. The Collected Works of Edward Schillebeeckx 2. London: Bloomsbury, 2014.

Schillebeeckx, Edward, 'The Role of History in What Is Called the New Paradigm', in *Paradigm Change in Theology: A Symposium for the Future*, edited by Hans Küng and David Tracy, translated by Margaret Kohl. Edinburgh: T&T Clark, 1989, pp. 307-19.

Schillebeeckx, Edward, 'The Sacraments: An Encounter with God', in *Christianity Divided: Protestant and Roman Catholic Theological Issue*, edited by Daniel J. Callahan, Heiko A. Oberman and Daniel O'Hanlon, translated by John L. Boyle. New York: Sheed and Ward, 1961, pp. 245-75.

Schillebeeckx, Edward, 'Sakramente als Organe der Gottbegegnung', in *Fragen der Theologie heute*, edited by J. Feiner, J. Trütsch and F. Böckle. Einsiedeln: Benziger, 1957.

Schillebeeckx, Edward, *The Understanding of Faith*, translated by N. D. Smith. The Collected Works of Edward Schillebeeckx 5. London: Bloomsbury, 2014.

Schillebeeckx, Edward, *Vatican II - A Struggle of Minds and Other Essays*, translated by M. H. Gill. Dublin: Gill, 1963.

Schillebeeckx, Edward, *World and Church*, translated by N. D. Smith. The Collected Works of Edward Schillebeeckx 4. London: Bloomsbury, 2014.

Schoof, Mark, *Breakthrough: The Beginnings of the New Catholic Theology*, translated by N. D. Smith. Dublin: Gill and Macmillan, 1970.

Schoof, Ted, and Jan van de Westlaken, *Bibliography 1936-1996 of Edward Schillebeeckx*, Baarn: Nelissen, 1996.

Schreiter, Robert J., 'Edward Schillebeeckx: His Continuing Significance', in *The Praxis of the Reign of God: An Introduction to the Theology of Edward Schillebeeckx*, 2nd edn, edited by Mary Catherine Hilkert and Robert J. Schreiter. New York: Fordham University Press, 2002, pp. 185-94.

Schreiter, Robert J., 'Pastoral Theology as Contextual: Forms of Catholic Pastoral Theology Today', in *Keeping Faith in Practice: Aspects of Catholic Pastoral Theology*, edited by James Sweeney, Gemma Simmonds and David Lonsdale. London: SCM Press, 2010, pp. 64-79.

The Social Concern of the Church www.catholicsocialteaching.org.uk/principles/glossary:structures.

Sokolowski, Robert, 'Creation and Christian Understanding', in *God and Creation: An Ecumenical Symposium*, edited by David B. Burrell and Bernard McGinn. Notre Dame, IN: Notre Dame University Press, 1990, pp. 179-92.

Sonderegger, Katherine, 'Anselmian Atonement', in *T&T Clark Companion to Atonement*, edited by Adam J. Johnson. London: Bloomsbury T&T Clark, 2017, 175-93.

Soskice, Janet Martin, 'Creation and the Glory of Creatures', *Modern Theology*, 29 (2013): 172-85.

Sperber, Nathan, and George Hoare, *Antonio Gramsci: His Life, Thought and Legacy*. London: Bloomsbury Academic, 2016.

Steinbeck, John, *The Grapes of Wrath*. Harmondsworth: Penguin Books, [1939] 1967.

Stokes, Philip, *100 Essential Thinkers*. London: Arcturus, 2006.

Swafford, Andrew Dean, *Nature and Grace: A New Approach to Thomistic Ressourcement*. Cambridge: James Clarke, 2015.

Tanner, Kathryn, '"Creation *Ex Nihilo*" as Mixed Metaphor', *Modern Theology*, 29:2 (2013): 138-55.

Taylor, Charles, *Modern Social Imaginaries*. Durham, NC: Duke University Press, 2004.

Te Velde, Rudi, *Aquinas on God: The 'Divine Science' of the Summa Theologiae I* Aldershot: Ashgate, 2006.

Te Velde, Rudi, 'God and the Language of Participation', in *Divine Transcendence and Immanence in the Work of Thomas Aquinas*, edited by Harm Goris, Herwi Rikhof and Henk Schoot. Leuven: Peeters, 2009, 19–36.

Thompson, Daniel Speed, *The Language of Dissent: Edward Schillebeeckx on the Crisis of Authority in the Catholic Church*. Notre Dame, IN: University of Notre Dame Press, 2003.

Townes, Emilie M., *Womanist Ethics and the Cultural Production of Evil*. New York: Palgrave Macmillan, 2006.

Trent, Council of, *The Canons and Decrees of the Sacred and Oecumenical Council of Trent*, translated by J. Waterworth. London: Dolman, 1848.

Turner, Denys, *Thomas Aquinas: A Portrait*. New Haven, CT: Yale University Press, 2013.

Vatican I: Dogmatic Constitution of the Catholic Faith, www.ewtn.com/library/COUNCILS.

Velecky, Lubor, *Aquinas' Five Arguments in the Summa Theologiae* 1a 2, 3. Kampen: Pharos, 1994.

Wahlberg, Matts, *Reshaping Natural Theology: Seeing Nature as Creation*. Basingstoke: Palgrave Macmillan, 2012.

Walsh, P. G., *Introduction, Translation and Commentary, Augustine De Civitate Dei Books I & II*. Oxford: Oxbow Books, Aris & Phillips Classical Texts, 2005.

Wang, Stephen, *Aquinas and Sartre: On Freedom, Personal Identity, and the Possibility of Happiness*. Washington, DC: Catholic University of America Press, 2001.

Wasington Valdez, Diana, *The Killing Fields: Harvest of Women: The Truth about Mexico's Bloody Border Legacy*. Burbank: Peace at the Border, 2006.

Weinandy, Thomas G., *Does God Suffer?* Notre Dame, IN: University of Notre Dame Press, 2000.

Williams, Thomas, 'Saint Anselm', in *The Stanford Encyclopedia of Philosophy*, Spring 2016 edn, edited by Edward N. Zalta. https://plato.stanford.edu/archives/spr2016/entries/anselm/.

Wippel, John F., *Metaphysical Themes in Thomas Aquinas*. Washington, DC: CUA Press, 1984.

Zahrnt, Heinz, *The Question of God*, translated by R. A. Wilson. New York: Harcourt, Brace & World, 1969.

INDEX

Adorno, Theodor 126, 155
Aeterni Patris 13, 15, 76
Alexandrian emphasis in Christology 89, 111, 112, 113
Annales model of change and continuity 2, 7, 8, 101, 102–5, 119, 128, 159, 192, 199
Anselm 3, 7, 24, 31, 87, 101, 192–3, 196, 211
anthropology, theological 6, 8, 17, 43, 46, 53, 54, 59, 95, 118, 148, 158, 161, 210
Antiochene emphasis 111, 112, 113
Aquinas 2, 5, 6, 7, 8, 13, 16, 17–21, 26, 29–30, 33–9, 43, 45–6, 76, 77, 78, 80, 82, 85, 91, 93–4, 97, 111, 112, 113, 127–8, 157, 181, 198–9, 211, 217
atheism 5, 33, 127, 201
atonement theory 4–5, 7, 46, 101, 144, 192–3
Augustine 110, 111, 131
Auschwitz 102, 126

Balthasar, Hans Urs von 14, 43–50, 52–6, 58–60, 64–6, 76
Benedict XVI 107
Boeve, Lieven 2, 9, 167, 195
  Catholic Dialogue School 214–16
  changed status of theology 204, 205
  context constitutive of theology 197
  detraditionalization 203
  European Values Study 201
  identity construction 9, 201, 215
  models of Catholic schools 212–14
  recontextualization 205, 208
  theologian's task 196
  Theology in a Postmodern Context 197
  university, church and society 201, 206
  religious studies 205, 209, 207–11
Borgman, Erik 14, 47, 74

Catholic Dialogue School 9, 195, 211–16, 219–20
Chalcedon 8, 85–6, 89, 94, 96, 97, 98, 106, 109, 111, 112, 113–15, 117, 121
Chenu, Marie-Dominique 16, 62, 91, 93, 94, 99, 198–9
Christology
  Alexandrian approach 112–13
  Antiochene emphasis 113
  Aquinas' creation faith, rooted in tenets of 13, 41
  Aquinas' *persona humana divinae naturae* 112–13
  Chalcedon, adherence to 112, 113
  Chalcedon, continuity with 8
  and identity of meaning 119–20
  and praxis of kingdom of God 140, 145
  is concentrated creation 7, 9, 110, 116–17, 161, 162, 218
  contingency, implications for 23
  continuity and change in Schillebeeckx's Christology 101, 125–6
  creation faith, basis in 2, 5
  dichotomized Christology 98
  divine and human in Jesus 111–12, 156
  dualistic Christology 114
  finitude, implications of 31
  God, meaning of, concentrated in Jesus 123
  inseparability of Jesus from God 142
  Jesus as representative 111, 115–16
  New Testament Christology 119
  paradox, Christology of 24–5
  relational dialectic, Christology of 25, 109
  soteriological Christology, constituents of 161–3
  Trinity and Christology 51
Ciudad Juárez 2, 8–9, 168–74, 178, 181, 183, 185–94, 219
Communio 44

Concilium 44
Constantinople, First Council of, 114, 121
contingency 5, 18, 19, 20–3, 28–30, 32–3, 55, 62, 126, 127, 133, 146, 150, 159, 173, 175, 180, 198
continuity and change 2, 7, 8, 73–5, 77, 79, 80, 85, 88–9, 91, 98–9, 101, 103–5, 119, 123, 128, 143, 192
covenant 66, 106, 116, 162, 173, 191, 198
creation, concentrated 2, 7, 9, 110, 111, 116–17, 123, 161–2, 163, 192, 218
creation faith 3, 5, 8, 13, 19, 20, 22, 26, 27, 28, 29, 30, 34, 39, 41, 43, 46, 47, 54, 101, 107, 109, 113, 117, 123, 133, 136, 148, 151, 167, 178, 190, 191, 197, 198, 205, 211, 214, 217, 218
critical theory, influence on Schillebeeckx 96, 123, 136, 147–51, 155, 159
crucifixion 3–4, 35, 41, 123, 131, 139, 142, 156, 176, 187, 193, 218

Darwinism 61–2
De Chardin, Teilhard 61
De Petter, Dominicus 14, 15, 17, 78, 95, 99, 157, 198
detraditionalization 203, 207, 208
dialectic (theological method) 36, 53–4, 74, 86, 90, 91 *see also* relational dialectic
divine freedom 19, 20,
divinization 3, 117–18
dualism 4, 17, 33, 113, 131, 132

Enchiridion 131

faith 2, 8, 9, 17, 18, 24, 29, 37, 38, 44, 45, 49, 60, 62, 63, 65, 66, 67, 73, 74, 75, 76, 77, 79–87, 89, 90, 93, 94, 98–9, 101, 116, 117, 120–1, 124, 125, 131, 136, 138, 144, 147–8, 150, 154, 158, 161, 167, 188, 195–6, 199, 200, 201, 205–9, 210, 211, 213, 215–16, 218
feminicide 2, 9, 168, 169–71, 180, 183, 184, 185–6, 188, 189, 191, 192–4
finitude 5, 21, 23, 26–8, 28–30, 31–3, 41, 54–5, 129, 135, 140, 145, 150, 152, 180, 181, 191, 217
freedom
  God's 19, 20, 48, 56, 133,

human 1, 2, 4, 20, 21, 23, 25, 26, 54, 56, 57, 58, 59, 65, 98, 106–7, 109, 129, 133, 134, 144, 159, 178, 180, 181, 183, 186, 188, 212
  Jesus Christ's freedom 4, 24, 25, 66
  Spirit, freedom in the 91
  unfreedom 149
Frankfurt School 96, 149, 155, 159

Garrigou-Lagrange, Reginald 16, 93
Gaudium et Spes 97, 158
Gilson, Etienne 17
Gnosticism 49, 91
grace 4, 15, 31, 82, 91, 97, 107, 108, 109, 114, 116, 118, 120, 128, 133, 140, 141, 144, 151, 152, 156–7, 200
grace-optimism 62, 136, 154
Gramsci, Antonio 147, 148, 174

hermeneutics 50, 80, 81, 88, 91, 92, 94, 97, 98, 115, 126, 141, 207
Hiroshima 102
historical-biblical criticism 91, 92, 98
Hoogeveen, Piet 111, 112
hope 27, 62, 92, 128, 136, 152, 153, 154, 168, 178, 179, 180, 181, 182, 183, 188, 191, 192, 194, 196, 216, 218
Horkheimer, Max 155
humanity
  distinction between God and humanity 58
  divinity and humanity of Jesus 24, 63, 64, 68, 98, 99, 118, 156, 157, 207
  environment/world and humanity 22, 35, 159
  fullness of humanity 2, 6, 27, 40, 69, 98, 113, 162, 218
  God and humanity 23, 26, 30, 48, 49, 57, 81, 82, 106, 152, 157, 161, 214
  God's self-revelation in humanity 8, 31, 39, 41, 45, 51, 52, 79, 98, 116, 118, 140, 172, 173, 190, 218
  Jesus' humanity 6–7, 23, 40, 41, 69, 97, 98, 107, 109
humanity and finitude 26, 28, 41
humanity and freedom 58, 133
humanity and God's honour 43, 63, 64, 69, 218

humanity's progress towards God 59, 61, 64, 69, 213
humanity and relationship with God 9, 38–9, 69, 98, 107, 116, 144, 219
sin and humanity 3, 45, 61, 62, 130, 134, 139, 142
true humanity 39, 40, 50, 56, 158, 159
humanum 159, 160, 161
Husserl, Edmund 17, 78
hypostatic union 113–14

identity 74, 87, 206, 209, 210, 212, 214, 215, 220
construction 9, 201, 202–3, 215, 216
of faith 83, 84, 90
of a human being 83, 148, 211
identity of meaning 74, 84, 86, 90, 119
identity of meaning, Christological 119, 120, 121
identity of meaning, evangelical 90, 119, 120
immanence 6, 32, 46, 47, 48–9, 91, 106, 109
implicit intuition of totality 14, 78, 95, 99
Incarnation 3, 4, 31, 39, 61, 66, 67, 97, 112, 139, 141, 152, 156, 198
individualism 203, 204
individualization 203, 207
Irenaeus 2, 6, 43–4, 46–69, 91, 115, 134, 148, 161

John Paul II 97, 137

Kant, Immanuel 17
Kennedy, Philip
Ansfried Hulsbosch's influence on Schillebeeckx 111, 113–14
on Aquinas' *rem* and *enuntiabile* 18, 77
on Aquinas' *in quo humana natura assumpta est* 7
on Christology is concentrated creation 8, 9, 218
on creation basis of Schillebeeckx's theology 18, 218
on Critical Theory and Schillebeeckx 123, 147
on humanity of Jesus 115
on praxis 6, 145
on *ressourcement* 93

on Schillebeeckx and existentialism 108
on Schillebeeckx and Irenaeus 43, 63,
on Schillebeeckx's continuity in metaphysical and epistemological fundamentals 95
on Schillebeeckx and humanity as fundamental symbol of God 157, 158
on Schillbeeckx and suffering 125, 126
kingdom of God 6, 23, 25–6, 27, 47, 55, 57, 63, 69, 96, 123, 128, 140, 142, 143–7, 151, 153–6, 158, 174, 194, 198
Kuhn, Thomas 101–2, 103, 104, 105, 126

Lamentabili 75
Leo XIII 13, 15, 76
Lukács, Georg 145, 147, 149, 150, 151

Manichaeism 131
Maréchal, Joseph 15, 78
Maritain, Jaques 17
Merleau-Ponty, Maurice 17, 78
method, theological 13, 50, 73, 88, 91–8, 99, 141–2, 157, 189, 196–7, 198, 206, 209–10, 219
modernism 75
Moltmann, Jürgen 142

NAFTA (North American Free Trade Agreement) 169–70
negative experiences of contrast 127, 136, 152, 177, 178, 188, 190
neo-scholasticism 16, 75–6, 78
neo-Thomism 13, 15, 75, 76
Nicaea, First Council of 121
Nicene Creed 112

Oosterhuis, Huub 112
original justice 127–8, 138–9, 151, 152
original sin 4, 123, 127–8, 130, 133–6, 138–9, 173, 175
orthopraxis 146–7

pantheism 109
paradigm change 102, 103–5
paradigm shift 102, 105
Pascendi 75
Pineda-Madrid, Nancy
Anselm's atonement theory 192–3

awareness of need for God 191
economic dimension to suffering in
  Ciudad Juárez 170
feminicide, definition of 168
'hegemonic world view' 173, 174–5
imaginal social existence 173
inductive method 189
recontextualization of suffering 191
salvation, endorsing and
  appropriating 192
salvation societal 169, 182–3, 194
social-suffering hermeneutic 173,
  180, 192
sociocide 169
stereotypes 174–5
suffering, analysis of 8, 169, 194, 219
theology of suffering 168, 178, 190, 191
Pius IX 13
pluralism 46, 55, 124, 125, 189, 203, 204
pluralization 196, 201, 203, 204, 207,
  212, 214
Poulsom, Martin
  on Burrell's defining of freedom 57
  on evangelical identity of meaning 84
  identifies Schillebeeckx's thinking
    as 'relational dialectic' 34, 53,
    91, 214–15
  on Irenaean idea of human life as
    participation in God's life 68
  on Irenaean 'ways of seeing God' 67–8
  on 'Kernel and its mode of
    expression' 86
  on praxis and practice used
    interchangeably 146
  on praxis as a 'way of becoming' 148
  on relational autonomy of dependence
    of creature on Creator 57
  on Schillebeeckx's conjunctural shift in
    what is genuinely human 158–9
  on Schillebeeckx's imagery of *Annales*
    model 103–4
  on Schillebeeckx's notion of praxis
    involving three terms 147
  on Schillebeeckx's relational dialectic of
    finitude and contingency 33
  on Schillebeeckx as a situational not a
    transcendental thinker 15
praxis 90, 123, 145, 146–8, 150, 151, 155,
  156, 167, 182, 206, 209, 220

praxis of the kingdom/reign of God 6, 57,
  123, 125, 138, 140, 141–2, 144, 145,
  147, 151–4, 155, 158, 174, 193, 219

Rahner, Karl 14, 44, 75
recapitulation 111, 115
Reconciliato et Paenitentia 137
reconfessionalisation 212–13
recontextualization 176, 178, 195, 197,
  205, 206, 208–9, 210, 211
relational dialectic 25, 33, 34, 54, 57, 79,
  86, 91, 104, 109, 116, 147, 179, 193,
  195, 197, 211, 214, 215, 219
relativism 212
religious studies 205, 207–11
ressourcement 2, 5, 6, 8, 17, 43, 44, 88, 93,
  99, 101, 108, 157, 208, 209, 218
resurrection 3, 5, 7, 22, 31, 37, 39, 51, 52,
  109, 110, 116, 117, 119, 120, 131, 140,
  157, 160, 162, 188
Robinson, John 199, 207
Romanticism 16

sacraments 93, 107–8, 109, 110, 114, 116,
  118, 157, 229
sacrifice 3–4, 24, 25, 34, 35, 36, 37, 123,
  139, 176, 187
salvation
  church as sacrament of 96
  church as servant of true salvation
    172
  in Ciudad Juárez 168, 189, 193, 219
  creation, link with 2, 39–40, 56, 69, 107
  cross and salvation 185
  death of Jesus and salvation 142
  definitive salvation is eschatological
    123, 156
  economy of, 14, 66, 67, 108, 110, 141
  emancipation from sin 151
  experienced in Jesus as directly from
    God 9, 31, 40–1, 67, 68, 97, 114, 120,
    123, 140, 142, 162, 175, 185, 192, 218
  faith 2, 19, 85, 161, 193
  followers of Christ, channels of
    salvation 37, 162, 185, 192
  God gives himself as our
    salvation 39, 56
  God wills salvation of humanity 145,
    161, 185

happiness, prosperity and well-being as salvation 63, 64, 65
Holy Spirit, salvation in power of 9, 52–3
hope and salvation 179
humanity's salvation is to God's glory and honour 63, 64, 65
Irenaeus' pedagogy of salvation 61, 64, 65
Jesus, 'essence of final salvation' 8, 66, 141
liberation from sin and suffering 140
life blood of human relationships 159
original sin and salvation 136
in praxis of kingdom of God 140, 141, 193
process of salvation 62, 64
recontextualization of salvation 176, 180
in relationship with God 41
revelation of salvation in world and time 49, 52, 177, 185, 186, 192
risen Christ, source of salvation 37, 140, 192
salvation history (*dispositio*) 7, 14, 46, 52, 64, 65, 66, 85
visio Dei and salvation 64
whole person, environment and society, salvation for 137, 159, 160, 162, 167, 182, 183, 194, 219
Sartre, Jean-Paul 20, 28, 127
Schoonenberg, Piet 113
Schreiter, Robert J. 18, 44, 189
secularization 45, 124–5, 153, 196, 199, 200–1, 202, 204, 208, 212
sin 1, 3, 4, 22, 27, 28, 31, 41, 54–5, 91, 118, 121, 123, 127–8, 129, 130, 133–40, 143, 144, 148, 149, 151, 156, 168–9, 173, 174, 175, 178–9, 180–1, 182, 183, 184, 187, 190, 191, 192, 193, 218, 219
social imaginary 173–5
Sollicitudo rei socialis 137
soteriology 3, 4, 19, 31, 46, 87, 140, 161–2, 167
Suarezianism 16
suffering
as caused by human behaviour 129–30, 169–70, 172, 179

in Ciudad Juárez 167, 190, 193
'crisis of history's suffering people' 153
and critical theory 149
feminicide, suffering of 219
finitude, suffering an element of 26, 28
God's opposition to 129, 140, 143–4, 172, 173–4, 218
grace of God through Jesus Christ needed to avoid inflicting suffering 133
Jesus is God's 'no' to suffering 144
Jesus saves people from suffering and sin 36, 140, 151, 190
media and suffering 179–80
moral suffering 129
natural suffering 128–9
and original sin 128
and praxis of the kingdom of God 158
resistance to 18, 178, 184–5, 188, 191
and responsibility 132, 179
social solidarity in resistance to 185
social-suffering hermeneutic 173, 180–2, 192
suffering and sin, personal and societal 137–8, 175, 182
talking about God through suffering and its opposite 125, 167, 172, 178, 190, 218
task is to overcome suffering 23, 26, 37, 130, 145, 191
terms 'suffering' and 'evil' 130–3

theiosis 58
theodicy 129, 189
Thomism 13, 15, 16, 75, 76, 78, 93, 97
tradition 7, 15, 31, 44, 45, 64, 67, 73, 74, 83, 86, 87, 88–90, 93, 94, 101, 119, 121, 156, 161, 167, 185, 195, 197, 203–4, 205–6, 208–9, 211, 214, 215, 216
transcendence 46–9, 52, 64, 91, 106, 109, 113, 152, 178
Trent, Council of 86, 91, 135, 139
Trinity 38, 46, 50–2, 79, 110–11, 112, 113, 114, 142

Vatican I 82, 203
Vatican II 7, 43–4, 75, 76, 85, 88, 95, 126
visio Dei 46, 63, 64, 66, 68

www.ingramcontent.com/pod-product-compliance
Lightning Source LLC
Chambersburg PA
CBHW062148300426
44115CB00012BA/2040